STREETS

For Jan Gijsbertus Ploem (1915–2001),
whose ever-curious spirit loved exploring the world's backstreets

STREETS
Exploring Hong Kong Island

Jason Wordie

香港大學出版社
HONG KONG UNIVERSITY PRESS

Hong Kong University Press
14/F Hing Wai Centre
7 Tin Wan Praya Road
Aberdeen
Hong Kong
www.hkupress.org

First published 2002
Reprinted 2003, 2008, 2009, 2011

ISBN 978-962-209-563-2

British Library Cataloguing-in-Publication Data
A catalogue record for this book is available from the British
Library.

10 9 8 7 6 5

Printed and bound by Liang Yu Printing Factory Limited, Hong Kong China

Contents

Foreword by Selina Chow   **vii**

Acknowledgements   **ix**

Users' Guide   **xi**

Introduction   **1**

Central   **12**
    Aberdeen Street   16
    Battery Path   21
    Chater Road   27
    Graham Street   34
    Hollywood Road   40
    Ice House Street   46
    Pedder Street   51
    Shelley Street   56
    Upper Albert Road   61
    Wellington Street   67

Peak • Mid-Levels   **72**
    Bowen Road   78
    Conduit Road   82
    Kotewall Road   87
    Lugard Road   91
    Old Peak Road   98

Wan Chai   **102**
    Cross Street   106
    Johnston Road   112
    Kennedy Road   118
    Lee Tung Street   122
    Queen's Road East   126
    Ship Street   131
    Stone Nullah Lane   135

Causeway Bay • Happy Valley   **140**
    Blue Pool Road   146
    Causeway Road   150

STREETS

Contents

Leighton Road	154
Shan Kwong Road	159
Tai Hang Road	163
Tung Lo Wan Road	168
Wong Nai Chung Road	173
Yee Wo Street	179
North Point • Shek O	**184**
Chai Wan Road	190
King's Road	194
Shau Kei Wan Main Street East	199
Shek O Road	204
Tong Chong Street	210
Southside	**214**
Stanley Main Street	218
Tung Tau Wan Road/Wong Ma Kok Road	223
Repulse Bay Road	228
Deep Water Bay Road	232
Aberdeen • Pok Fu Lam	**236**
Aberdeen Main Road	242
Pok Fu Lam Road	246
Victoria Road	253
Wong Chuk Hang Road	259
Western	**264**
Belcher's Street	270
Centre Street	275
Des Voeux Road West	279
High Street	284
Ladder Street	289
Tai Ping Shan Street	294
Western Street	300
Bibliography	**307**
Photograph Credits	**315**

Foreword

Whether we are those who think we know Hong Kong well, or those who just love to visit, Jason Wordie's fascinating stories of the many gems that make our city unique will open our eyes even further to the layers of experiences that it offers. Meticulously researched, helpfully presented and touchingly told, they charmingly demonstrate the many facets of this place, its history, its sights and its people woven into the mesh of the not-quite-perfect fusion of East and West. It will silence the critics who spread the false impression that 'Hong Kong has few attractions'. For those of us who believe in the magic of Hong Kong, Jason Wordie has given us the words to prove it.

Selina Chow
Chairman 2000–2007
Hong Kong Tourism Board

Acknowledgements

R ichard Abrahall, Tony Hedley and John Lambon undertook the photographic work for the book with unfailing cheerfulness and great thoroughness, often revisiting a site numerous times to get just the right shot. Without their skill, enthusiasm and dedication, this would have been a very different book — if indeed it had appeared at all.

Streets: Exploring Hong Kong Island derives in part from an idea by Susan Sams, Associate Editor (Features) of the *South China Morning Post*, for a series in the newspaper's *Post Magazine*.

No one writing on subjects related to local history in Hong Kong can fail to acknowledge the tremendous debt we all owe, whether directly or otherwise, to the pioneering work undertaken by the Reverend Carl T. Smith, for decades the doyen of Hong Kong's archival researchers. Likewise encouragement of Dr Elizabeth Sinn, presently Deputy Director of the Centre of Asian Studies at the University of Hong Kong, has been of great assistance to many people, myself included, over the years. Dr Patrick Hase, formerly a Hong Kong government administrator and a scholar with a special interest in the New Territories, read the manuscript with a keen eye to detail and pointed out a number of errors and inconsistencies that I had overlooked.

The *Journal* of the Hong Kong Branch of the Royal Asiatic Society has been a tremendous resource, with many obscure and otherwise hard to find local details hidden within its volumes.

My friends Peggy Elenbaas Ploem and the late Jan Gijsbertus Ploem have always been very supportive of decision to write for a living.

Wong Nai-kwan, Curator of the Hong Kong Police Museum and a fund of detailed local history knowledge, has been a great deal of help in numerous practical ways in the preparation of this book

Edward Stokes, Sarah Draper-Ali, David and Evangeline Ollerearnshaw, Peter and Sarah Cunich, Vaudine England, Ko Tim-keung and Jennifer Day have all provided a great deal of encouragement and sound advice in their own way at various times — in a few cases without fully realizing it.

STREETS

Acknowledgements

Wee Kek-koon was very encouraging and supportive throughout, as always, and provided considerable practical assistance as the book came towards publication.

My own research on various subjects over the years has been greatly enriched by the friendship and enthusiasm of numerous long-time residents of Hong Kong — both past and present — who between them have given me insights into local life and society that I would never have otherwise obtained. In this connection, I would especially like to thank Gloria d'Almada Barretto, the late Lady May Ride, Arthur E. Gomes, Nina Bieger and Irene Garfinkle (nee Smirnoff), Mrs Irene Braude, John R. Harris, and Tony and Liz Hewitt.

Colin Day, Ada Wan and Clara Ho at Hong Kong University Press have been tremendously encouraging and continuously patient with a project that has proven exceptionally complicated.

Numerous participants on the various historical walking tours I have taken out over the last few years for various local organizations — it would be impossible to name them all individually — have provided many off-hand insights into backstreet life in Hong Kong and a great deal of intellectual stimulation along the way. These walks started out as a cool-weather diversion for me and have gradually become a most enjoyable undertaking.

Users' Guide

The series of localized walks starts in Central and takes in the Mid-Levels and the Peak, then moves eastwards towards Wan Chai, Causeway Bay, North Point and Shau Kei Wan. It then follows around the southern coast to Shek O, Stanley, Repulse Bay and Deep Water Bay, and on to Aberdeen and the Pok Fu Lam coast, finally finishing in Western district.

Transport options is listed in order of accessibility. It is assumed that one will pick up public transport such as buses and trams from a closely defined, easily accessible centralized start point such as the Star Ferry or Exchange Square bus terminus. For locations such as Pedder Street or Ice House Street that are so close to the Star Ferry that walking would be the quickest option, I have included transport options to get there from further afield. I have assumed in all cases that only public transport will be used, and so have not listed convenient parking facilities for private cars.

Like Hong Kong itself, what at first glance will appear a disordered mélange of sights and places has an inner logic that makes it work. Areas such as Causeway Bay and Stanley and Pok Fu Lam appear as they would moving eastwards and then around the island from Central. Within these areas, locations such as Yee Wo Street or Tung Tau Wan Road and Victoria Road follow the same sequence. Individual places in or around the specific location, such as a temple, shop or whatever, flow in a logical sequence for a pedestrian alighting from transport at a designated start point. These are always indicated by a 'No. 1'. Some aspects of an area or individual location mentioned in the text are quite subjective — like Mid-Levels traffic or market atmosphere in Wan Chai — and may or may not be immediately apparent to the first-time visitor.

Romanizing Cantonese street names — or anything at all — is a difficult and inherently flawed undertaking, as the language is tonal and diacritical marks should properly be used to indicate where these should properly be used. Making these pronunciation aids intelligible to the non-specialist would involve the introduction of complex tone scales and approximation charts that have no place in work like this. The aim of romanizing destinations in the 'How To Get There' section is to facilitate communication between a non-Cantonese speaker and a taxi-driver with minimal English and get the passenger where they want to go. As anyone accustomed to taking taxis in Hong Kong will realize, taxi miscommunications can make for some rather fraught experiences; while the aim of the 'How To Get There' romanizations is to minimize such confusions, it will not, alas, completely eliminate them.

The aim is to dip into the book, and use it as a guide to forming your own impressions.

Many apparently obvious 'sights', such as Flagstaff House, the Star Ferry and Lan Kwai Fong, are not included in this book. As a general rule of thumb, if a place appears in standard guidebooks or local tourist literature, it will not be found in *Streets: Exploring Hong Kong Island*. This book aims to cover the lesser-known, more generally overlooked elements of Hong Kong and its culture, and not the usual visitors drawcards which are extensively documented elsewhere. Where more widely known features are incorporated, such as Statue Square or Government House, their inclusion is to provide a different view to well-known sights, and perhaps in the process help peel away the layers of urban myth that have come to surround them over the years.

The views expressed in this book are my own, and will not be everyone's version of either Hong Kong or specific parts of it.

Introduction

E ven for those who have lived for many years in Hong Kong, the place and its people continue to fascinate, beguile, infuriate and disgust. Behind the hubris of Hong Kong's recent self-designation as 'Asia's World City', a glitzy depiction easy enough to be seduced by in certain areas, numerous images abound; and an abundance of clichés.

Thronged city streets pulsing with energy, thronged with buses, trams, taxis, private cars and people, people ...

Quiet backstreet courtyards shaded by spreading banyans and heavily fragrant *pak laan* trees (*Michelia alba*), with a garrulous foursome playing mah-jong somewhere in the afternoon shade.

The curling rooflines of venerable Chinese temples wreathed in sandalwood-scented incense smoke, their walls blackened and dark with years of accreted dust and soot.

Crowded squalid back alleys, smelling of roasted pork, diesel fumes, market sweepings and washing hung out to dry.

Undeveloped, almost wild countryside, only a short distance away from the heart of one of the world's most overcrowded cities.

Gleaming steel and glass office towers, the modern day's temples to trade, banking and property speculation; sharp-suited office-workers scurrying in and out, clutching their mobile phones all the while.

Money-making machine masquerading as a legitimate society; noisy politicians gesturing pointlessly for the watching television cameras; government officials responsible only, it sometimes seems, to themselves alone.

Bone-thin old people, pushing trolleys stacked high with waste cardboard and discarded aluminium cans slowly up the hillsides into the dusk.

Fantastic, unlikely, glittering Manhattan East skyline, backed by sheer, towering, jungle-covered mountainsides where the solitary hiker can walk for hours and see almost no one, then clamber down the cliffside and swim off magnificent beaches in the open sea.

Dinners simple, extravagant or anything in between, followed by the latest Hollywood film, or a performance of brightly painted opera singers first down from Szechwan (Sichuan); gazing out across Victoria Harbour's myriad lights into the midnight sky.

Few places in Asia can have changed so much over the last few decades; the remarkable thing is just how many links to the past still linger on in Hong Kong, amid all the glitz and modernity. Staggering too just how much has gone forever.

Attractive, integrated civic precincts like the formerly gracious surrounds of Statue Square have been completely transformed — some would say obliterated — over the past half-century, with only a few isolated remnants like the old Supreme Court and the Cenotaph to remind us of what once was a very attractive downtown area. That element of the past has gone. It has vanished, been thrown away. It no longer exists. Central involves many adjectives, but pleasant is seldom one of them.

Some places, remarkably, have changed little or nothing with the passage of time. A St John's Cathedral parishioner or a student from the University of Hong Kong, returning after half a century or so away, would find little changed in either old building or their immediate surroundings. But these, notably, are amongst the few exceptions.

Of the best of Hong Kong's old urban buildings, hardly any still remain. Tsim Sha Tsui's Kowloon-Canton Railway Station, Central's Hong Kong Club and General Post Office, Causeway Bay's Lee Theatre or the marvellous Repulse Bay Hotel — the list of lost heritage-grade buildings that only live on in picture books and fading memories is almost endless; everyone has a favourite example of a place now vanished.

And all of these buildings mentioned above were only demolished after — not before — a dedicated Antiquities and Monuments Office was established in 1976. They were lost because even when Hong Kong's, admittedly toothless, protective legislation was enacted, few local residents cared enough to publicly demand preservation of what still remained.

As a direct result, Hong Kong's ever-present combination of entrenched vested interests, private greed and public apathy has ensured that very little built heritage now remains in the urban areas to pass on to coming generations. And of course, on the more frequented streets of areas such as Central and Causeway Bay, virtually nothing remains from the past. And what does still precariously hang on becomes a locally renowned 'antiquity', eagerly pointed out to those, especially newcomers to Hong Kong, who aver that nothing now remains from the past.

A flight of stone steps lit top and bottom by brackets of wrought-iron gas lamps, say, or an incongruously surviving bronze statue, marooned pathetically out of time and context, become local marvels. Featured in guidebooks and tourist pamphlets and eagerly pointed out to sightseers as evidence that Hong Kong still cherishes its links with the past, few, if any, of Hong Kong's 'monuments' would be considered notable anywhere else in the world. But here they are made much of, and that fact in itself provides interesting and unexpected insights into Hong Kong's psyche.

Perhaps most obviously, the lavish attention devoted to these scraps and fragments is a tell-tale marker of Hong Kong's remarkably inward-looking nature and, by extension, just how ice-thin the city's layer of 'internationalism' really is. Hong Kong's heritage sites are seldom openly benchmarked against similar sites in other 'world cities' — the comparison would just be too marked.

But in a backhanded sort of way these scattered oddments really *are* monuments to Hong Kong's past, yet in ways very few care to think about. Their enduring presence are testaments to the city and its people's prevailing lack of civic awareness, to its wanton disregarded sense of how what went before elementally shapes what Hong Kong is like now, and the quite chilling unconcern for what the place would eventually be like for future generations.

This indifference often parallels a striking, sometimes stunning, ignorance on the part of many Hong Kong people of all races, of the place that they have lived in all their lives. It's almost too easy to say, as many local residents do, that Hong Kong has no history, and a truism that for so much of its history the future was so uncertain as to be unfathomable. As a direct result, for many Hong Kong people, the city lives only in and for the present.

An interested backstreet wanderer looking to know more about the city's past is not often served by asking other Hong Kong people for clues. For the most part, Hong Kong people don't know anything much about it either, and most can't quite understand why anyone should take much any interest in a heritage not their own. Far better to sip cappuccinos in the air-conditioning somewhere and talk about life in Sydney, New York or Vancouver, they imply, than poke about in local backstreets among the dirt and the smells where after all, there's really nothing much to see or do anyway.

What often forcefully strikes newcomers to Hong Kong is how extraordinarily little knowledge, or even curiosity, most people born and brought up here seem to have about the place they've lived in all their lives. Cynics frequently sneer that if Hong Kong people can't make money out of something, sing into it, eat it or hang a designer label off it then they feel it's not worth knowing about. While there is unfortunately some truth in this, the underlying reasons why so many have ended up knowing so little about the place they have lived in all their lives are deep-rooted and complex.

Before the late 1960s, very few people of any race, with the partial exception of the local Portuguese and Eurasians, a small section of the Chinese population and a smaller still number of Europeans, and a scattering of Parsees, Jews and others, really *were* local, in the sense of being lifelong residents, born, raised and educated in Hong Kong. The overwhelming majority of the population came here to earn a living, **not** make a home. Almost everyone was from somewhere else, and fully intended to go back there in time.

To speak of *Heung Kong Yan* (Hong Kong People) before that time, in the sense that the term would be understood by many today, has virtually no meaning, and is a little like referring to sixteenth-century Italians, or nineteenth-century Singaporeans; there just weren't any. Tuscans, Genoese and Neapolitans in Italy, or Hokkiens, Tamils and Bugis Malays in Singapore, yes, but the distinctive, shared inter-communal identity which we recognize today in those places came much later, as it did to Hong Kong as well.

With little shared heritage and so much discontinuity after the Pacific War, what was here before 1949 was largely irrelevant to those who came afterwards. In the 1950s almost no sense of a shared Hong Kong community existed. Instead, there was a collection of different communities who lived side by side but seldom if ever mingled. Cultivating a common Hong Kong-based heritage through the study of local history and encouraging the sense of patrimony that develops as a result was a non-starter when, for most residents, there was simply no common legacy to begin with.

Hong Kong wasn't a place that those who eventually became 'Hong Kong People' had grown up with, and they didn't really expect — much less hope — that their children or grandchildren would ever come to feel deeply for the place. Hong Kong's only value was as a haven of refuge from disorder elsewhere, a temporary way station for people who never lost the feeling that ultimately they were just stopping off on the way to somewhere else.

Given this transient situation, why should anyone bother to care for the place, or want to know more about it than they needed for day-to-day living? If graceful old buildings were heedlessly destroyed, beautiful scenic vistas irretrievably ruined, the harbour and beaches fouled almost beyond redemption and the New Territories countryside squandered and lost, well, ultimately it didn't matter — or so the flawed reasoning went.

For after all, Hong Kong wasn't really home; it was just a place to make enough money to buy an emigrant's visa to Canada, Australia or the United States, just as three generations earlier Hong Kong represented little more than the opportunity to save up for a comfortable retirement elsewhere in one of the scattered Pearl River Delta towns, or in one of the more picturesque English villages, depending on where one had originally hailed from.

The conscious development of a distinct Hong Kong identity was never encouraged; it still isn't largely because it would be interpreted by the mainland government (a fact they themselves have admitted) as the colonial authorities trying to create a separate, ultimately self-governing entity out of Hong Kong, similar to Singapore's political development at this time, which they would never tolerate. And today, as we are constantly reminded, the concept of 'One Country' is paramount, whatever the rider about 'Two Systems' might once have been taken to mean. But the end result of both policies has been the same — a Hong Kong identity has evolved by default and somehow managed, in spite of so many obvious faults and flaws, to survive and flourish against the odds.

In the future we may come to see that the distinct, widespread,

Hong Kong identity, no less real for being flawed, belonged only to a thin slice in time, falling somewhere between the turmoil of the late 1960s and the turn of the twenty-first century, a few years after the handover. Shanghai ceased to be a meaningful exchange between China and the rest of the world by the mid-1950s as China turned inward and in many ways Shanghai ceased to exist as an identity distinctly separate from the rest of the mainland. A similar convergence appears to be happening in Hong Kong, always a very inward-looking place anyway. And as China continues to modernize and look outward, the formerly stark disparities in lifestyle and expectations between Hong Kong people and their mainland contemporaries can only further narrow with each passing year.

The not-so-slow diaspora of Hong Kong people in the 1980s and 1990s, the steady hemorrhaging of Hong Kong's best and brightest to Canada, Australia and elsewhere in the post-Joint Declaration, and especially post-Tiananmen years, is perhaps one of the clearest markers of this. The genuinely middle class — as distinct from the merely affluent — have not, sadly, returned to Hong Kong in any great numbers. They have left permanently, and local society shows their loss in many less obvious ways.

Those who have come back, regrettably, are for the most part as opportunistic as those who never left in the first place, perhaps even more so. Their sense of commitment to Hong Kong, if it even exists at all, is even more tenuous than it was before; now they and their children no longer *have* to stay here, come what may, if doing so doesn't really suit them in any way. And so there is little incentive to work for a better Hong Kong for tomorrow's generation — their day can dawn elsewhere. For these people it really *doesn't* matter now, if it ever did anyway, whether Hong Kong gets further trashed, polluted, built over, and despoiled. They've got their bolt hole; here is only for now. Why bother about anything else?

The disregarded past, nevertheless, is still lurking about, but increasingly it takes some looking for in most places. Wandering about Hong Kong Island's backstreets, in places like Kennedy Town, Shau Kei Wan or Wan Chai, one can sometimes feel like an archaeologist of the modern-day working without a shovel, piecing together isolated fragments from what was here until almost yesterday to build up a picture of a very different place.

Glimpses of earlier times remain here and there, and in some corners audible echoes as well, but for many, what went before is at best partially buried, even somewhat obscure. But learn what to look and listen for, and an otherwise everyday scene can completely change.

Market streets are still raucous places of vendor's cries, and not so long ago the clip-clop of wooden slippers (*mook kek*) was a common and distinctive sound heard all over Hong Kong. Over the last forty years *mook kek* have steadily given way to rubber-soled shoes, and their once common available presence has vanished into the past. But they are still sold in a few shops here and there, and very occasionally one will hear someone wearing them, probably an old person, clattering along the pavement in the late afternoon in search of a fresh fish and some green vegetables to prepare for the family's evening meal.

At moments like that, one can think that the city's distinctiveness hasn't completely vanished, not just yet anyway, and that there are still echoes — audible at quite a distance in this case — of what Hong Kong used to be like. Or it can seem like that, for those who care to listen. And so, wandering around Hong Kong's backstreets, one needs to look for other elements from the past, more cultural and lasting, and identify links between them and the present. One's historical imagination takes over, and this is perhaps the best part of a wander around Hong Kong.

A foundation stone here, a statue there or from time to time that rarest of local sights — a well-preserved old building — give subtle hints to Hong Kong's past. Names on streets give a few such intimations of the past and lead on to other lingering signposts that point the way towards vanished people, long lost places and almost completely altered ways of life. But not too many clues lead to ready answers and their presence poses as many questions about contemporary Hong Kong's attitude to its past as they lay to rest.

In recent years heritage trails in both the urban and rural areas have attempted to write something of their area's past back into public consciousness, but like many such initiatives, sadly, they all too often seem like a case of too little and far too late for any meaningful impact on public awareness to be possible.

Let's take an example of one such walking trail, well researched and seemingly well thought out, with considerable sums of public money spent on implementation. What does Dr Sun Yat-sen, revolutionary 'founder' of modern China, and the *gai see* (wet market) on Central's Bridges Street, smelling of dried vegetables, wet feathers and fresh chicken blood, possibly have in common? On the surface of it, nothing. Nevertheless, this unremarkable, rather grubby spot forms an integral part of the Central and Western District Board's Sun Yat-sen Heritage Trail — a series of marker plaques at various locations connected with Dr Sun's student years in Hong Kong and subsequent revolutionary activities, when he used the British colony as a base and relatively safe haven.

For marker plaques are all that remain; almost everything else that was in any way connected with Sun Yat-sen's time in Hong Kong has long since been demolished. As with other heritage trails created in the urban areas in recent years, the inscriptions here record, in effect, that 'on this site, three or four buildings ago, there used to be something interesting or significant.' But beyond that, nothing from the past remains for the ambler to encounter. There is virtually nothing at all to see as you walk along, beyond a usually unremarkable modern building and a small marker plaque.

The Central and Western Heritage Trail, laid out by the Antiquities and Monuments Office, follows a similar pattern to the Sun Yat-sen Trail. Out of thirty-five 'sites of interest' depicted on official brochures publicizing the Sheung Wan Route, nineteen of them are only marker plaques. While some of the sites covered, such as the Man Mo Temple, are of considerable historical and cultural interest, others are of, at best, tenuous importance. While well-meaning, the historical significance of these sites is often so unconvincing that all but the most hardened history fanatic, whose sole aim and purpose is to gaze at the site of the long-vanished stall where Dr Sun habitually took his breakfast congee, can be enthused by any of them.

One such tenuous 'heritage site' is the public park on Caine Road, the claim to prominence of which is that it is where a row of Police Married Quarters once stood. Built in 1920 of red brick and stucco and less than sixty years old when torn down, they were of no great architectural merit; in Sydney, Calcutta, Manchester or Singapore, buildings such as these would literally not have warranted a second glance. The pamphlet might just as well read, 'On this site, more than twenty years ago, there once stood a row of fairly unremarkable buildings, since demolished.' The tower block on Seymour Road, immediately behind and overlooking the park, stands on the site of *Idlewild*, the rather more impressive town residence of early compradore Sir Robert Hotung. By the logic employed concerning the park's inclusion there should perhaps be an entry for that as well, but there isn't.

All of this, though, sadly demonstrates just how bare the bottom of the local heritage barrel has been scraped. When 'sites' like the park on Caine Road have been deemed worthy of inclusion in literature promoting 'heritage', it is impossible not to suspect that it was only for sheer want of anything better.

Heritage is generally a rather subjective concept; what has meaning and significance for one group can be — and all too often is — completely irrelevant to others. Hopefully here on these pages, various kinds of Hong Kong people, from the recently arrived to those whose families have lived here for generations, can recognize elements of the place that are significant to themselves.

Perhaps the most famous sight in Hong Kong, an image well-known to generations the world over, is the sight of the city itself, layered upon the lower slopes of Victoria Peak, with the green-clad mountainside itself providing a majestic silhouette and unchanging backdrop to the constantly evolving scene below it. Of all aspects of Hong Kong's heritage, this view is one that everyone across the full racial, socio-economic spectrum, from Shanghainese tycoon to Cantonese taxi-driver, Pakistani watchman to Peakite *tai tai*, has at some point gazed at and admired, even if only unconsciously.

In a few short years that view will be gone. Super-high office buildings, that most pernicious present-day example of greedy vested

9

interests prevailing over the wider, less immediately tangible public benefit, are steadily obliterating the very view of the Peak itself with an impenetrable wall of glass and steel. And now it is too late to stop.

Like most of Hong Kong's built heritage in the past, this view is being lost without pathos, without protest, and almost without comment. No one in authority, it seems, has ever thought of the uninterrupted Hong Kong skyline as an invaluable part of Hong Kong's collective heritage, of equal value to Chinese, Europeans, Eurasians, Parsees, Portuguese, Indians and every other nationality who ever settled here, which must be preserved at all costs. As a result, possibly the only element of Hong Kong's heritage that is common to all groups is shortly to disappear forever.

Part of the reason for this lies in the blindly commercial nature of Hong Kong and many of its people who, as the cliché appropriately runs, know the price of everything and the value of nothing. Another cause perhaps is the weary acceptance by both concerned parties and one suspects, the general public, that the unsubtly expressed wishes of powerful vested interests would inevitably prevail, over this as every other issue, whatever protest may have been made. This is what has always happened in the past, and so, perhaps, there seemed little or no point in even trying.

Future generations of residents and visitors may gasp in delight at many things in Hong Kong, but the majestic sight of Victoria Peak, rearing massively unimpeded above the heights of the city will, alas, not be one of them.

In this book I have tried to show Hong Kong as it really *is*, or at least as it is to me, rather than present an idealized version of how it was, or could be. Featured within these pages you will find the beautiful, the modern, the stylish and the graceful, placed immediately next to scenes of squalor, poverty, decay and stupidity. For this is how Hong Kong is; the magnificent and the tawdry, the distressing, the agreeable and the mindless, all somehow managing to coexist side by side, and overlapping most of the time as well.

Some corners of Hong Kong depicted here are prosaic and everyday, and reflect elements of Hong Kong life that are repeated all over the territory; others are more obscure, and many are completely area-specific. Many locations are sharply focused while others contain more diffuse images, impressions and evocations. Aspects of Hong Kong life and Hong Kong people that I've selected, as well as my comments about them, will be controversial; maybe even embarrassing or offensive at times.

Some places are a hidden embarrassment of little-known riches while others contain not much more than the street names themselves and a few stories to point the way towards what once was found there. In these localities I have tried to show things that aren't there anymore, and try to give a flavour, a smell, and a sound of what it once was like, or might have been like.

Like Hong Kong itself, it is a deliberate but at times seemingly random selection, an often contradictory blend of sights, sounds, smells, and images. Hong Kong is like that too. It is not the same place for everyone, and neither should it be.

Above all *Streets: Exploring Hong Kong Island* is an intensely personal book. This is *my* Hong Kong, written as *I* see it. It is a view of Hong Kong seen through the eyes of a long-term resident — myself — whose image of the place and its varied peoples constantly oscillates between fascination, disgust, amusement, irritation, pride and delight, all emotions experienced in the course of an average day and often within an hour or two. But nevertheless I still go to bed every evening loving the place as much as ever. And I still don't quite know why I feel that way.

Mine will not be everyone's version of Hong Kong. It will certainly seem be obscure for some, and for others locations that should seem the most familiar will be almost unrecognizable. But within these boundaries I hope readers will identify elements of Hong Kong that are familiar to them as well, stimulate a wish to explore others that are more unknown, or simply cause them to nod with recognition and then say quietly to themselves, 'Yes, that's how I see it too.'

Generally referred to these days as either Central or *Chung Wan* (Middle Circuit), in official documents the district is still known by its early designation as the city of Victoria. Often thought of as a completely modern commercial area, a high-rise urban jungle with virtually nothing left to remind the present of its past, Central still reveals surprising traces of its history — if one knows where to look.

The British landed and took possession of Hong Kong on 26 January 1841. The capital of the new colony was named Victoria and in time grew until it extended over much of what is now Sheung Wan, Central and Wan Chai. Marker stones were set up to establish the town limits from Happy Valley to Pok Fu Lam; some are still there today.

Central District was the first area of planned urban development in Hong Kong. At land sales held in June 1841 (six months after the British flag was raised at Possession Point), 51 lots of land were sold to 23 merchant houses to build offices and godowns. Prominent European and American-owned firms who bought property at that time included Jardine, Matheson and Co. still prominent today, and its then rival Dent's and Co., which was wiped out in the slump of 1867, as well as others such as Russell's and Olyphant's. Spacious office buildings with broad verandahs and shutters — a style common in present-day Macao — were built along the waterfront, which later became known as Praya Central and later, after major reclamation, as Des Voeux Road Central. Other offices were built between the Praya and Queen's Road as far west as Central Market, the site of which was designated for use as a public market in 1842.

In November 1841, the ridge of land between Albany Nullah (now Garden Road) and Glenealy Nullah (now Glenealy) was set aside for Crown use and was subsequently known as Government Hill. The Colonial Secretariat, Government House, Albany Government Quarters and St John's Cathedral were all built on this slope.

The area extending eastwards between Government Hill and Wan Chai was designated for military use. Victoria and Wellington Barracks were built, and the area remained reserved for military use until the late 1970s. This officially created division between the Central and Wan Chai areas meant in effect that additional residential and commercial area could only be

• Aberdeen Street	• Hollywood Road	• Upper Albert Road
• Battery Path	• Ice House Street	• Wellington Street
• Chater Road	• Pedder Street	
• Graham Street	• Shelley Street	

developed to the east of the military cantonment, the area now covered by Queen's Road East.

The slope below the present-day Central Market developed into a crowded Chinese-populated area known as the Middle Bazaar. After 1843 the area was cleared following a number of fires, those resident there moved to Tai Ping Shan further west and the Middle Bazaar vicinity became a predominantly European area. However, by the late 1860s numerous Chinese merchants had bought up European-owned property around Cochrane, Wellington and Pottinger Streets, transforming the area. By the 1870s backstreet Central had gradually developed into the general street layout that still prevails today.

In the 1840s, the backstreet areas around Lyndhurst Terrace, Hollywood Road and Aberdeen Street were predominantly European residential areas. From the 1870s onwards, however, increasing numbers of Chinese merchants bought properties in this area, converting the buildings into tenements. From this time onwards European residents moved up the hill to the Caine and Robinson Road areas, and away from Central, marking the beginnings of residential development on the Mid-Levels as well as accentuating racial separateness.

While Western became an important commercial centre, especially for Chinese businesses, Central became the principal European business district with the eventual construction of the Hongkong and Shanghai Bank headquarters symbolizing this.

STREETS

Central

As Hong Kong further developed and prospered in the latter quarter of the nineteenth century, the available land area in the Central district became insufficient for further development. A proposal for a large-scale reclamation in Central was first proposed by Sir John Bowring (Governor, 1854–59), though this was opposed by a number of prominent merchants on the grounds of expense, and the proposal was shelved.

Central became not only the financial but also the cultural heart of Hong Kong between 1860 and 1880, with the construction of a substantial City Hall which had a well-stocked library, a Theatre Royal which often had artists performing from overseas, reception rooms and so on. In those days, however, Hong Kong did not have a separate municipal administration, and responsibility for the City Hall devolved upon the Hong Kong government.

Most of the City Hall was demolished in the 1880s to make way for the Hongkong and Shanghai Bank Building; as is so often the case in Hong Kong civic spirit swiftly yielded precedence to commercialism, and the public had to wait another eighty years before a new City Hall was built. However, a part of the old City Hall still stood until the 1940s, when it was finally demolished to make way for what is now the old Bank of China.

In 1887 the wealthy Armenian financier Sir Paul Chater proposed a reclamation project for the central business district which was accepted after some discussion. Along with J. J. Keswick, Chater was co-founder of Hong Kong Land, still the major commercial landlord in the area. The Praya Reclamation Scheme commenced in 1890 and when it was completed in 1904, it added 59 acres of land to the Central waterfront; Statue Square was subsequently laid out on this open area.

Soon after its completion, grand new buildings were completed around the square and surrounding streets. A massive, red-brick and granite General Post Office, ornate new premises for the Hong Kong Club, a Supreme Court, and the commercial Prince's, Queen's, King's, York and St George's Buildings were all constructed. Except for the Supreme Court (now used as the Legislative Council Building), all have since been demolished and only the name of two — Prince's Building and St George's Building — still persist in a modern incarnation.

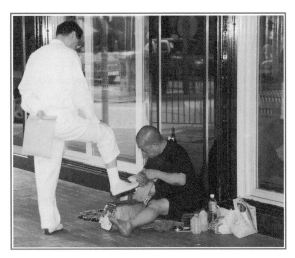

By the 1920s the Crown Colony — with the attractive Central area at its heart — had acquired an air of settled permanence, with an open civic area on the habour complete with a Cenotaph modelled directly on that in Whitehall. Unlike Macao, which developed an attractive tree-lined waterfront Praya, Hong Kong's waterfront remained resolutely commercial, with local, riverine and Macao ferry piers dotted along its length and sampan moorings and warehouses extending along the western end. The sole exception was around Statue Square, which attained an air of Edwardian civic dignity that has been now completely lost.

With its physical outline transformed by successive waves of reclamation, Central's appearance altered completely through the 1970s as most old buildings were heedlessly demolished; some, such as the General Post Office and the Hong Kong Club, were torn down after, **not** before, heritage legislation was enacted. Central these days gives an appearance of overwhelming glitz and modernity, but a wander around the backstreets, or even the main streets, still reveals a surprising amount about the area's past if you know where to look and what to look for.

Massive reclamations in the 1990s for Airport Railway core projects have further transformed Central, placing the original waterfront Praya now several hundred metres inland. Further new mega-storey buildings currently under construction seem set to change the area's appearance even further in coming years.

This steep street, so precipitous it could almost be in San Francisco, extends from Caine Road down to Wellington Street. It was named after Lord Aberdeen, Foreign Secretary at the time of Hong Kong Island's cession to Great Britain. The small fishing port of Shek Pai Wan, also known as Heung Kong Jai (Little Hong Kong), was renamed for him as well, and not, as the popular urban myth has it, after the other fishing port in Scotland.

Aberdeen Street's steepness can be read as a metaphor for both the range of social classes of residents and the range of building styles that once very clearly marked the divide between the Mid-Levels, which properly begins at Caine Road, and the lower city. Distinctions have blurred somewhat in recent years; real estate agents often describe flats as being in 'the Mid-Levels' — properly above Caine Road — when they are nothing of the sort. And in a telling break with past perceptions, the size and quality of residential accommodation located higher up the hillside is no longer automatically superior to that found below.

Caine Road, which crosses the top of Aberdeen Street, was named after Major William Caine, Hong Kong's first Police Magistrate; he was later appointed Lieutenant Governor from 1854–59. In the late nineteenth century, this sleepy, tree-lined thoroughfare was the site of substantial homes for Hong Kong's

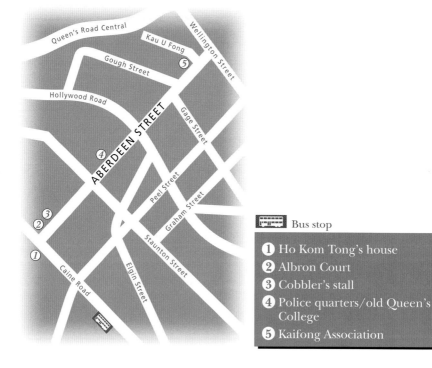

Bus stop

1 Ho Kom Tong's house
2 Albron Court
3 Cobbler's stall
4 Police quarters/old Queen's College
5 Kaifong Association

developing merchant class and a quiet residential area with extensive views over the harbour. This was in every respect different from the rather ugly concrete canyon permanently choked with taxis, goods-vans and minibuses that it is today — a fate Caine Road shares with other once pleasant, tree-lined roads further up the hillside. But in spite of the sweeping changes nearby in recent years, Aberdeen Street and the surrounding lanes still retain much of the character of old Hong Kong, particularly at the lower end around Hollywood Road.

1 Ho Kom Tong's house

This substantial red-brick house with granite pillars and wrought-iron balconies was built in 1914. It is one of the very last survivors, sadly, of the opulent mansions that once lined the roads up through the Mid-Levels — almost all the others have been demolished for tower blocks. Formerly the residence of wealthy businessman Ho Kom-tong, younger brother of the Eurasian millionaire Sir Robert Hotung, the building was used for a time by the Japanese Army during the years 1942–45.

Ho Kom-tong died in 1950 and his family sold the house in 1959 to the Cheng family. They subsequently sold it a year later to the Church of Jesus Christ of Latter Day Saints, in whose hands it still remains. The Mormons now use it as a church, as well as a cultural and educational centre. As with other similar houses along here, *Kom Tong Tai* — as it is known to the Cantonese — once had a stunning view of the harbour below, now almost totally obscured by tall buildings and, on many days, by blanketing grey smog as well.

2 Albron Court

Caine Road was once the site of many substantial mansions, and marked the dividing line between the Mid-Levels, an area of spacious villas surrounded by gardens, and the crowded, closely packed city below. This rather pathetic-looking granite gatepost is all that remains of Albron Court, a substantial two-storey mansion built in the 1870s for the wealthy Parsee opium trader and businessman, H. N. Mody. Mody Road in Tsim Sha Tsui is named after him, and he was also an early beneficiary of the University of Hong Kong paying for most of the construction costs of the Main Building on Bonham Road.

At one time Albron Court had turrets and a small tower, ornamental plasterwork, and windows made of small, multicoloured glass panes shaded by wooden shutters, while the front garden had a huge old frangipani tree seasonally filled with yellow and white flowers, its branches so high that they reached almost up to the roof.

By the mid-1970s the house had fallen into a very dilapidated condition and the roof was shored up by wooden beams. As with so many other historic buildings that were lost around that time, Albron Court was demolished without comment, and replaced by the featureless high-rise apartment block that one can see on the site today. For some obscure reason one of the old gateposts on Caine Road was retained, and it still stands there incongruous, next to the steps leading up to the

Wellcome supermarket, while all else that reminds us of this historic old house and its former occupant has vanished without trace.

③ Cobbler's stall

The old man at this street-side cobbler's stall under the tree on the side of Aberdeen Street didn't want to give his name, but volunteered that he has been there since well before Albron Court was demolished in the late 1970s. Repairs to shoe-soles average $60 (he wouldn't say what he charged in the old days) and although business has quietened down in recent years — due most likely to the advent of the throw-away society — he still gets a few clients. Mostly

these days it is older people and the poor who come by for repairs. On some days, he admits, there is very little work to do at all.

Other vanishing trades and traditional crafts can still sometimes be seen in the vicinity, a lingering reminder of a past Hong Kong when things were made to last and mended when worn rather than immediately thrown away and replaced. One such tradesman to look out for around here is an itinerant knife and scissor grinder. Now, like the cobbler, quite elderly, he travels about the area, with his sharpening stone and tools slung on two poles, calling his distinctive cry to attract customers. When someone has given him a task he sits down on his portable bench and gets to work — a mere ten minutes or so later the job is done, and both the knife-grinder and his portable workshop are on their way again. Honing that blunt kitchen chopper or putting a new edge on your dressmaking shears costs less that $20, and the edge is so keen you could almost shave with it.

4 *Police quarters/old Queen's College*

The government-funded Central School was established in 1862 to provide an education in English for promising local boys, who could then use the skill by becoming clerks and interpreters in either government or the larger firms. Most of the early students were Eurasians, though in due course they were joined by growing numbers of Chinese attracted to the school by the advantages perceived in knowing English and a few European boys whose families could not afford to educate them in Britain. The Central School moved to this site in 1889, and was renamed Queen's College.

A noteworthy early pupil of the Central School was Sun Yat-sen, who later went on to study at the Hong Kong College of Medicine and in due course became a Chinese revolutionary and 'Father of Modern China'. Another old Boy who did very well for himself was Sir Robert Hotung, who after an early career in the Chinese Maritime Customs later became compradore of Jardine, Matheson and Co. Eventually he branched out on his own, becoming one of Hong Kong's first indigenous multimillionaires and living on into his nineties. He died in 1956.

The substantial old three-storey school buildings, with Corinthian pillars and ornamental urns along the parapet were torn down when Queen's College was relocated to Causeway Bay in 1950 and the present police quarters built in their place. On the Shing Wong Street side of the site a marker plaque indicates what once was — sadly all too often the only evidence of the past to be found in older areas of Hong Kong. Queen's College still remains one of Hong Kong's most sought-after government schools, and its old boys continue to fill the higher ranks of government and the business worlds.

The Police Married Quarters have been recently sold for redevelopment, but the enormous banyan trees clinging to the retaining wall and trailing aerial roots across Hollywood Road have been here since Queen's College days; is it too much to hope for that a developer will spare them and incorporate them into the new building?

(5) *Kaifong Association*

Kaifong associations (street committees) were — and still are — found all over Hong Kong and are important indicators of grassroots public opinion. Last century members of local *kaifong* were not themselves elected by anyone at all. They were simply groups of civic-minded, status-seeking citizens resident in a particular area of the city who set themselves up and voted themselves in as a public body. Accepted or at least tolerated by the general public because they were either affluent or 'fixers', none of their 'constituents' ever actually picked them; they chose themselves. Until recently a dilapidated two-storey building stood at the lower end of Aberdeen Street. Shored up by steel girders, this was formerly the Central District Kaifong Association. The premises themselves have now been demolished, sadly just days before they were due to be photographed for inclusion in this book.

How To Get There

By Bus:	No. 13 from Central Star Ferry Pier, alight on Caine Road at the bus stop immediately after Hong Kong Baptist Church. Walk about 50 m in the direction of the traffic until you come to the junction of Caine Road and Castle Road.
By Taxi:	'Wai Seng Doh, Kam Tong Dei' ('Castle Road, Ho Kom Tong's Residence').

Battery Path
砲台里

This pleasant, attractively green area above Queen's Road Central, on the lower side of what was once called Government Hill, stretches up to St John's Cathedral, the Central Government Offices. Battery Path has changed very little in several decades, and is perhaps Hong Kong's last remaining real heritage precinct, if we define such a concept by having an integrated number of old buildings surrounded by attractive open spaces. Other areas elsewhere in Hong Kong that were once like this — Statue Square immediately comes to mind — have long since been lost to concrete and demolition squads.

Battery Path recalls the old Murray Battery, a fixed-gun emplacement overlooking the harbour located roughly where the Court of Final

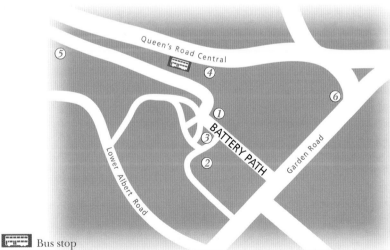

Bus stop

1 Old French Mission Building
2 St John's Cathedral
3 Roy Maxwell's grave
4 Beaconsfield Arcade
5 Central Government Offices
6 Cheung Kong Center

STREETS

Appeal now stands. This was erected in 1841, shortly after the British took possession of Hong Kong Island and named after Sir George Murray, Master General of the Ordnance from 1841–46. Still in place in 1882, when it had five gun positions, Murray Battery was removed in the late nineteenth century as the military developed newer emplacements in more remote areas. Long forgotten, the memory of this early gun battery still persists; *Pau Toi Lei*, the Chinese name of this pleasant path leading up to St John's Cathedral, means Gun Battery Lane.

Old postcards and photographs from the early twentieth century show the junction of Battery Path and Ice House Street thronged with sedan chairs, their bearers resting for a while between fares under the shade of spreading banyan trees. Those same trees are still there today, though the last sedan chair bearers vanished from the streets of Hong Kong in the early 1960s.

① Old French Mission Building (Court of Final Appeal)

Foreign missionaries frequently used the British colony as a base for their China activities, or as a rest and recuperation post for missionaries based for long periods in the interior provinces. This imposing red-brick, white-domed building was originally built as a residence for the Imperial Russian Consul in Hong Kong, and was later lived in by the *taipans* of Augustine Heard and Co., a prominent early trading firm, originally based at Canton (Guangzhou) and Macao, that went bankrupt in 1876.

In 1915 the mansion was sold to the French *Missions Etrangères de Paris* who extensively rebuilt it, adding a chapel in the north-west corner, and reopened it in 1917; a plaque above one of the doors bears this date. During these renovations a whitewashed dome was added and the building was refaced with red bricks, substantially altering its original appearance. At this time the building came to be known as the 'French Mission Building', which still persists today. The *Missions Etrangères de Paris* also had premises at Pok Fu Lam.

Immediately after the Japanese surrender in 1945, a provisional government was established by the Colonial Secretary Mr F. C. (later Sir Franklin) Gimson, with headquarters in this building. Gimson went straight from the internment camp at Stanley to Central and got the civil administration going again a fortnight before the British Fleet arrived.

After the war, the building was used as the Victoria District Court for many years, and then housed the Government Information Services for a time. It temporarily housed the High Court in the early 1980s, and is now used as the Court of Final Appeal.

(2) *St John's Cathedral*

St John's Cathedral, next to the French Mission Building on Battery Path, is another survivor from earlier times, incongruously set amongst modern tower blocks. The cathedral grounds are the only piece of land in Hong Kong with a freehold title, bestowed to the Anglican church when Hong Kong became a Crown Colony. All other land in Hong Kong is held on a variety of long-term leases. The cathedral dates from 1847, and a memorial stone on the Garden Road side records a visit by HRH The Duke of Edinburgh KG on 16 November 1869.

Inside the cathedral the large, beautifully executed, stained glass East Window was installed after the Second World War, the gift of local millionaire financier Noel Croucher. The original window had been lost during the Japanese occupation from 1941–45, when St John's Cathedral was used by the Japanese as a social club.

The South Transept houses a number of plaques and a Roll of Honour to those killed during the war years in Hong Kong. Hanging from the ceiling are the tattered remains of the Hong Kong Volunteer Defence Corps Colours, secretly buried to avoid their capture by the Japanese and only uncovered during building works in the late 1950s.

St John's Cathedral remains a popular church, with several well-attended services held each Sunday, including some in Tagalog, and the quiet, tree-shaded grounds are a peaceful, welcome respite from the jostling, noise and crowds only a few metres below on Queen's Road Central.

③ Roy Maxwell's grave

Within the grounds of the cathedral, under a spreading tree and surrounded by a low chain railing, lies the grave of Private Roy Maxwell, a local Eurasian serving in the Hong Kong Volunteer Defence Corps, who was killed in Wan Chai on 23 December 1941, two days before the British surrender to the Japanese.

Maxwell was buried here shortly afterwards by three of his fellow Volunteers who were with him when he was killed. Surrounded by a low chain-mail fence, Maxwell's is the only known grave in the cathedral precinct. Maxwell has another gravestone at Sai Wan Commonwealth War Cemetery, which records that he is buried within the cathedral grounds.

④ Beaconsfield Arcade

Beaconsfield House, immediately below Battery Path, recalled its earlier predecessor Beaconsfield Arcade, which was built by Emmanuel Ralph Belilios, a prominent early Jewish businessman and property developer who named the building after Lord Disraeli, the nineteenth-century politician and only Jew ever to become British Prime Minister. Belilios was also a philanthropist; Belilios Public School which he endowed is still in existence today.

There once stood an ornamental fountain in front of Beaconsfield Arcade, donated to the public in 1864 by the long since vanished trading firm of Dent's & Co., an early rival of

Jardine, Matheson & Co. that collapsed during a slump in 1867. The fountain was eventually removed in the mid-1930s when an earlier Hongkong and Shanghai Bank Building was demolished.

All these things are now in the distant past and almost beyond living memory now. Everything mentioned above has long since been demolished, rebuilt or forgotten, as has the successor building Beaconsfield House. These days the site of Beaconsfield Arcade is used for nothing more imaginative than a public lavatory — albeit a remarkably clean and well-situated one.

5) Central Government Offices

The East and West Wings of the Central Government Offices, just to the south-west of Battery Path, replaced the earlier Colonial Secretariat, a porticoed, high-ceilinged building from the early 1850s, that was pulled down a century later. Some of the large mature trees nearby predate the present Central Government Offices by several decades, and feature in old photographs of the area. The present buildings were designed by John Charter, a government architect who with his wife had been an internee at Stanley during the Japanese occupation.

Before 1997, the Central Government Offices grounds above Battery Path and along Lower Albert Road were completely open and the public could freely walk through to the cathedral precinct below, and mount a protest on the way through if they felt like it. High iron fences with sharply pointed railings were installed all around at the time of the handover, completely surrounding and isolating the government offices from the public, a move that left many people drawing disquieting symbolic conclusions both about the future of open government in Hong Kong and the highly defensive, bunker mentality that often seems to prevail among our leading civil servants.

6) Cheung Kong Center

One of Central's latest gleaming-new, steel and mirror-glass skyscrapers, Li Ka-shing's flagship Cheung Kong Center was designed to have a substantial area of open space surrounding it. A large banyan tree that stood near the entrance was deliberately spared, and is still there today; a large open space surrounds the very tall building, largely unshaded, forbidding-looking, and completely without trees, seats or anything to make the precinct inviting to weary pedestrians. Perhaps unsurprisingly, few want to do more than hurry through. Sit on one of the polished granite edges and security guards will hustle out and very swiftly move you on. Perhaps the idea of the design all along was to discourage idlers ...

For over 120 years this large site at the bottom of Garden Road was used as a parade ground for Murray Barracks across the road; along with the nearby cricket ground — now the concrete expanse of Chater Garden — the parade ground was one of Central's largest flat, or nearly flat, open spaces. The British military relinquished the site in the early 1960s, and the Hilton Hotel was built there.

The Hilton, popularly nicknamed the Stilton because of the unusual mottled concrete design, remained one of Hong Kong's most popular — and conveniently located — gathering places till the mid-1990s, when in turn the hotel was pulled down and Cheung Kong Center built in its place.

How To Get There

By Bus:	Buses that stop on Queen's Road Central at the bus stop behind HSBC Building – 5X, 6, 6A, 6X, 12, 12A, 12M, 13, 23A, 40M, 61, 66, 309, 681, 930, 962, A11, E11, M21 and N11.
By MTR:	Central MTR Station Exit K. Walk towards and then under HSBC Building. Cross Queen's Road Central and when you reach the bus stop, walk up the steps to Battery Path.
By Taxi:	'Pau Toi Lei, Chung Sum Fat Yuen' ('Battery Path, Court of Final Appeal').
By Tram:	Take any east-bound or west-bound tram (except those shuttling between Kennedy Town and Western Market) and alight in front of the HSBC Building, walk under it, cross Queen's Road Central and walk up the steps to Battery Path.

Sometimes it seems that Hong Kong lacks a real civic precinct, defined by open public space surrounded by genuinely impressive public buildings. The city once had such a precinct after the first major Central reclamation was completed in 1904. This created two blocks of new land between Des Voeux Road and Connaught Road. The formerly waterfront Des Voeux Road was known prior to reclamation as Praya Central, and when Connaught Road became the new waterfront, the old Praya was renamed after Sir William Des Voeux, governor of Hong Kong from 1887–91.

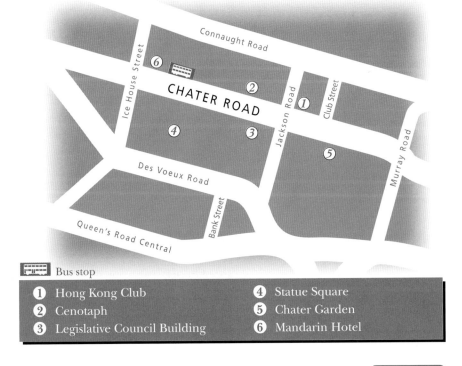

Bus stop

1 Hong Kong Club
2 Cenotaph
3 Legislative Council Building
4 Statue Square
5 Chater Garden
6 Mandarin Hotel

Chater Road

The road down the centre of the new area was named after Sir Paul Chater, the driving force behind the reclamation scheme. An Armenian businessman who came to Hong Kong in 1864 as a bank clerk, he later became a currency exchange broker and in time diversified into numerous business interests. In partnership with J. J. Keswick, Chater was co-founder of Hong Kong Land, which remains the major commercial landlord in the area.

Ardently Anglophile, Chater named the open area in the centre of his reclamation Royal Square, and commissioned a statue of Queen Victoria to grace the middle of it. In time she was joined by other British kings and queens, as well as — perhaps appropriately for a city where the civic and commercial worlds so often seamlessly blend — the Chief Manager of the Hongkong and Shanghai Banking Corporation.

Gradually Royal Square became known as Statue Square, which it remains today. The commercial buildings surrounding the square were named Prince's Building (same name, newer building), Queen's Building with a small domed tower (now the Mandarin Hotel), Alexandra Building (named after the then Princess of Wales) and the Kadoorie family's St George's Building (since replaced but still bearing the same name). When Chater died in 1926 he was eulogized as one of the city's founding fathers, and the physical shape of the city today still owes much to his combination of civic vision and an eye for the main chance.

(1) Hong Kong Club

The original Hong Kong Club was built in 1846 at the bottom of Wyndham Street and in 1897 moved to a magnificent new home on the present site. The old four-storey Hong Kong Club building had high ceilings, impressive entrance columns and broad verandahs shaded with canvas awnings with vantage points overlooking the square, the harbour and the cricket ground.

For the next eighty years the club building stood there like a relic from the Victorian era, with — according to some — social attitudes to match, for the first century of its existence the Hong Kong Club retained a

Europeans-only membership policy, which debarred Chinese, Eurasians, local Portuguese and other Asians from membership. This policy was repealed, apparently after some very heated discussion amongst the members, shortly after the end of the Pacific War.

Sadly the gracious old building was demolished in 1981 — at about the same time as so many other landmarks elsewhere in Hong Kong were lost — and replaced by the present fairly anonymous multi-storey building. The Hong Kong Club still retains four floors, as previously, with the others rented out commercially, and the original entrance arches are incorporated within the upstairs foyer of the new building.

2 *Cenotaph*

The well-built Hong Kong's war memorial is an almost exact replica of the Lutyens-designed Cenotaph in Whitehall. It was unveiled in 1923 and was facing the harbour across Connaught Road. The British Concession at Tientsin (Tianjin) also had a Cenotaph commissioned around the same time, as did the International Settlement at Shanghai, though these were removed after the communist takeover of both cities in 1949.

Initially built to commemorate the dead of the First World War, following Hong Kong's liberation from the Japanese, the dates 1939–45 were added to honour victims of the later conflict. Much later, in the 1970s, the Chinese characters meaning 'May their martyred souls be immortal, and their noble spirits endure' were carved on the side as a belated recognition that the struggle against the Japanese had been a Chinese war as well.

For some years before the handover in 1997, soldiers from the barracks at nearby HMS *Tamar* raised flags at the Cenotaph in the morning and lowered them at sunset, though this practice has been discontinued. National flags are still raised on the Cenotaph on national days. The lawns around the Cenotaph are immaculately kept, and surrounded by railings, mainly to keep off the crowds that would otherwise sit there, especially on a Sunday when the area is thronged by thousands of off-duty Filipino domestic helpers.

③ *Legislative Council Building (Old Supreme Court)*

The foundation stone of the Supreme Court was laid in 1903 by Governor Sir Henry Blake, and the extensive domed building was finally completed in 1912. Designed by the British architectural firm of Webb and Bell, the Supreme Court made extensive use of *fa gong shek*, the attractive black-flecked Hong Kong granite once extensively quarried in the hills of eastern Kowloon and around the harbour areas.

During the Japanese occupation the Supreme Court building was the Hong Kong Island headquarters of the Gendarmerie, the Japanese version of the Gestapo. Hated and feared even by the Japanese themselves, some of those who were taken into the building for questioning did not come out alive. On the Chater Garden side bullet and shrapnel damage sustained during wartime bombing raids can still be seen; badly repaired in places, the scars are still clearly visible.

The Supreme Court moved to Queensway in the late 1980s, and the building was extensively restored and renovated to house the Legislative Council. In spite of Hong Kong's retrocession to China, the Imperial Crown on the top of the dome is still there, perched on top of Hong Kong's post-colonial law-making assembly. As the building is a declared monument, it cannot be removed.

④ *Statue Square*

Statue Square half a century ago was very different in every respect from the rather grey, fume-choked area that we have today. Many mistakenly assume that the 'Statue' in the square refers to the one facing the Legislative Council, a frock-coated Victorian gentleman named Sir Thomas Jackson, at one time Chief Manager of the Hongkong and Shanghai Banking Corporation. It's a fair assumption, as Jackson's is the only statue still remaining there, but it is not the case.

The Chinese characters for Statue Square reads 'Empress' Statue Square', and recall a time when, in the middle of the square, under an ornate cupola, stood a seated bronze statue of Queen Victoria. The four quadrants of the square surrounding the statue were closely trimmed ornamental lawns and flower-beds, surrounded by low railings to keep off passers-by.

The Queen's statue was removed by the Japanese during their occupation of Hong Kong from 1941–45. After being recovered from Japan at the end of the war, she was repaired and put on a plinth in Victoria Park, where she still is today.

Immediately across Connaught Road from Queen Victoria's statue was the colonnaded entrance to the Star Ferry. In all, the square was an attractive, green civic precinct surrounded by substantial buildings fronting onto the harbour, with an uninterrupted view of the Kowloon hills beyond. The ferry piers were relocated following reclamation in the 1960s, and are soon to be relocated yet further away to the north.

⑤ *Chater Garden*

Once upon a time, what is now Chater Garden was a cricket ground — Hong Kong's smaller version of Singapore's Padang — which provided both the venue for numerous parades and civic occasions and one of the few open spaces in the city centre.

Photographs taken during the 1967 riots show the Bank of China Building behind bedecked with Mao pictures and loudspeakers blaring revolutionary slogans, while unperturbed Englishmen in immaculate cricket whites hit it for six on the lawn in front of them.

In the more socially aware spirit of the early 1970s introduced by Governor Sir Murray Maclehose (1971–82), the Hong Kong Cricket Club's exclusive use of the grounds was seen as too much a symbol of colonial elitism in the downtown area. After negotiation the club was relocated to Wong Nai Chung Gap and the grounds in Central turned over to the public. While few would dispute this admirable, civic-minded sentiment, it nevertheless is a pity that greater imagination could not have been given to the subsequent use of the space.

Instead of the green lawns of yesteryear — admittedly off-limits to the general public but nevertheless *there* — we are left today with a rather grubby concrete sitting-out area and a few dispirited-looking, diesel-blackened shrubs. Chater Garden, due to its proximity to the Legislative Council, is a popular venue for protests of all kinds, but as an attractive civic venue the site is almost completely wasted.

⑥ *Mandarin Hotel*

The discreetly elegant Mandarin Hotel was built in 1964 on the site of the old Queen's Building, and remains, arguably, Hong Kong's finest hotel. Joyce Ma, doyenne of Hong Kong's fashion scene, opened her first boutique there some thirty years ago. Along with the Peninsula, the Mandarin is Hong Kong's answer to the grand hotels in London, Paris and New York. About as conveniently located

as it is possible to get in Central, for decades film stars, ambassadors, famous authors and the simply wealthy have regarded it as a home from home. Jan Morris and Margaret Thatcher regularly stay there. Perennially popular with the denizens of the local social pages, the Mandarin at lunch-time is where the ladies who lunch go to see, be seen and compare each other's new handbags — as well as to lunch.

Dinner at the Mandarin Grill is superb, and while it is *very* expensive — even by Hong Kong standards — the experience is worth it now and then for a real treat.

How To Get There

By Bus:	Buses that stop at Chater Road Statue Square bus stop – 5, 5A, 5B, 10, 12A, 23A, 26, 40M and 103. Buses that stop at Connaught Road Central Statue Square bus stop – 29R, 47A, 70, 115, 260, 603, 619, 720, 780, 781, 788, A12 and M590.
By MTR:	Central MTR Station Exit J3.
By Taxi:	'Tse Dah Doh, Heung Kong Wui Sor Dai Ha' ('Chater Road, Hong Kong Club Building').
By Tram:	Take any east-bound or west-bound tram (except those shuttling between Kennedy Town and Western Market) and alight in front of the HSBC Building. Walk along Des Voeux Road Central towards the Legislative Council Building. Turn left into Jackson Road after walking past Legco. Walk along Jackson Road until you reach the Hong Kong Club Building.

Graham Street
嘉 咸 街

Situated directly across from the mirror-walls and constantly changing disco-light colours of The Center is Graham Street and its daily fresh food *gai see* or street-market. This narrow lane remains — for now anyway — an earthy and vital slice of the 'real' Hong Kong, rapidly vanishing in other places. Some of the buildings along this steep little backstreet have stood here for a century or more, but all of this is soon to change as the area is slated for eventual demolition and redevelopment.

Many of Central's office-workers stop off here on their way home to pick up some really fresh bean curd, fish and vegetables for dinner, instead of settling for the frequently stale produce on offer in the supermarkets.

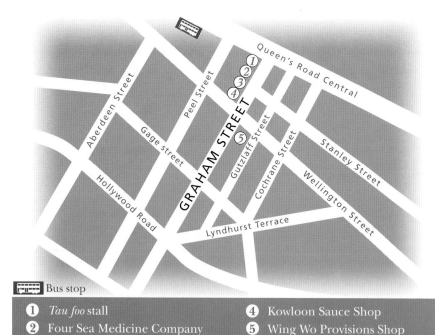

Bus stop

1. *Tau foo* stall
2. Four Sea Medicine Company
3. Frozen meat shop
4. Kowloon Sauce Shop
5. Wing Wo Provisions Shop

Graham Street is almost continually damp and slippery and it's very easy to come a cropper ambling along here. Most of the wetness comes from the stalls along the edges of the street, as the vegetables are frequently splashed down to keep them fresh in the summer heat. To this slurry is added, throughout the day, an unappealing mixture of café slops, market leavings and rubbish dropped by passers-by. By early evening, whatever the season, Graham Street is almost completely deserted, as with much of Central, as the last weary office-workers head for home and the stallholders that cater to them pack up and go.

1 *Tau foo stall*

Almost permanently clad whatever the weather in white T-shirt, grey shorts and black cloth slippers, the cheery old proprietor of this long-running stall on the corner of Graham Street and Queen's Road Central has been plying the bean curd trade here for decades; when pressed for details he says he just can't remember how many it is any more.

Ah Sook (uncle) and his cheery wife sell excellent *tau foo fa* (sometimes described as 'silken bean curd') soft bean curd, sliced in thin pieces and served with sticky home-made ginger syrup and a generous spoonful of *wong tong* (ochre-yellow, crumbled-up Chinese cane-sugar) sprinkled over the top.

Served hot or cold, the price is the same, a bargain at $5. For regular customers, the empty bowl will be filled up with sweet *tau cheung* (soya bean milk) after you've finished eating at no extra cost. They also stock various grades of fresh, pressed, dried or deep-fried bean curd, as well as bean sprouts. Quality is some of the best in the street.

② *Four Sea Medicine Company*

This little medicine shop has a remarkable array of patent medicines on display. Some are made in Hong Kong, while others are imported from Singapore, Malaysia or elsewhere. One popular remedy is Sea Coconut Cough Mixture, a bargain at $16 a bottle. The potion is manufactured in Hong Kong but has contents and instructions printed in Malay, Chinese, Tamil and English — obviously with the Singapore and Malaysian market in mind. The perennially popular Madam Pearl's Cough Mixture comes in two sizes ($12 and $16) and will both relieve that nagging cough and put you to sleep at the same time.

Menthol-based embrocation oils such as Axe Universal Oil range from a couple of dollars a bottle to under $20 for a large one that will last the average family for years. Rub it on your body to relieve aches and pains, on the head and under the nose for headaches, and on the stomach to dispel wind. It works — really! Penang-made Nutmeg Oil with a few strands of mace in the bottom of the bottle serves the same purpose, and while a little bit more expensive than the others, it certainly smells a great deal nicer.

Four Sea also stocks the usual array of pre-packaged Chinese herb mixtures and some everyday household items such as soap powder, dishwashing liquid and powdered bleach — all very competitively priced. Green nylon scouring pads for example are a bargain at $5 for a bundle.

3) *Frozen meat shop*

You can buy anything in the frozen meat line here from a few slices of luncheon ham or a chicken leg to half a bullock's worth of steaks. Much of the beef on offer comes from Brazil and is much cheaper, says one of the workers, than that obtained from Australia, New Zealand or the United States. You can just taste that disappearing Amazonian rainforest with every bite you take.

For those without environmental hang-ups, or the simply budget-conscious, a 2 kg roll of admittedly very tender Scotch fillet goes for $60, while frozen ox tongues, just the thing for making your own cold meat, are about $30 each.

If you require, the staff will happily cut a steak off the frozen slab with a broad-axe sized meat-cleaver while you wait, weigh it and take your money as you go out. Frozen fish and seafood are a major item as well, with large fillets of flounder or sole going for $12–15 each. There is a fair amount of passing retail trade, they say, but most business goes wholesale to restaurants in Central and elsewhere.

4) *Kowloon Sauce Shop*

This little shop sells their own brand of really tasty *ho yau* (oyster sauce), a snap at between $15 and $30 a bottle depending on the size, ideal for serving with some fresh greens from one of the stalls outside. In spite of repeated enquiries no one seemed to know just where the oysters came from — let's hope they were *not* plucked from the turgid waters of Deep Bay in the northwest New Territories ...

Bottles of *tau baan cheung* (yellowish fermented soya bean sauce) and *laat chiu yau* (chilli oil) stand packed in cartons in front of the shop, and none are over $10 each. Staff are friendly and also supply wholesale to the restaurant trade. They also stock a range of mainland-made *jeet cho* (black or red vinegars), the tastiest of which are made with glutinous rice, and some cooking-grade Chinese rice wines like the cheap and ever-popular Kwangtung Miju.

5 Wing Wo Provisions Shop

One of the few remaining *jaap for poh* (sundry goods shops) in the area, Wing Wo Provisions Shop still manages to do a brisk business — even when the very building is in danger of falling down around the proprietor's ears. This decrepit-looking two-storey building, now more than a century old, is shored up with iron girders on the corner of Graham and Stanley Streets. Stand under the awnings of this one at your own risk!

Various sizes and varieties of eggs are in the front of the shop, with fresh hen's eggs imported from the mainland going for $9 a dozen. Duck's eggs are slightly more. Black paste-covered *haam daan* (salted eggs), great in summer soups, and the incomparable *pei daan* (so-called 'hundred-year-old' eggs with the yolk inside rendered a gooey yellow-green) coated in dried mud and rice-husks are a dollar or so each.

Sharp-tasting, *jee geung* (pink-coloured pickled ginger, just the thing to eat with a slice of *pei daan*) is $5 a jar. Both sweet and salty varieties of *mui choy* (preserved vegetable), delicious steamed with minced pork, water chestnuts and black mushrooms, are in piles out in front, and you can buy a few pieces for dinner or an entire case of the stuff if you want.

How To Get There

By Bus:	No. 91 or No. 94 from Central Ferry Piers, alight on Queen's Road Central at the bus stop immediately after the Central Escalator. Walk against the direction of the traffic until you come to Graham Street.
By MTR:	Central MTR Station Exit D1. Turn right at the exit and walk along Pedder Street towards the junction with Queen's Road Central. Turn right into Queen's Road Central and continue walking until you reach the Central Escalator. Graham Street is on the left about 50 m further on.
By Taxi:	'Wong Hau Dai Doh Chung, Gaa Haam Gaai gaai see' ('Queen's Road Central, Graham Street market').
By Tram:	From anywhere in Central, take any west-bound tram marked 'Kennedy Town', 'Western Market' or 'Whitty Street', and alight on Des Voeux Road at the Hang Seng Bank Building. Walk towards Central Market and on its left is Jubilee Street. Walk up Jubilee Street until you reach the junction with Queen's Road Central. Graham Street market is across the road.

Hollywood Road
荷李活道

Extending from Central Police Station to Queen's Road West, Hollywood Road has a lot of interest to offer both residents and visitors. Beyond the Man Mo Temple, 'international'-flavoured Central gradually tails off and overwhelmingly Chinese Western District begins.

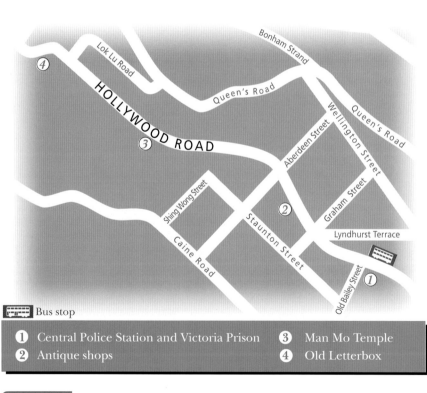

Bus stop

① Central Police Station and Victoria Prison

② Antique shops

③ Man Mo Temple

④ Old Letterbox

Gentrified somewhat since the Mid-Levels escalator opened in the early 1990s, Hollywood Road and the surrounding streets have a lot more to offer than the plethora of antique shops and cutting-edge, up-to-the-second eateries which immediately spring to mind. But all the same there are plenty of those, to suit all tastes.

Hollywood Road was built, like most major roads in Hong Kong's early years, by the Royal Engineers, and named by Hong Kong's second governor Sir John Davis after his family home at Westbury-on-Trym near Bristol, England. The naming of the thoroughfare — contrary to the tourist myth — has nothing whatever to do with the Californian film capital, but all the same it has been used for 'authentic' location shots many times over the years. Generations of tourists have felt slightly daring as they poked about in dusty antique shops in search of hidden treasures, peered into unfamiliar back alleys, and gingerly explored the Man Mo Temple's incense-darkened recesses. So this is Hong Kong ...

Hard as it may be to believe today, mid-nineteenth-century Hollywood Road had numerous attractive private residences along the eastern end, as well as a few European-staffed brothels along nearby Lyndhurst Terrace and Elgin Street, while the western end was almost a no-go zone for Europeans, leading as it did into the foul, disease-ridden Tai Ping Shan slums beyond the Man Mo Temple.

① *Central Police Station and Victoria Prison*

Central Police Station's oldest part dates from 1864 and adjoins the Victoria Prison complex on nearby Old Bailey Street.

Originally three-storey high, an additional floor was added in 1905. In 1919 a magnificent new extension was built on the Hollywood Road  frontage, classical in style, rendered in plaster and faced with specially procured red Formosan bricks. The Police Training School (now at Wong Chuk Hang, near Aberdeen) was located here from 1920–23. During the Japanese occupation from 1941–45, Central Police Station was used as the Central District headquarters of the feared and hated *Kempetai* — Japan's answer to the Gestapo.

Central Police Station has been known to generations of Hong Kong policemen as *Dai Gwoon* (big station). Lines of police uniforms can often be seen drying further in the sun, adding a homely touch to an otherwise very institutional building. The entire station complex was recently declared a monument, which means that unlike so many other historic buildings it will be preserved — at least in some form — for future generations to appreciate.

Built in the 1850s and substantially renovated since, Victoria Prison is one of Hong Kong's oldest buildings and a declared monument. Until then remote, purpose-built Stanley Prison was built in the late 1930s, Victoria Prison was Hong Kong's main lock-up, housing everyone from pickpockets to axe-murderers. And until Stanley opened, the gallows were located here as well.

In the early days turnkeys were notoriously corrupt (often ex-criminals themselves), who sometimes allowed inmates out of jail for a while if the price was right. Eventually European warders were replaced by specially recruited Indians — there are still many serving in the Correctional Services Department today.

Still very grim-looking and forbidding today behind high granite walls, Victoria Prison is now used mainly for visa overstayers and has a high South/South-east Asian and West African population. The walls along Chancery Lane, behind the prison, are topped with broken glass, a very effective method of keeping people out — or in this location inside — widely used elsewhere in Asia. From time to time, proposals are mooted to close Central Police Station and Victoria Prison and give over the site to other uses, but for now, the complex retains its original function.

(2) Antique shops

Hollywood Road's antique shops have been popular with both the curio-curious and the serious collector for decades. Merchandise on offer along Hollywood Road ranges from seriously expensive, museum-quality Ming and Ching furniture to good-quality reproductions of popular items.

Some shops stock pieces made from *huang hua lei*, the lustrous honey-coloured wood much used in north China for cabinet making, while others specialize in *shuen tsi* (blackwood), traditionally very popular among the southern Chinese both in China and in emigrant communities in South-east Asia.

Along with old posters and repro 'old Hong Kong' photographs, quite scarce and valuable books and manuscripts can still be found in some shops; more than a few gullible tourists over the years have been mightily deceived by the air of Confucian integrity and scholarly quiet that prevails in many of these places. On the other hand, many of China's cultural treasures over the years — and those of other Asian countries as well — have found their way into the hands of private collectors both in Hong Kong and abroad via Hollywood Road's antique shops and their extremely knowledgeable cabal of dealers.

Many antique shops along here stock an astonishing array of high-grade furniture and metal polishes, hard to obtain elsewhere in Hong Kong. Pure Beeswax and Turpentine Polish, for example, is $170 for a large tin, and gives a gloriously lustrous sheen to any dark wood furniture. You — or your amah — will never use the supermarket generic brands again after trying these!

3) Man Mo Temple

One of Hong Kong's enduringly popular tourist spots, permanently and photogenically wreathed in incense fumes, is the Man Mo Temple, on the corner of Ladder Street and Hollywood Road. This old temple, always popular with worshippers of all ages, is dedicated to the Gods of Literature and War.

A permanent temple building was first erected here in 1847, on a site originally granted by the government as premises for a school. Whilst the buildings were generally used as a temple, a school may also have been conducted there, as was common with temples elsewhere in China at the time.

In 1850 the building was renovated and enlarged to its present size. A later addition is the *kung sor,* or public meeting hall, which adjoins the temple next to Ladder Street and dates from 1862. The carved stone lions in the forecourt were presented to the temple, according to the inscription on their plinth, by the Pork Butcher's Guild in 1851, enduring testimony that for some at least in early Hong Kong, business was prosperous.

The newly elected Directors of the Tung Wah Group of Hospitals meet here annually to confirm their acceptance of responsibility for the welfare of the Chinese community. In assuming this responsibility the Tung Wah Hospital Committee is in fact the successor of the nineteenth-century Man Mo Temple Committee. This was composed of prominent Chinese who through their committee were able to relay community issues and concerns to the Hong Kong government, long before Chinese representation on the Legislative Council or the Secretariat for Chinese Affairs (now Home Affairs Department) existed.

A nineteenth-century Imperial Chinese plaque housed inside the temple commends the committee for its hard work and dedication assisting flood relief in China. Whenever a major natural disaster such a flood, earthquake or famine occurred on the mainland, the Hong Kong public were quick to assist and donated very generously — an underappreciated trend which has continued down to the present day.

There are a number of other Man Mo Temples in Hong Kong, including a very interesting one at Tai Po, but this remains the best-known one. Often used as a film set, scenes from the 1950s' movie *The World of Suzie Wong* were shot around here. And there are English-speaking fortune-tellers! Legions of tour buses pull up in front all day long, making the Man Mo Temple a very busy place most of the time.

4 *Old Letterbox*

Yanked out in most other locations around Hong Kong in the frenzy to be politically correct just before the handover, a few old cast-iron letterboxes like this one, that have weathered war, Japanese occupation, redevelopment all around and decades of typhoons, still precariously survive here and there in quiet corners of the city.

Until quite recently a letterbox bearing King Edward VII's Cypher stood outside the historic Man Mo Temple; placed there somewhere between 1901 and 1910, this heritage item — one of the few originals in the area — was removed without comment and replaced with the functional green box one sees there today. More a lingering vestige of the past in a city that conspicuously lacks very many than a 'humiliating symbol of another country's sovereignty', one laments that there are not a few more boxes like this one still scattered about Hong Kong's backstreets, and that more careful thought — and less pettifogging bureaucracy — went into decisions concerning their removal or retention.

How To Get There

| By Bus: | No. 13 from Central Star Ferry Pier, alight on Hollywood Road right in front of the Central Police Staton. |
| By Taxi: | 'Ho Lei Wood Doh, Chung Keui Ging Chue' ('Hollywood Road, Central Police Station'). |

An otherwise unremarkable alley running off Queen's Road Central, Duddell Street was named after two brothers, George and Frederick Duddell, early landholders in Hong Kong who relocated from Macao after the British colony was established. Both were members of the first Volunteer corps raised in Hong Kong in 1854. Frederick Duddell, and his wife Harriet, are both buried in the Old Protestant Cemetery in Macao.

Parallel to Duddell Street for part of the way uphill, Ice House Street recalls — believe it or not — a large nineteenth-century ice storage depot that formerly stood at the street's junction with Queen's Road Central. The Hong Kong Ice Company, established in 1845, sold natural ice imported in insulated vessels. The government provided the site to the company free of rent for 75 years on condition that ice was provided to hospitals at cost price. The trade in imported ice continued until 1874, when an ice manufacturing plant was established at Causeway Bay.

Little remains of these early days to remind us of this period in Hong Kong's history, except the Bishop's House above Ice House Street, the Victorian-era gas lamps on Duddell Street and the name of Zetland Street, commemorating the long-since-removed Masonic Lodge. Both were named after the Second Earl of Zetland, Grand Master from 1844 to 1870.

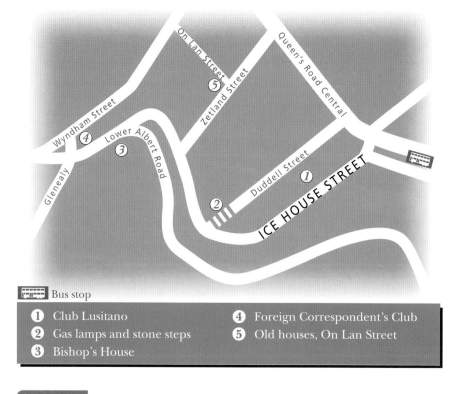

🚌 Bus stop

❶ Club Lusitano
❷ Gas lamps and stone steps
❸ Bishop's House
❹ Foreign Correspondent's Club
❺ Old houses, On Lan Street

1 Club Lusitano

The Club Lusitano, gathering place of Hong Kong's Portuguese community for over 130 years, has a longer continuous occupancy of a site than any other club in Hong Kong. Previously located in Shelley Street, the local Portuguese community have had premises (now under reconstruction)

on Ice House Street since 1866. Descendants of the original building's donors are still active members today.

As the local Portuguese community was very large in the early twentieth century, the social life of the club was extensive and popular. A Portuguese sporting club, the Club de Recreio, later opened in Kowloon and was also very popular. The new Club Lusitano building, with a prominent Portuguese cross on the roof, has recently been rebuilt.

2 Gas lamps and stone steps

Look in tourist literature promoting Hong Kong heritage and one of the must-see 'sights' of Central is this flight of stone steps at the top of Duddell Street. Somehow it seems very sad that of all that once stood in the nearby streets, these are almost all that have been preserved for the future; possessing no commercial value whatsoever, the flight of stairs was saved by default.

Attractive wrought-iron gas lamps at the top and bottom date from 1883 and are still lit every evening and maintained by Towngas, successor company to the Hong Kong and

China Gas Company that originally provided all of Hong Kong's streetlighting before electricity superceded it. Of the more than two thousand gas lamps which once lit Hong Kong's streets, over a dozen were still being used in the early 1950s.

③ Bishop's House

Official residence of the Bishop of Victoria for more than 130 years, the quietly imposing Bishop's House above Ice House Street with its distinctive round tower, now rather marred by air-conditioning boxes, is one of the oldest surviving buildings in Central. Part of the garden was used to build a Juvenile Care Centre, which opened in April 1953.

The initiative for the centre came from the socialistically inclined Bishop R. O. Hall (sometimes unkindly referred as the 'Pink Bishop' because of his humanitarian views). Finding premises unavailable and government unforthcoming with a site, he gave over part of the grounds for the building, construction of which was fully funded by local stockbroker Noel Croucher.

Ice House Street

Central

4 *Foreign Correspondent's Club (old Dairy Farm Building)*

Hong Kong has few archaeological sites of note, and almost the only ancient ruins to be seen — at least in the downtown area — are either proffering a beggar's bowl or clutching a glass around a club bar. One of the best spots in Hong Kong to view that fast-vanishing species — the 'Old China Hand' (or those who fancy that they are) — is the Foreign Correspondent's Club. The food served is rather good and reasonably priced, as are the drinks, and as the guest of a member the people-watching here is some of the most interesting in town. This is the place to go when you want to eavesdrop on those who believe that they *really* know what's happening in Hong Kong.

The off-pink stucco and red-brick detailed buildings were used for decades as cold storage and distribution premises for the Dairy Farm Ice and Cold Storage Co. Ltd. (now Dairy Farm) originally established in 1892. They were extensively renovated in 1913, which accounts for the date to seen on the Wyndham Street side of the premises. As well as accommodating the FCC and its denizens, part of the building is used for the Fringe Club, one of Hong Kong's more popular alternative theatres.

49

STREETS

⑤ Old houses, On Lan Street

Surviving more by accident than conscious plan, these balconied terrace apartments on On Lan Street date from the early twentieth century. Two are in good condition, while the others obviously require some care and attention. Perhaps a sympathetic property developer could turn these terraces into highly desirable serviced apartments right in the centre of the city, rather than just allowing them to decay further and eventually pulling them down?

How To Get There

By Bus:	Buses that stop on Queen's Road Central at the bus stop behind HSBC Building – 5X, 6, 6A, 6X, 12, 12A, 12M, 13, 23A, 40M, 61, 66, 309, 681, 930, 962, A11, E11, M21 and N11. From there, walk about 200 m in the direction of the traffic until you reach Ice House Street. Buses that stop on Ice House Street at the bus stop in front of New Henry House – 23A and 26.
By MTR:	Central MTR Station Exit D1. Turn left at the exit and walk along Pedder Street until you come to the junction with Queen's Road Central. Cross Queen's Road Central and walk against the direction of the traffic until you come to Ice House Street.
By Taxi:	'Chung Waan, Suet Chong Gaai' ('Central, Ice House Street').
By Tram:	Take any east-bound or west-bound tram (except those shuttling between Kennedy Town and Western Market) and alight on Des Voeux Road Central in front of The Landmark. Walk on The Landmark side of Des Voeux Road Central against the direction of the traffic and turn right at the first corner into Ice House Street.

This crowded thoroughfare, one of the busiest streets in Central, was named after Lieutenant William Pedder, a Royal Navy officer who arrived in Hong Kong in 1842 while serving on the gunboat HMS *Nemesis*. Pedder stayed on and was appointed Hong Kong's first harbour-master and marine magistrate. In the nineteenth century the street ended where the harbour began, at the present Des Voeux Road, and photographs dating from this time show both sides of Pedder Street lined with trees, all long since cut down.

At the junction of Queen's Road and Pedder Street there once stood a clock tower, its timepiece allegedly rather unreliable, that was donated to the colony by one-time watchmaker turned shipping magnate Douglas Lapraik; the tower remained a local landmark for decades until it was finally demolished as a traffic nuisance during the First World War. Douglas Castle, Lapraik's country house in Pok Fu Lam, still stands. A student hall of residence, it is better known today as University Hall.

In the 1920s it was possible to park one's car in the middle of Pedder Street — without charge — and cross to the now demolished Gloucester Hotel for lunch or a drink; a very different world from today's impossibly thronged pavements.

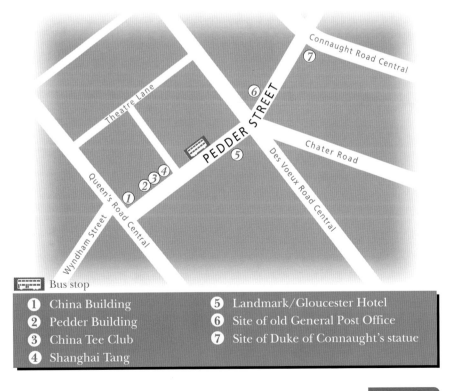

🚌 Bus stop

❶ China Building
❷ Pedder Building
❸ China Tee Club
❹ Shanghai Tang

❺ Landmark/Gloucester Hotel
❻ Site of old General Post Office
❼ Site of Duke of Connaught's statue

1 China Building

Back in the 1930s there used to be a cafe on this spot called the *Blue Bird*, a favourite rendezvous point among Hong Kong's then tiny middle class. The *Blue Bird Cafe* was locally famous for — believe it or not — ice-cream sundaes. Now an everyday item, there once was a time when eating an ice-cream was a real treat, to be indulged from time to time in comfortable surroundings with a few close friends. Until the 1940s few except the wealthy had refrigerators and instead relied on ice-chests with daily deliveries of ice to the door in large blocks. In those years there was a well-known Chinese restaurant known as *Tai Tong* found on the top floor, a popular lunch-time rendezvous for Chinese businessmen to meet and cut deals.

In place of the long-since-vanished *Blue Bird Cafe*, there is a Hongkong and Shanghai Bank branch on the corner of Queen's Road Central, housing what must be some of Hong Kong's busiest ETC machines.

2 Pedder Building

This is the very last survivor of the old pre-war office buildings that once lined either side of Pedder Street. Built in 1923, Pedder Building has somehow managed to survive when many far newer buildings in the immediate area have been levelled. The original walls were finished with Shanghai plaster, a now obsolete mixture of cement and sand. When the building was given a face-lift in 1993, it proved impossible to find artisans who could work in this medium.

Unlike many newer buildings, Pedder Building has a covered sidewalk, enabling pedestrians to keep on the move in spite of occasional cloudbursts. Anyone watching how people are forced to cower in doorways elsewhere in Central during a rainstorm will surely realize just how sensible these arcades were. Perhaps future architects will reintroduce them?

③ China Tee Club

In spite of its name, the China Tee Club high in Pedder Building is accessible to the general public. A very pleasant venue for nostalgia seekers of a sort, it is a delightful respite from the relentlessly 'international' and 'upmarket' places a few blocks away in the grubby backstreets of 'SoHo' or 'The Fong'. Gently circling ceiling fans don't significantly affect the powerful air-conditioning, and the tables and chairs are more akin to a backstreet *kedai kopi* (Straits Chinese coffee shop) in Penang or Singapore than anything that ever existed in Hong Kong. China Tee Club has a Straits-inspired menu to match, with *laksa*, satay, nasi goreng and other similar fare, all consistently good and reasonably priced.

④ Shanghai Tang

Want to fantasize for a while that it's circa 1932, you're dancing cheek-to-cheek with a slinky White Russian nightclub hostess in a smoky nightclub just off Bubbling Well Road in old Shanghai, but just don't have the gear to recreate the part? Then head straight for this place.

A commercial extension of its flamboyant cigar-smoking owner, David Tang, Shanghai Tang has certainly made an impact since its opening in the early 1990s. A brightly coloured pastiche of 1930s' Shanghai-style stereotypes, right down to the red-turbaned Sikh manning the front door, it is impossible to miss this place — even if you wanted to. Quality is high at Shanghai Tang, but then so are the prices.

Few passers-by realize that some serious old Hong Kong money is behind the venture, artfully concealed behind the nouveau-riche aura that seems to cling to the place. The owner's great-grandfather endowed the Tang Chi Ngong School of Chinese at the University of Hong Kong in the early 1930s (which is still there today and bears his name) while his grandfather Sir Tang Shui-kin was one of Hong Kong's greatest public benefactors, donating schools, clinics and hospitals, many of which bear his name as well.

⑤ Landmark/Gloucester Hotel

Back in the 1920s, at the Des Voeux Road end of Pedder Street stood the old Hong Kong Hotel, home to the bar known as the 'Gripps'. Pre-war this was Hong Kong's best-known drinking place, where sooner or later just about everyone went. The name of this long vanished local institution is perpetuated in another bar at the Omni Hong Kong Hotel on the Kowloon side, but unlike the original bar which was famous throughout the Far East, even in Hong Kong most people have never even heard of the latter one.

The Hong Kong Hotel was partially gutted in a fire in 1926 and replaced by the Gloucester Arcade and Hotel. It in turn was demolished in the mid-1970s and the Landmark complex built in its place. Gloucester Tower, one of the office blocks that make up the new complex, recalls the memory of the earlier building on the site.

⑥ Site of old General Post Office

The old red-brick and granite General Post Office, first built in 1911, was demolished in 1976. Massive Doric-topped columns that stood astride the main doors on the Pedder Street/Des Voeux Road corner ended up at Kadoorie Farm in the New Territories, where they are still to be seen today, stranded halfway up the hillside. Heavy stone fireplaces, timber panelling and flooring were ripped out and went to private houses elsewhere in Hong Kong — sad but at least better than just filling up a landfill somewhere.

Central's long-gone old General Post Office, like the old Kowloon-Canton Railway Station on the Tsim Sha Tsui waterfront, often features on tourist images depicting 'old Hong Kong', another worthwhile building lost to 'progress'. In its place we now have the black mirror-walled World Wide House, packed with small shops selling Philippine produce and remittance and freight agents.

(7) *Site of Duke of Connaught's statue*

A statue of the Duke of Connaught, one of Queen Victoria's younger sons, once stood gazing across the water at the harbour end of Pedder Street. Like so many other statues around the Central area, this one was taken down and hauled away by the Japanese during their occupation of Hong Kong and presumably melted down for scrap. Very few local residents now remember that the long dead Duke's statue ever existed, and one has to search old photographs carefully to even find a glimpse of it. Connaught Road was named after him to commemorate his visit in 1890 to invigorate the Central reclamation, and not, as the urban myth has it, the place in Ireland. Until the late 1960s' reclamation, it remained the harbourfront thoroughfare popularly known as the Praya.

How To Get There

By Bus:	Buses that stop on Pedder Street – 6, 6A, 6X, 11, 12, 12A, 13, 15, 15C, 25, 61, 64, 66, 75, 90, 90C, 97, 309, 681, A11, M21 and N11.
By MTR:	Central MTR Exit D1.
By Taxi:	'But Dah Gaai, Wah Yan Hong' ('Pedder Street, China Building').
By Tram:	Take any east-bound or west-bound tram (except those shuttling between Kennedy Town and Western Market) and alight on Des Voeux Road Central in front of The Landmark. Walk on The Landmark side of the road in the direction of the traffic until you reach the junction with Pedder Street.

Shelley Street
些 利 街

This very steep street extends up to Robinson Road from Hollywood Road and is named after A. E. Shelley, an early Hong Kong government administrator. Shelley arrived unemployed in June 1844 with vague letters of recommendation from Lord Stanley, then Secretary of State for War and the Colonies and — in the absence of anyone else suitably qualified — was soon after appointed Auditor-General. Shelley's appointment was not a great success; Hong Kong's second governor Sir John Davis described him in a report as 'dissipated, negligent, unreliable and in debt'.

Until the hillside escalator was built in the early 1990s, Shelley Street — along with other streets in the vicinity — remained just another precipitous Hong Kong Island backstreet, of little interest to anyone other than the people who lived there. The Central Escalator helped change all that, and today the once unremarkable area is the thriving home to a growing number of fashionable bars, interesting shops and high-quality cafés — all with prices to match. But how many remember that, well over a century before the aspirational term 'SoHo' was invented, Shelley Street and surrounding lanes were known by the many local Portuguese who made their homes in the lanes near the mosque as *Matto Moro*, 'Field of the Moslems'?

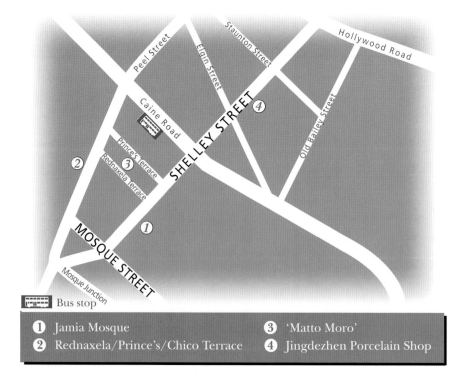

Bus stop

❶ Jamia Mosque

❷ Rednaxela/Prince's/Chico Terrace

❸ 'Matto Moro'

❹ Jingdezhen Porcelain Shop

STREETS   56

① *Jamia Mosque*

Incongruous among the tower blocks that completely surround it, the green-washed Jamia Mosque is reached through an elaborate wrought-iron gate and a flight of stone stairs.

Cool and tranquil, surrounded by a small garden and some massive old trees, this quiet old place of worship seems a world away from the ever-busy Central Escalator running up the hill alongside it. The nearby streets of Mosque Street and Mosque Junction take their name from this attractive relic of the past.

The first mosque on the site was built in 1849 and at that time was commonly known as the Lascar Temple — a name still perpetuated today in the Cantonese name *Mo Lo Miu* (Moslem's Temple).

Rebuilt and extended in 1915, the

Jamia Mosque was the first Moslem place of worship to be built in Hong Kong; there is now a much larger and more elaborate one on Nathan Road in Kowloon. For decades most worshippers here were policemen, many stationed just down the hill at the Central station on Hollywood Road. Pre-war Hong Kong had a sizeable contingent of Punjabi Moslems serving in the Hong Kong Police. Recruitment ceased after the Japanese occupation ended, and the last of them retired in the mid-1960s.

② *Rednaxela/Prince's/Chico Terrace*

Now completely rebuilt, these once dingy terraced streets running off Shelley Street provided 'cheek-by-jowl' terraced accommodation early last century for the less well-off members of Hong Kong's local Portuguese community. Mostly lacking private sanitation, this was where the 'clerical' class made their homes, a convenient walking distance to their places of employment in the business district further down the hillside.

Many of the Portuguese families who lived in this area were clerks in the leading British firms, such as Jardine Matheson and Co., and in the banks and shipping companies. In the years before the Pacific War, most of the Hongkong and Shanghai Bank's clerical staff were local Portuguese.

Their knowledge of Cantonese, and the fact that they were educated in English at a time when most of the local population were not, made them invaluable to local businesses in an intermediary role. There were not many firms of any size before the war which did not employ the Portuguese in some capacity. Others rose to prominent positions in the medical and legal professions. There were few areas of employment open to local people, except the most menial, in which they were not fully represented.

After the Kowloon peninsula was ceded to Great Britain in 1860, Tsim Sha Tsui gradually developed as an alternative place of residence. By the early twentieth century ferry services had greatly improved and many local Portuguese families moved across the harbour; gradually Chinese tenants took their place, and the Portuguese presence became a receding memory.

'Rednaxela' is Alexander spelled backwards, and the corner street sign was once a popular one for thieves to steal; replacements disappeared regularly, and no doubt a few have become 'funky' or 'eclectic' home décor items somewhere over the years.

③ 'Matto Moro'

Up until the early years of the twentieth century, it was mostly the local Portuguese who inhabited the area of small terraces extending up the hillside, between Caine and Robinson Roads, near the Jamia Mosque. Manners and habits from earlier times, with strong roots in Macao, still persisted in this area until early last century.

In the years before the First World War, some very old local Portuguese women still wore *kebaya* (a long-sleeved, Malay-style blouse), an enduring legacy of the long past Portuguese presence in Malacca. Other cultural influences that had travelled over the generations from there to Macao, and thence to Hong Kong, still found expression in people's daily lives. Women's activities centred around the home and the church, with many attending Mass twice a day in the Cathedral further along Caine Road. Generally they appeared in public wearing a *dô*, a long cape-like costume, generally black, as a general coverall. Wryly described by some as a garment designed to conceal all sins, it was very distinctive and local Portuguese women wearing it were immediately recognizable. Like *kebaya*, the *dô* had vanished by the end of the First World War.

Before relocating to Ice House Street in 1866, the Club Lusitano — Hong Kong's Portuguese club — had premises on Shelley Street below Caine Road, and was a popular meeting place for (mostly) the male members of the community. Amateur theatricals, cards, drinking and conversation were the norm; many local Portuguese were very musical, and *tunas* (recitals) and other performances were very popular.

4 Jingdezhen Porcelain Shop

Named for the famous porcelain kilns found near the town of the same name in Jiangxi Province, which has been famous for porcelain production for hundreds of years, various interesting, high-quality porcelain items can be obtained at this shop at very reasonable prices. *Famille rose* or *famille verte* coffee sets, with half a dozen small cups, coffee-pot, milk jug and sugar bowl go for $550. Teasets of all shapes and colours, attractively painted flowerpots of various sizes, along with plates of all shapes and functions are on offer. High-quality reproductions of museum-quality vases are also available, and some are very beautiful. The vivid Tang-dynasty-inspired *sancai* (three-colour) glaze ware is especially attractive; reproduction Sung celadon with its cracked green glaze remains a firm personal favourite.

Central backstreets, like Shelley Street have been popular browsing places for decades for old furniture, carved ivory, mah-jong sets, various types of porcelain and other 'curio' type items; prices are generally more competitive than in tourist areas like Tsim Sha Tsui, but with the increasing gentrification of 'SoHo' this comparative advantage, like much else in the area, seems set to change in the coming years.

How To Get There

By Bus:	No. 13 from Central Star Ferry Pier, alight on Caine Road at the bus stop immediately after Hong Kong Baptist Church. Walk back to the Central Escalator and go uphill until you reach the mosque.
By MTR and Central Escalator:	Central MTR Station Exit D1. Turn right at the exit and walk along Pedder Street towards the junction with Queen's Road Central. Turn right into Queen's Road Central and continue walking until you reach the Central Escalator. Go up the Central Escalator until you reach the Jamia Mosque.
By Taxi:	'Boon Saan Keui, Mo Lo Miu Gaai' ('Mid-Levels, Mosque Street').

Hong Kong has two 'Albert Roads', Upper and Lower. These winding roads, criss-crossing what was once known as Government Hill, were named after Queen Victoria's Consort Prince Albert of Saxe-Coburg-Gotha. Most of the buildings located on them are for 'Establishment' use, a rare continuity with the past not often found in other parts of Hong Kong.

Government Hill extended — as it still does — between Garden Road on the east and Glenealy ravine to the west, and was used for government offices, St John's Cathedral (then the Established Church), Government House and senior government staff quarters. More spacious and unhurried than the business areas below, Upper and Lower Albert Roads tend to symbolize the differences in outlook between commercial and administrative Hong Kong.

The Central Government Offices on Lower Albert Road (formerly the Colonial Secretariat) have occupied the same site since the early 1850s, as has Government House on the rise above it, though there are plans to eventually build a large new government offices complex somewhere on the massive new Central reclamation.

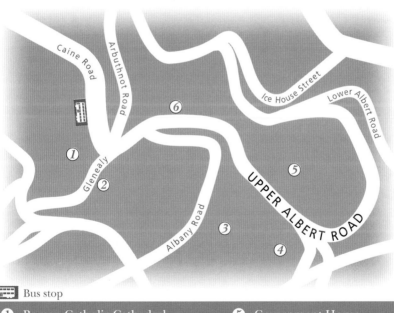

🚌 Bus stop

1. Roman Catholic Cathedral
2. Glenealy
3. Zoological and Botanical Gardens
4. Memorial Gate at Botanical Gardens
5. Government House
6. Church Guest House

① Roman Catholic Cathedral

The Roman Catholic Cathedral of the Immaculate Conception at the western end of Upper Albert Road, built in 1888, replaced a much earlier, smaller building at the junction of Pottinger and Wellington Streets. For years the Roman Catholic Cathedral's whitewashed tower was a prominent local landmark, but is now almost totally obscured by the Caritas buildings fronting onto Caine Road below.

Most early parishioners here were local Portuguese, who lived on the hillside terraces off Shelley Street near the Jamia Mosque known among themselves as *Matto Moro*. Many were very devout, especially the women, and attended church services several times a day. Otherwise the Roman Catholic community in Hong Kong was quite small, with relatively few British members. In addition to the local Portuguese, there were a number of Irish Catholics in the congregation. Irish orders were prominent in education, and Jesuits from Ireland were very active in local educational institutions such as Wah Yan College.

For well over a century, right up until the 1960s, Hong Kong remained an Italian bishopric, and the Italian missionary contribution to Hong Kong, especially in the field of education, remains quite pronounced to this day. The Sacred Heart Canossian College, very close to the Roman Catholic Cathedral along Caine Road, was until 1937 named the Italian Convent and it is still known by this name among many older residents. The land upon which it was built was donated to the church by the prominent local Portuguese d'Almada é Castro family in 1860.

For many years the Italian Convent contained three different schools, one English, one Portuguese and one Chinese. The Chinese school was completely independent of the others and until 1941 was known as Pui Ching School. After 1945 Pui Ching merged with the others into one school which took boarders until about 1960. The attractive, expansive 115-year-old convent was demolished in 1976 and replaced by functional new buildings, completely lacking any of the character and grace of the old.

② *Glenealy*

Glenealy, the steep path leading down from Robinson Road to Wyndham Street was known in the early days as Elliot's Vale, a rare reminder of Captain Charles Elliot, the man behind the British occupation of Hong Kong in 1841. The name commemorating Hong Kong's founder didn't stick for long however, and by the 1880s the ravine had become known as Glenealy — as it still is today — after a private house that once stood on the site of today's Roman Catholic Cathedral.

These days no one remembers the previous designation Elliot's Vale at all, and the only commemoration of the long-since-demolished Glenealy itself is the name of this shady path down through the ravine into the city. Elliot himself has no memorial in the city he helped found, either in street name, mountain, building or statue, and as far as modern Hong Kong is concerned, it is as though this much-maligned man never even existed.

③ *Zoological and Botanical Gardens*

First established in 1861, the Hong Kong Botanical Gardens — like others created around the same time at Penang, Singapore, Ceylon and elsewhere in Asia — were originally set up to determine what plants could best grow in the local soil and climate. In time, all became places of considerable beauty as well as valuable open spaces for the growing cities.

After generations of deforestation by villagers Hong Kong did indeed appear in the early 1840s, as British Prime Minister Lord Palmerston dismissed it, as a 'barren rock with hardly a house upon it'. However, by the late 1920s most of the formerly denuded hillsides have been changed into a heavily wooded hiker's delight. Most of these early plantings were cut for firewood during the Pacific War, but have since gradually been replanted.

The Botanical Gardens eventually became a popular recreational facility for the general public, which they remain to this day. An ornamental wrought-iron bandstand located on the upper level paid for by the Parsee community was one

STREETS

of the most popular features in the nineteenth century, with military bands from nearby Victoria Cantonment providing free entertainment to strolling visitors on Sunday afternoons.

These days the gardens are very popular with early morning walkers, *tai chi* practitioners and office-workers who escape to the relative quiet of the gardens from the teeming streets a few blocks below. The Botanical Gardens also houses a small and well-kept zoo with an amazing pink flamingo enclosure and what must be one of the world's biggest — or rather fattest — captive orangutans, named Datu.

(4) *Memorial Gate at Botanical Gardens*

The inscription on this Torii-shaped memorial gate at the lower entrance of the Botanical Gardens records Chinese loyalty to the Allied cause during the Second World War. In some respects the inscription can be seen as a barbed reference to shifting loyalties, as many socially prominent people, including several Executive and Legislative Council members, remained anything but constant to the erstwhile government, collaborating as enthusiastically with the Japanese as they ever had with the British before them.

Knighthoods and other British honours were conveniently ignored and sedulously not used, yet when peace came in 1945 and the British returned, the local elite changed their spots once

again and were for the most part reinstated into their former positions; proving that as far as the local power-brokers are concerned, some things in Hong Kong never change.

⑤ *Government House*

Hong Kong's first purpose-built Government House was erected on this site in 1851 and was designed by Charles St George Cleverly, Government Surveyor in the 1850s. Prior to that date the governor lived in rented accommodation in various other places including, for a time, Spring Gardens in Wan Chai.

Government House formerly enjoyed a commanding view of the harbour and town below before it was hedged in by tower blocks and flyovers. By the mid-1930s the original building, battered by decades of typhoons and infested with dry-rot, beetles and borers, was rapidly becoming unstable; some exterior walls were even shored up with girders. Plans were made to demolish the building, turn the site over to commercial uses and relocate Government House to another site higher up on Magazine Gap.

The Pacific War intervened before a final decision could be made, and in 1942 the Japanese demolished the crumbling structure and rebuilt it in their own style, though mainly retaining the original floor plan. The gatehouses are original; still being structurally sound they were retained and incorporated into the new complex.

The Japanese fitted out Government House with Formosan pine panelling, *tatami* mats, *shoji* screens and other quintessentially Japanese decorative features, which the pre-war governor Sir Mark Young, returning to Hong Kong after over three years as a prisoner-of-war, ordered removed. Since then an English 'country house' décor has largely prevailed, with some attractive *chinoiserie* added by Chris Patten during his tenure in office.

A purpose-built, fully integrated world unto itself, Government House has a communications centre, hotel-style kitchens, private and public rooms, offices, tennis courts and extensive, beautifully maintained grounds. With the dagger-like, I. M. Pei-designed Bank of China Building poised at it, Government House now also has atrocious *fung shui;* a reason that was advanced for so many political problems in the late colonial era, and allegedly the reason why the present Chief Executive Tung Chee-hwa chooses not to live there.

6 Church Guest House

Popular author Han Suyin once lived here, and vividly described both the building and its occupants in her autobiographical novel *A Many Splendoured Thing,* set in Hong Kong in the late 1940s. In those days foreign missionaries were slowly being squeezed out of China by the communists, and many initially stayed here on their arrival in the colony before finding other homes or moving overseas.

Church Guest House remains a rare reminder of what many old apartment houses in the area once looked like, in the days before high-rise blocks turned the pleasant tree-lined roads of the Mid-Levels into fume-filled concrete canyons. Still owned by the Anglican diocese, some of the apartments are rented for residential use, while others are used as Diocesan offices.

How To Get There

By Bus:	No. 13 from Central Star Ferry Pier, alight on Caine Road at the bus stop immediately after Caritas House. Walk back towards Caritas House and turn right.
By Taxi:	'Geen Doh, Ming Oi Chung Sum' ('Caine Road, Caritas House').

Just one street behind Queen's Road Central, Wellington Street — named for the Iron Duke — is a different world to the 'international' areas a short distance away; for those who feel that there isn't much left to experience of the 'old Hong Kong', a stroll along this interesting backstreet

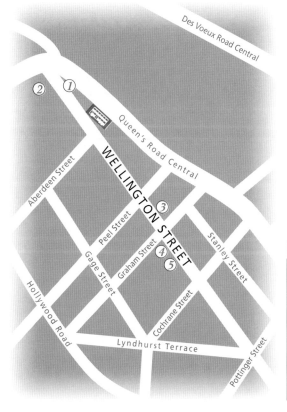

Bus stop

1. Public bathing facilities
2. Old houses
3. Wing Cheung Ivory and Majong Shop
4. Wah Fung *Siu Laap* (roasted meat) Shop
5. Backstreet scenes

should convince them otherwise. But watch out for some of the minibuses when you're ambling along here — they drive like utter maniacs and seem to regard pedestrians as fair game!

Wellington Street is one of Central's oldest thoroughfares, and — remarkably for a demolition-crazed place like Hong Kong — there are quite a few old buildings still standing along here; it also retains a completely Chinese feel, quite unlike the 'international' flavour that is rapidly developing a few streets further up the hillside. At the eastern end of Wellington Street lies Lan Kwai Fong with its bars, restaurants and endless etcetera. Towards the Western end, only a few hundred metres away, a quite different world awaits.

(1) *Public bathing facilities*

For all the noise we hear these days about Hong Kong being a modern, international, 'world' city, there are still many aspects of Hong Kong life that remain completely — and given the SAR's wealth shamefully — of Third World standards. Public sanitation is perhaps the most obvious of them. Many crumbling old tenement houses — like these on the corner of Wellington Street and Queen's Road Central (see below) still lack even basic indoor sanitation.

Public lavatories and bathhouses were first built in the 1920s in tenement areas to improve sanitation and reduce the spread of epidemics, and were constructed underground in a few places to help conserve space. Some have since been filled in, but others, like this one located right in the business heart of 'Asia's World City', still serve a vital community function.

2 Old houses

Right at the junction of Queen's Road Central and Wellington Street a few tenacious survivors from the past somehow manage to hang on. With narrow balconies filled with washing, plants and household junk, these decrepit pre-war tenements still provide homes for people, even if they *are* shored up with iron girders to prevent them from collapsing. An absence of bathing facilities in these buildings — there is no interior sanitation — isn't a great problem as the public facilities are located just across the street.

3 Wing Cheung Ivory and Majong Shop

The international trade in ivory has been banned for quite a few years now, but wander along here and you'd be immediately forgiven for thinking otherwise! And if the shops can't get any more ivory, then where *does* the abundant profusion of very new-looking ornaments come from? Ask the staff in the shops along here and they'll tell you that they're 'using up old stocks'. Hmmm ... Make up your own minds on that one!

Long, elegantly carved cigarette holders — you'll feel like Noel Coward with one of these — go for $160 or so. They also do a wide variety of bone-carving as well — much more ecologically sound these days than ivory. An attractively carved cow-bone mah-jong set backed with bamboo goes for $350 or so — a little less if you haggle.

4 Wah Fung Siu Laap (roasted meat) Shop

Selling crispy *siu yuk* (roasted pork), juicy *char siu* (red barbequed pork) and abundantly calorific *siu ngor* and *siu ngaap* (roasted goose and duck) *siu laap po* (roasted meat shops) like this one are found all over Hong Kong. As it's reasonably priced and there is no preparation involved, there would be few families that didn't eat *siu laap* with the evening *soong* (dishes to go with the rice) at least occasionally.

Wah Fung roasted meat shop on Wellington Street is a long-established concern and the roasted meat on offer is of excellent quality and reasonably priced. One of the cheapest items are roasted pork bones which go for about $10 or so for a few. Simmered for a few hours with *choy gon* (dried kale) these bones make an excellent and very healthy family soup.

5 Backstreet scenes

Wander up a backlane off Wellington Street and you're likely to find well-tended pot-plants, overhanging balconies and a remarkably village-like feeling, quite at variance with the fact that it's right in the heart of one of the planet's most densely

populated urban conurbations. These
back corners are perhaps one of Hong
Kong Island's most unlikely and
pleasing sights, but few ever seem to
venture in and notice them.

How To Get There

By Bus:	No. 91 or No. 94 from Central Ferry Piers, alight on Queen's Road Central at the bus stop immediately after the Central Escalator. Walk in the direction of the traffic until you come to the corner of Queen's Road Central and Wellington Street.
By MTR:	Sheung Wan MTR Station Exit A2. Turn left at the exit and walk along Wing Lok Street until you reach the junction with Man Wa Lane. Turn right at the junction and walk along Man Wa Lane until you reach the junction with Bonham Strand. Turn left and keep walking until you reach the junction of Bonham Strand, Queen's Road Central and Wellington Street.
By Taxi:	'Wong Hau Dai Doh Chung, Sun Gei Yuen Kwong Cheung' ('Queen's Road Central, Grand Millennium Plaza').
By Tram:	From anywhere in Central, take any west-bound tram marked 'Kennedy Town', 'Western Market' or 'Whitty Street', and alight on Des Voeux Road Central near Sincere's Department Store. Turn into Wing Wo Street and walk towards the junction with Queen's Road Central.

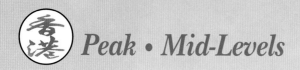
Hung Heung Lo, meaning Red Incense Pot, was a name given to Hong Kong Island in the eighteenth century. Victoria Peak is sometimes described in Cantonese as *lo fung* (incense bowl's peak), hence Victoria Gap is known as Lo Fung Hap (Incense Bowl Gap).

British colonies developed hill-stations wherever possible, as a refuge from the lowland heat and the tropical diseases that claimed so many lives. In spite of its small size, Hong Kong was no exception. Starting in the 1860s, wealthy Europeans began building bungalows or summer houses near the sea at Pok Fu Lam, to escape the heat and congestion of the city after office hours. In time the Peak District, 1,200 feet above sea level, became more popular and many built houses there instead. Other than on foot, the only means of getting to and from the Peak was to journey up and down by sedan chair and so every Peak resident kept one. Not to be outdone, eccentric Jewish entrepreneur Emmanuel Ralph Belilios (whose first home stood on the site of Peak Galleria) was kept supplied with necessities by pack-camel.

The Peak was the local answer to Simla, summer capital of British India, and developed a rarefied atmosphere that aimed to match it on a smaller scale. Living there came to symbolize social arrival in colonial days, and in many suburban minds it still does. From 1867 until after the Pacific War, the governor had a home there, right at the summit. At the very apex of the colony, at its highest geographical point, stood Mountain Lodge, the governor's summer residence.

Right from the start, Mountain Lodge was not a great success. Plagued with fog and damp for half the year, it was frequently damaged by the typhoons that came every summer. Remote, isolated and difficult of access, its only advantage was the refreshing change of climate it offered in the days before fans or air-conditioning. Many of the governor's wives in particular hated it. They felt isolated by the remoteness of the house, before the Peak became built-up, and were disturbed at night by the winds that howled around the bare scrubby hills.

The governor's hill-station residence went through three separate incarnations. The first Mountain Lodge was a three-roomed bungalow, forming part of the military sanatorium. The next, purpose-built in 1867, was in the architectural style popularly described as 'Wild West Swiss'. Of timber construction with elaborately fret-worked shutters and eaves, it resembled the hill-station residences then being built everywhere from Mussourie to Penang, and still to be seen in these places today. It was promptly attacked by termites, periodically damaged by typhoons, and finally demolished as unsafe in 1897.

The last Mountain Lodge, like its predecessors, was not very well-built. As with Government House in the city below, a combination of shoddy materials and the climate gradually took their toll. By the 1930s both buildings were in a very unstable condition. Mountain Lodge, being much more exposed to winds and damp, was in a particularly bad way; it was infested with wood-borers, bugs and beetles, it often stood unused for months on end. The governor's other alternative residence, Fanling Lodge in the New Territories, was much preferred by this time. Surrounded by pleasant open country and right near the golf course, it came to be used far more than the Peak house for weekend breaks away from town.

One governor who did maximize use of Mountain Lodge was Sir Frederick Lugard, the distinguished African administrator who lived in Hong Kong from 1907 till 1912. His wife, the well-known journalist Flora Shaw, described her first view of the house by sedan-chair, moving '... up and up round the sides of the rocky but flower-covered hills, through pure air which grew cooler every moment, across little dips and cuttings each giving us a more exquisite view than the last of seas and islands, till finally we were marched abreast through the gates'. Lugard pronounced his hill retreat 'exquisitely situated with views of green islands set in a blue sea far below'. Both were clearly captivated, as many have been, by the great natural beauty of Hong Kong. But even that had its drawbacks. 'It is dreadfully damp,' he continued, 'worse than Nigeria in the rains, envelopes all glued together, and cigars like bits of sponge.'

When Governor Sir Mark Young returned to Hong Kong in 1946 after being a prisoner of war, he made inquiries about the renovation of Mountain Lodge. The advice he received from the Public Works Department indicated that the building was beyond repair, and 'the rehabilitation of Mountain Lodge would be perpetuating an out-of-date, uncomfortable and expensive house'. Mountain Lodge was demolished, contrary to the urban myth that the Japanese destroyed it, but the foundations are still there today, along with the gatehouse and remains of the gardens.

In 1885, The Hong Kong High-Levels Tramway Co. was incorporated to link

STREETS

the city with Victoria Gap, and in 1888 the line was completed, greatly improving access to the city below; unfortunately the following year the tracks were partially destroyed by torrential rains and landslides but repaired soon afterwards. The funicular railway was the first tramway to be built in Hong Kong: trams were not introduced into the urban areas for another sixteen years. A second funicular route was proposed before the First World War to cope with increased traffic, but the rapid introduction of motor vehicles defeated the scheme. Originally steam-powered, the tramway was eventually electrified and, for more than a century, the Peak Tram has remained one of Hong Kong's most popular attractions for both domestic and overseas visitors.

Situated at Victoria Gap where the Peak Tower stands today, the Peak Hotel, 1,250 feet above sea level, commanded extensive views of the teeming harbour, the mountains on the mainland New Territories and the islands; it also had a branch in town, known as the Victoria Hotel. Under joint Parsee–Chinese ownership, the manager in the 1890s was nevertheless a European, William Farmer.

The Peak Club began in temporary accommodation in 1893 and in 1902 moved to permanent premises on Mount Austin Road. Open to British men and women of the 'right type', the Peak Club soon became a popular rendezvous for tea dances and bridge parties. Sir Thomas Jackson, then Chief Manager of the Hongkong and Shanghai Banking Corporation — a statue of him stands in Central — was behind the Peak Club's establishment and served as its president until his retirement in 1902.

One contemporary writer described the views from the Peak as overlooking 'brown, arid-looking hills of the mainland ... [and the Pearl River Delta's] wide expanse of blue water set with opalescent-looking islands, [which] stretches as far as the eye can reach'. Hilly terrain and striking natural beauty — still so much in evidence today — saw walkers briskly striding along Peak-side paths before breakfast, walking stick in hand and dog at heel, as much part of the landscape as they would be in Surrey.

'Betty', an entertaining — if pseudonymous — chronicler of European life in Hong Kong, described the Peak and the suburban snobbery that developed there in 1905; 'a would-be mountain, dotted over with bungalows and villas, where live the elect ... The Peak looks down on everything and everybody. The lower levels look up to the Peak.' Some contemporary observers might aver that while the buildings have mostly changed, little else has since then.

In *A Many Splendoured Thing*, her autobiographical novel set in Hong Kong, Han Suyin acidly wrote of its European residents: 'Their aim is to attain that chimerical upper stratum of birth and financial security which only exists in the English middle-class mind, but which, in the Colony, is still so doubtfully symbolized by that eminence called THE PEAK.'

One of Hong Kong's most persistent myths, like pre-war Shanghai's infamous, completely non-existent 'No Dogs or Chinese' signpost, is that before the Pacific War Chinese were not allowed to live on the Peak. Potent symbols of 'colonial racism' such as this one are more often remembered in Hong Kong than the often rather different facts from which they derive.

The 1890s had seen serious bubonic plague outbreaks in Hong Kong, epicentred around the overcrowded, filthy Tai Ping Shan tenements where little effective government control existed over sanitary matters. Partly as a result, in 1904, the Peak Reservation Ordinance was gazetted, introduced principally to guarantee that only European-style (meaning detached) residences were built. Building restrictions by extension meant that better sanitary measures would be maintained. This was especially important as mosquitoes breeding areas — malaria was a scourge of Hong Kong in those times — and other infectious diseases such as cholera and plague bubonic, were difficult to control in densely packed areas. It was further explained that, 'The reservation of this district is desirable ... that a healthy place of residence may be preserved for all those who are accustomed to a temperate climate and to whom life in the tropics presents the disadvantage of an unnatural climate.'

The ordinance further stated that: 'It shall be lawful for the Governor-in-Council to exempt any Chinese from the operation of this Ordinance on such terms as the Governor-in-Council shall think fit.' In later decades, these included such personalities as China's First Lady Madame Chiang Kai-shek, who also lived on the Peak for a time just before the Japanese invasion.

By 1904 the Peak had developed into a purely European area which further exaggerated the separation of the European population to a greater degree than had been the case in the colony's early years; the ordinance effectively formalized what had already taken place, and further segregated the European and Chinese sections of the population.

In time the only non-Europeans who spent the night on the Peak were servants, labourers and the millionaire Sir Robert Hotung and his family — and they were Eurasians, *not* Chinese. Hotung's family home, *The Falls*, still stands in extensive gardens just below Victoria Gap.

Europeans living on the Peak led a somewhat schizophrenic existence: spending the day in the overwhelmingly Chinese, yet still socially segregated, world of work in the city below, and returning at night to a very English 'Peak-side' world, far removed in every way from life lived several hundred feet below. It was also an abnormal world, principally composed of children, young and middle-aged males, married women and a few grown-up daughters brought out at a marriageable age, with few elderly residents; as now, most Europeans tended to leave Hong Kong on retirement. And for many European residents, however long they lived in Hong Kong, the Peak was virtually the only part they ever really knew.

Mid-Levels

Extending from the Caine Road–Bonham Road level as far up the precipitous hillside as May Road, the Mid-Levels (*boon shan kui*) have for well over a century been one of Hong Kong's most desirable places to live.

Hong Kong's physical geography can sometimes be seen as an allegory for its social life; the higher one gets up the hill, the more rarefied the atmosphere becomes in every respect. Mid-Levels was where the merely wealthy lived; unlike the Peak which was de facto a European enclave — with the exception of the wealthy Eurasian Hotung family — the Mid-Levels had a much more racially mixed population. Armenian businessman Sir Paul Chater's palatial mansion Marble Hall, overlooking the city from its eminence above Conduit Road, was perhaps

the most impressive private home in Hong Kong in its time. There were numerous other substantial houses — Parsees like H. N. Mody, endower of the University of Hong Kong, as well as wealthy local Portuguese, Chinese, Europeans, Sephardic Jews and a few Indians all made their homes here.

Until the late 1950s, the Mid-Levels was a place of winding tree-lined roads with gracious mansions set on terraced gardens, all with spectacular views of harbour, islands and the city below. One author described the night view of harbour lights and neon as being like 'the hoard of a jewel-thief'.

Gradually as the demand for property became more acute, the old mansions were sold for redevelopment and apartment blocks were built in their place. Some were reasonably attractive; many were ugly and anonymous, built with an eye to a swift return for — after all — who knew what the future would bring. Almost none of the old Mid-Levels houses still remain, and many of the earlier apartment blocks have in turn given way to newer tower complexes, each one flashier and more pretentious than the last.

During the property-crazy mid-1990s, it seemed easier to buy an apartment or hire a maid than get a loaf of bread along these roads; that frenzy seems to have subsided somewhat these days as property prices have dropped. The rapid pace of development has diminished the area's attractiveness over the last thirty years, but while several other parts of Hong Kong have become just as desirable an address and far more expensive, Mid-Levels still remains, for many, the only *possible* place to say that they live.

Part of the reason for the area's continued popularity is the close proximity to Central, a fifteen-minute walk — though few Mid-Levels residents ever *do* walk — or a few minutes by car. The Central Escalator, linking Queen's Road Central with Conduit Road, did much to transform the once unfrequented backstreets above Hollywood Road, but has not significantly reduced traffic congestion in the Mid-Levels at all, despite that aim being one of the main reasons behind its construction in the first place.

This gently meandering stretch of hillside road must be one of Hong Kong Island's most popular — because easiest — walking trails. On a clear day, Bowen Road has wonderful views of the harbour and the Kowloon hills beyond. Continue along Bowen Road on to Black's Link for stunning views of the southern islands, or turn and head steeply uphill along Wan Chai Gap Road to the Police Museum and on to the Peak.

Bowen Road is named for Sir George Bowen, governor of Hong Kong from 1883–85. Colonial administrators got around the world a lot in those days; prior to his service in Hong Kong, Sir George Bowen was governor of Queensland, where a town on the northern coast — justly famed for the excellence of its mangoes — is named after him.

① Bowen Road Hospital

Built in 1903, this massive red-brick three-storey building at the junction of Bowen and Borrett Roads has been a local landmark seen from the harbour ever since. Bowen Road Hospital even stayed in use as a functioning military hospital — still

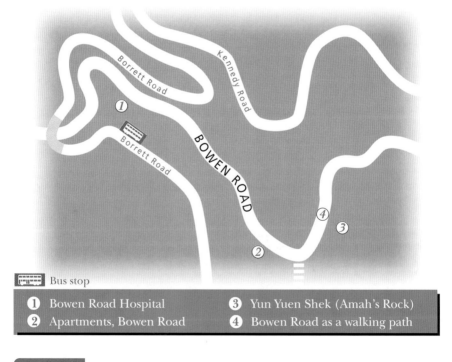

Bus stop

| ❶ Bowen Road Hospital | ❸ Yun Yuen Shek (Amah's Rock) |
| ❷ Apartments, Bowen Road | ❹ Bowen Road as a walking path |

staffed by British Army personnel — right through the Japanese occupation until March 1945. It remained in continual use as a British Military Hospital until 1967. For many years afterwards the buildings were used as premises for Island School, one of the English Schools Foundation's leading secondary schools, now located in new premises across the road.

The imposing stone gatehouse and steps on Bowen Road are almost completely overgrown with bougainvillaea and vines these days, making the steps up to the hospital buildings look like a wall at Angkor Wat, slowly giving way to buttressed roots. Sympathetically restored and refurbished, the ex-BMH building would make a wonderful museum or exhibition space, and a preservation order has recently been placed upon it.

2 *Apartments, Bowen Road*

Residential apartments on Bowen Road are highly sought after, as the road is quieter than most of the Mid-Levels due to no through traffic. Blocks of flats are mostly built on the foundations of older houses demolished in the 1950s and 1960s — and often the stone stairs leading up to them and part of the retaining walls are original. One attractive old house still remains standing along Bowen Road; partly hidden by shrubbery and guarded by barking dogs and equally ferocious amahs, it must be a wonderful and secluded place to live.

(3) Yun Yuen Shek (Amah's Rock)

The access path up the 'Amah's Rock' has now been closed off, as it is deemed 'unsafe', along with the slope nearby. A number of these 'Amah's Rocks' look out over the sea elsewhere in Hong Kong; two other well-known examples are at Sha Tin and Lamma.

Legends endlessly retold in generations of tourist literature record heart-rending village tales; of anxious fisherman's wives who come up to these high vantage points to watch for their husband's return home from the sea. The unstoppable torrent of grief and weeping that followed when she learned her *lo gung* (old man) would return no more turned the poor lass to stone.

A good tale to be sure, and the tourists love it. But the shape of the rocks themselves — they are all remarkably phallic-looking — combined with the earthy humour of peasants everywhere, point towards a much more basic original version; 'Waiting for Husband' stones? Work it out for yourself!

(4) Bowen Road as a walking path

Bowen Road is very popular with walkers, be they the vigorous early-morning, this-is-good-for-me walker, the gentle afternoon stroller or the tuned-out, listening-to-the-Walkman variety. Scenic, easy to get to and from, and for the most part fairly level, a turn along here represents exercise without too much effort. Dog-owners use it in droves as well, but unfortunately seldom clean up after their charges; perhaps the mysterious and still uncaught 'Bowen Road poisoner' simply stepped on one dog-turd too many and lost it ...

5) *'Matilda', Bowen Road and perceptions of social arrival in Hong Kong*

For some at least, Bowen Road wasn't quite the most desirable address in town early last century, as this little rhyme from the period neatly illustrates. A telling statement about suburban snobbery in Hong Kong, the only fault that could be found with a Bowen Road address was its altitude relative to the Peak.

> *Before she arose to the Peak*
> *Matilda was timid and meek,*
> *But she now condescends*
> *To her Bowen Road friends*
> *With a smile that is cutting and bleak.*

How To Get There

By Bus:	Minibus No. 9 from Central Star Ferry Pier, alight in front of the Carmel School on Borrett Road.
By Taxi:	'Bo Loh Doh, Yau Tai Gaau Kwok Tsai Hok Hau' ('Borrett Road, Jewish International School').

Named for the water pipeline (or conduit) that runs along this level of the hillside from Pok Fu Lam Reservoir, Conduit Road is one of Hong Kong's more desirable addresses, though a brief wander along here does make one wonder why, as apartment blocks along Conduit Road — and elsewhere in the Mid-Levels — can be described as

being like 'a fur coat and tattered knickers'; meaning head-turningly opulent on the outside, and disappointingly tawdry beneath.

Cracked, roughly laid concrete sidewalks lead to ornate gold-painted gateways that would almost put Windsor Great Park to shame and grand, hotel-style marble foyers gradually give way, after you've gone up in the lifts out of public view, to poky, poorly designed flats with all too often a multimillion-dollar view over — you guessed it — another monolithic block of flats.

The Hillside Escalator terminates here after snaking its way up from Queen's Road Central and even though it was meant to alleviate traffic, Conduit Road can

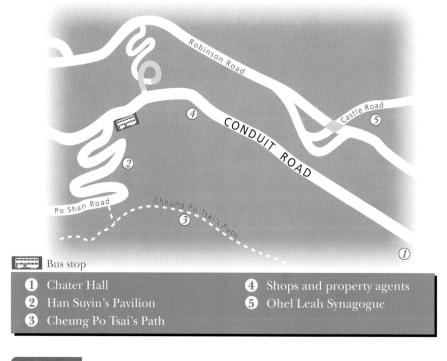

Bus stop

① Chater Hall

② Han Suyin's Pavilion

③ Cheung Po Tsai's Path

④ Shops and property agents

⑤ Ohel Leah Synagogue

still get quite congested along here at rush hour; most residents would be completely lost without taxis or private cars.

Perhaps hard to believe today, until the 1950s this then scenic stretch of mountainside road was notable for breathtaking views in every direction and numerous attractive pre-war mansions, all set in large terraced grounds overlooking the harbour. Gradually throughout the 1960s these gracious reminders of earlier, less-hurried times were torn down to make way for today's anonymously flashy tower blocks, and almost none of them now remain.

Peak • Mid-Levels

(1) *Chater Hall*

This rather unremarkable block of government flats was once the site of what was probably Hong Kong's most magnificent private house, Marble Hall, home of Armenian businessman Sir Paul Chater. Born in Calcutta, Chater came to Hong Kong in 1864 as a young man and lived here till his death in 1926. Involved in numerous commercial enterprises, perhaps his most lasting memorial is Central's large open area Statue Square, and Chater Road which bears his name.

Built in the late nineteenth century, Marble Hall was faced with marble and fitted out extensively within with the same substance. Under the terms of Chater's will, Marble Hall and most of its contents was bequeathed to the Hong Kong government but could be used by his widow for as long as she wished to live there. Despite Lady Chater's permanent departure from Hong Kong in the late 1920s, the bequest did not finally take effect until her death in 1935.

Following its takeover by the Hong Kong government, the building was used by the Royal Navy as the residence of its Commander-in-Chief, China Squadron, until the outbreak of the Pacific War. Badly damaged by fire not long after the Japanese surrender in 1945, Marble Hall stood semi-derelict for several years and was finally demolished in 1953; the present utilitarian apartment building — itself one of the oldest buildings still standing along Conduit Road — was then built on the site.

② Han Suyin's Pavilion

The heavily romantic 1950s' film *Love Is A Many Splendoured Thing* was partly filmed in a large mansion on Conduit Road, used at the time as the Foreign Correspondent's Club, though watch the film today and you would think it was set almost anywhere in the world but Hong Kong, so great have been the changes over the last few decades.

The old mansion was eventually demolished in the late 1960s and the candy-striped apartment complex known as Realty Gardens — where each tower block is named after a European city such as Paris and Venice — was built on the site instead.

Behind the apartment complex there is a small pavilion which can still be seen, almost hidden among the trees, where in real life author Han Suyin and her boyfriend, *Times* correspondent Ian Morrison, used to meet up on the sly, before he was finally killed in Korea and Han wrote her autobiographical novel about their relationship; the lilting, Academy Award winning theme song remains a Hong Kong anthem for many of the film's generation.

③ Cheung Po Tsai's Path

Just above the pavilion, along the hillside, there is a little-known and unremarked path, sometimes used by hikers, but otherwise overgrown. According to local legend, this track marks the route of Cheung Po Tsai's Path, a track around the side of the Peak used as a coastal lookout by the pirate band led by Cheung Po-tsai, several decades before the British settled in Hong Kong. After the pirates were pacified — they were never actually defeated in battle, being too powerful in the waters around the Pearl River Delta — the local Qing officials co-opted their leaders, including Cheung, into their administration.

Following their switch in allegiance Hong Kong, which like most others in the region was little more than a remote, rocky island frequented only by fishermen and pirates, was renamed Tai Ping Shan (Great Peace Mountain), though some scholars dispute the role Cheung's pacification played in the island's redesignation. Cheung Po-tsai is also commemorated elsewhere in Hong Kong; the Tin Hau Temple at Stanley still possesses a bell and drum donated by him.

4 *Shops and property agents*

Hong Kong's property-crazy, bubble-economy of the mid-1990s is perhaps nowhere better exemplified than along here, as buying an apartment or hiring a maid was almost easier to do along Conduit Road — and in many other parts of the Mid-Levels — than getting in a few groceries. Flats along here start at about $4

million for something vaguely reasonable in an older block, and spiral dramatically upwards for anything spacious with a decent view, and well-appointed as opposed to merely lavish.

Many property agents advertise themselves as 'specializing in expatriates', meaning that it doesn't matter that they charge a small fortune for their services, as the home office — wherever that may be — will ultimately be footing the bill and many clients have little knowledge of Hong Kong realities either. And this is not an entirely unfair assessment; for many present-day 'expatriates', the over-priced, over-hyped concrete canyonland of the Mid-Levels, like overcrowded workaday Central just down the hill will, sadly, be almost the only Hong Kong they ever get to know.

5 *Ohel Leah Synagogue*

Built in 1901, the Ohel Leah Synagogue on Robinson Road is one of the few remaining Edwardian buildings still extant in Hong Kong and still in regular use. Funds for the synagogue's construction were provided by Jacob Elias Sassoon, then head of the prominent firm E. D. Sassoon and Co., which mostly traded in Indian opium and cotton. It was named Ohel Leah (Abode of Leah) after Leah Gubbay Sassoon and built by the leading local architectural firm Leigh and Orange

Peak • Mid-Levels

— still prominent today — that was responsible for many other public buildings found elsewhere in Hong Kong and the Treaty Ports.

Now dwarfed by tower blocks, Ohel Leah Synagogue was saved from demolition and extensively restored in the early 1990s; perhaps ironically, prominent local Jewish interests were the most vocal around that time in calling for the building's destruction and redevelopment.

Originally many of Ohel Leah's congregation were Orthodox Sephardic Jews, most of whom were originally from Baghdad. These Jews settled on the China coast after moving on from Iraq to various locations in British India, principally Bombay and Calcutta. These days Hong Kong's Jewish community comes from all over the world, with Americans and Israelis being particularly well represented. Various types of Kosher food — some of which is imported all the way from New York — are available in the Jewish community centre attached to the synagogue.

A number of interesting old Jewish artifacts are contained within the synagogue's collection, including some early Chinese items that may originally have come from Kaifeng in Henan Province, home of the Chinese Jews for more than a millenia.

How To Get There

By Bus:	Minibus No. 3 from terminus on the harbour side of Prince of Wales Building, alight on Conduit Road when you see the signs 'Realty Gardens' and 'Haddon Court' on your left. Walk up the hairpin bends until you reach the pavilion.
By Taxi:	'Gon Tak Doh, Luen Bong Fa Yuen' ('Conduit Road, Realty Gardens').

Attractive, tree-shaded, or pleasant are not adjectives that immediately come to mind when describing much of the Mid-Levels these days. Four decades of overdevelopment have transformed — some would say almost completely blighted — a once delightful area. Despite these widespread changes, the tree-shaded precinct around Lyttelton Road, Park Road and Kotewall Road, at the western end of the Mid-Levels near the University of Hong Kong, still retains a flavour of what much of the Mid-Levels used to look and feel like before the tower blocks took over.

Kotewall Road was named after former Executive Councillor Sir Robert Kotewall. Of mixed Parsee and Chinese descent, Kotewall

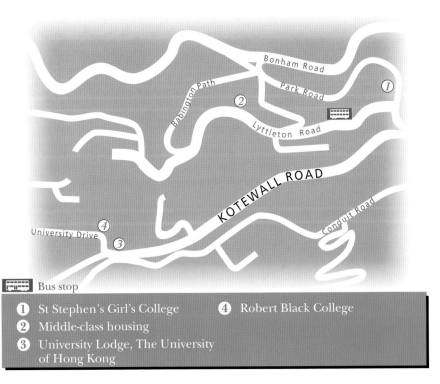

Bonham Road

Babington Path

Park Road

Lyttleton Road

KOTEWALL ROAD

Conduit Road

University Drive

🚍 Bus stop

❶ St Stephen's Girl's College
❷ Middle-class housing
❸ University Lodge, The University of Hong Kong
❹ Robert Black College

started life with the Hong Kong government and later branched out into various business enterprises. Appointed to the Legislative Council in 1923, Kotewall was knighted for his services to the colony in 1938. Despite being Senior Member of the Executive Council when the Japanese invaded the colony, Kotewall — in a remarkable display of political expedience — attended the Japanese victory parade, shouted *banzai*, made a florid congratulatory speech welcoming the victors and encouraged others to do likewise. For the duration of the war Kotewall worked closely with the Japanese, being known by his Chinese name Lo Kuk-wo. With the return of the British after the war ended, he again restyled himself Sir Robert Kotewall, and died in 1949.

(1) St Stephen's Girl's College

One of Hong Kong's most prestigious girl's schools, St Stephen's Girl's College on nearby Lyttelton Road, was founded in 1906 by the overseas missions of the Anglican Church, assisted by donations from prominent local businessmen such as Legislative Councillors Ho Kai and Tso Seen-wan. In 1908 the school shifted to Caine Road, and in 1922 moved to its present attractive premises on Lyttleton Road. The foundation stone of the present building was laid by the Prince of Wales (later the Duke of Windsor) when he visited Hong Kong as part of an Empire world tour. The school itself was opened two years later in 1924 by Lady Stubbs, wife of Governor Sir Reginald Stubbs.

Of the 1923 pioneer batch of graduates, four went on to study at the University of Hong Kong. This was quite remarkable, given both the size of St Stephen's Girls College and the University of Hong Kong in those days, and wider social mores concerning higher education for women.

Just before the Pacific War there were 22 members of staff and 386 students. During the Japanese occupation, the school was closed and the premises used as an espionage training centre. In 1967 the college ceased to be a boarding school and became a day school. One of the few schools to still retain its original campus, St Stephen's Girl's College remains one of Hong Kong's most sought-after local girl's schools.

2) *Middle-class housing*

In evidence everywhere in Hong Kong these days are all the more materialistic markers of 'middle-class' prosperity; a striking change from even thirty years ago when the middle layer was really quite thin.

The pleasant tree-lined streets around Lyttelton Road were always solidly upper-middle-class residential areas, centred around good schools and the nearby university, with as much open space as the steep Hong Kong hillsides allowed. Apartment buildings in the area are mostly older, dating from the 1950s and 1960s, and consequently are much larger than the average modern flat. Many have large balconies and a glance upward along here shows that they are generally filled with outdoor furniture and flowering plants, rather than the drying laundry and domestic overspill so commonplace in many other parts of Hong Kong.

3) *University Lodge, The University of Hong Kong*

Built on the site of the long-vanished nineteenth-century Victoria Battery, the Vice-Chancellor's residence at the University of Hong Kong replaced an earlier structure, a little down the hillside, that was built when the university opened in 1912. Most of the university buildings were extensively damaged during the Japanese occupation by looters, who stripped out all accessible timberwork to burn for firewood. Deemed not worth repairing, the old Vice-Chancellor's Lodge was demolished and the present attractive residence built in 1950. Extensively renovated inside and out a few years ago, this is just about the only remaining period building still in existence around here.

Standing silently in the back garden is a massive 9.2-inch naval gun, remnant of the site's earlier role. Until a few decades ago, it looked out across the western harbour and the island-studded sea beyond, but now it points impotently out over the undistinguished tower blocks that make up both the university campus and most of its formerly stunning view.

4 *Robert Black College*

This attractive postgraduate college, set around Chinese-style courtyards with numerous mature trees, shrubs and flowering plants, was built in 1967 and named after Sir Robert Brown Black, governor of Hong Kong from 1958–64. Major donors to the project included prominent philanthropist Sir Tang Shiu-kin and the Swire conglomerate. Until Robert

Black College was built, the University of Hong Kong had no residential facilities for postgraduate students and visiting overseas scholars, who had either to make their own arrangements elsewhere or be accommodated as house guests of other academics or the Vice-Chancellor.

For some years a rather British-themed collegiate flavour prevailed under one of the wardens, with self-consciously formal dinners, port-passing rituals and so on, but at present a more casual regime persists and accommodation prices at Robert Black College — for those with academic accreditations — are some of the most reasonable in Hong Kong.

How To Get There

By Bus:	No. 13 from Central Star Ferry Pier, alight at bus stop after the bus turns into Lyttelton Road.
By Taxi:	'Sing See Tai Fan Neui Tsz Chung Hok' ('St Stephen's Girl's College').

Lugard Road
盧吉道

One of Hong Kong's most splendid promenades, Lugard Road has been a prime walking spot for generations. The road is semi-circular and links with Harlech Road to surround Victoria Peak. Both roads combine to make a very popular walking path, as it is completely impossible to get lost; just keep on walking and eventually you'll get back to the Peak Tram

station. Recent shotcreting efforts have blighted some once pleasant sections, but for the most part the views are still stunning in every direction.

Too narrow in most places to really be a road, for much of its length Lugard Road is more like a path winding past stands of wild banana, fragrant flowering creepers and all sorts of tropical vegetation. Densely shaded for most of its length,

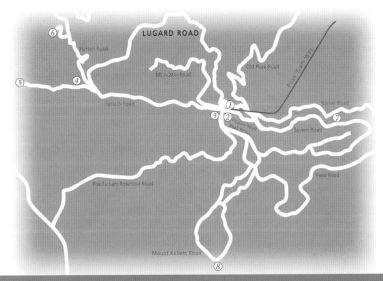

❶ Peak Tram Terminus, Victoria Gap		❺ Pillbox, High West
❷ Peak Galleria		❻ Pinewood Battery
❸ Peak Lookout		❼ Victoria Hospital
❹ Playground/rifle butts, corner of Lugard and Harlech Roads		❽ Matilda Hospital/Mount Kellet

STREETS

Lugard Road enjoys stunning vistas of the harbour, distant islands and closely packed city beneath. This is a place to come to when you need to put the jostling crowds and packed streets below into their proper context. As seen from here, most of the surrounding countryside is made up of extensive green hills with few buildings, an aspect of Hong Kong Island all too easily forgotten a couple of hundred metres further below.

Many roads in Hong Kong recall former governors, colonial secretaries and commanding generals and this one, named after Sir Frederick Lugard, governor from 1907–12, is no exception. Hong Kong formed a brief Far Eastern *interregnum* in Lugard's career as a long and distinguished African administrator, and he is most well remembered today for the creation of Nigeria. Along with his wife, the well-known journalist Flora Shaw, Lugard was also instrumental in establishing the University of Hong Kong.

While there are a number of houses at various points along its length, Lugard Road — perhaps surprisingly given its majestic harbour and island views — is not one of the Peak's more sought-after residential addresses. The road is too narrow for cars to pass in most places, the cliffsides for much of its length are too steep to build anything on, and the houses scattered along its length are often considered remote and difficult of access.

1) Peak Tram Terminus, Victoria Gap

The Peak Tram has been trundling its way up to the Peak since 1888. The High Level Tramway, as it was first called, was the first cable railway in all of Asia. Soon after followed by another on Penang Hill, it still remains one of the steepest in the world. In 1888 a Peak-bound tram left the lower terminus near St John's Cathedral every fifteen minutes, the journey took eight minutes and the gradient in places was one in two. It is exactly the same today, albeit with new vehicles, and remains one of the few elements of Hong Kong that has changed little with the passage of time.

The Peak Tram remains one of Hong Kong's enduring favourites, ever-popular with residents and tourists alike. As with the Star Ferry, there

cannot be a visitor to Hong Kong who has not taken a ride on the Peak Tram at least once. The trams are Swiss-made, and pass each other on the way up or down. There are four stops along the way, at Barker Road, May Road, McDonnell Road and Kennedy Road. Though few passengers alight at intermediate stations these days, they are a reminder of the time when the tramway, for Peak residents, was as much an everyday commuter service as the MTR.

② *Peak Galleria*

This expansive shopping complex, very popular with tourists and other visitors, was once the site of Peak Mansions, a medium-sized residential block for medium-grade expatriate civil servants. It was used as headquarters for the Hong Kong Volunteer Defence Corps for a time during the fighting for Hong Kong, and was also badly damaged by shelling during that time. Renovated after the war, Peak Mansions was repaired and resumed its original function as government housing until it was demolished in early 1989 and the Peak Galleria built on the site.

In front of the shopping complex there is a splashing cybernetic fountain, apparently one of the 'must-be-photographed-in-front-of' locations for mainland visitors to Hong Kong, or so it appears, given the large numbers standing and snapping away in front of it at any hour. Most of the shops inside are aimed straight for the tourist market, as the T-shirts and other merchandise on offer attest. After wandering around the Peak for a few hours on a hot day the Haagen-Daaz shop on the ground floor, with its wonderful variety of ice-creams and sorbets, is just the place to relax for a while and cool off.

③ *Peak Lookout*

The Peak Lookout is a low, bungalow-style building, and has counterparts in other old British hill-stations in the region, such as Fraser's Hill near Kuala Lumpur and Penang Hill. For decades the Peak had a highland village feel to it, with very little traffic and no crowds. The nearest the place came to bustling activity before the war was at the old Peak Hotel next to the Peak Tram, which served cream teas and hot buttered crumpets on foggy winter afternoons. For many local families in the 1950s, a trip up to the Peak followed by an ice-cream or lunch at the Peak

Cafe — as it was then known — remains a well-remembered Sunday treat, and one of the few outings available.

For decades very little changed at the cafe, either the menu, the décor or the prices. As the local population's tastes and expectations expanded, the old-style Peak Cafe lost its appeal and gradually declined in popularity. Threatened with demolition in the early 1990s, a spirited campaign to save it resulted in a face-lift, new management and greatly renewed popularity. Increased prices reflected the changes, but the attractive old building had an atmosphere lacking in many newer places. It has since changed hands as well as changed its name, and the interior design has been completely altered.

(4) Playground/rifle butts, corner of Lugard and Harlech Roads

This quiet, tree-shaded sitting out area at the corner of Harlech and Lugard Roads is one of the few places along here that has a public toilet. And being relatively remote, they're almost always very clean, unlike the ones close to the Peak Tram that are invariably foul. The well-equipped children's playground here seems

unplayed in for the most part, and the vegetation becomes quite thick towards the flat area to High West. Remarkable as it may seem today, in the 1920s this site was considered sufficiently far away from houses to be used as a small firing-range; a few elderly residents can still recall the sharp crack of rifle fire coming from here on a weekend afternoon. The target butts were located facing High West and the hillside, and were no longer used after the Pacific War.

(5) Pillbox, High West

Harlech Road, as much a country lane as Lugard Road, winds out towards High West from the junction near the playground. The sides of the path have not — as yet anyway — been stripped of vegetation and blighted with shotcrete and are usually thick with vivid purple-flowered *melastoma* in the summer months.

Out at High West the views over sea and islands are stunning when the pollution isn't too bad, and even on a weekend it is possible to have the place almost entirely to yourself. An old abandoned pillbox that once watched over the East Lamma Channel has been partially refurbished, and a scale map placed on top, so visitors can tell what they are looking down upon. Sit on one of the benches and enjoy the panoramic view of hills and islands, with High West, shrub-covered, rocky and dramatic, rearing up behind.

6 *Pinewood Battery*

Construction of a gun battery started on this remote hillside west of Lugard Road commenced in 1903, but in 1910 the emplacement was designated surplus to requirements and the guns removed. After standing abandoned for over a decade, it was reactivated in the mid-1920s as an anti-aircraft

emplacement. After being bombed and badly damaged in the early stages of the Japanese attack on Hong Kong it was abandoned, and never refortified after the war. Some of the shells fired at the battery from Stonecutter's Island after its capture by the Japanese fell short and landed among the University buildings on the hillside below, some of which were in use as a Field Ambulance hospital.

The Pinewood Battery site has been converted into a popular picnic area, with magnificent views on a clear day out over the East Lamma Channel and the sea beyond. A little difficult to get to, it is usually relatively clean on Monday mornings, unlike most barbeque sites elsewhere in Hong Kong. Located just up the hill from the University of Hong Kong, the abandoned bunkers and gun-battery are a popular haunt for students to come up and sit out under the trees. Watch out for the comically camouflaged weekend warriors who besiege this and other wartime sites, such as nearby Mount Davis on weekends, and public holidays, randomly firing plastic pellets from air-rifles, shouting mock commands and generally enjoying themselves — and leaving a tremendous mess behind them afterwards.

(7) Victoria Hospital

Built by public funds to celebrate Queen Victoria's Diamond Jubilee in 1897, the red-brick Victoria Hospital on Barker Road was originally known as the Victoria Hospital For Women and Girls, and had 41 beds when it opened.

Situated some 1,000 feet above sea level, the hospital was considered healthier for seriously ill patients than those in the lower town. More egalitarian than the Matilda, the Victoria Hospital admitted 'private patients, wives of Government servants, children and natives', and was later considerably enlarged.

(8) Matilda Hospital/Mount Kellet

Opened in January 1907, the Matilda Hospital at Mount Kellett, still one of Hong Kong's most respected private hospitals, was built and endowed by Mr Granville Sharp in memory of his late wife. Sharp's bequest specified — given the attitudes of the day — that the hospital was intended for the treatment of any nationality 'other than Chinese or Portuguese'; happily the hospital now takes patients of

any race. The Matilda remains one of Hong Kong's most popular private hospitals, and like the others, standards are world-class and fees are very high.

The hospital organizes an annual sedan chair race to raise money for charity; the last place in Hong Kong where these now obsolete modes of transportation can still be seen in use.

How To Get There

By Bus:	No. 15 from Central Star Ferry Pier, alight at final stop at Peak Galleria.
By Taxi:	'Saan Teng Kwong Cheung' ('Peak Galleria').
By Peak Tram:	From lower terminus at Garden Road to final stop.

STREETS

Old Peak Road
舊山頂道

At one time Old Peak Road was the only route up to the Peak. The slow and rather strenuous climb was only undertaken by hikers in search of exercise or coolies bearing loads of everything from coal to ice. Rest stations for heavily laden labourers were built along here by those pricked with at least a little social conscience, and now they serve just as well for hikers. Keep on going steadily upwards past the last apartment blocks; gradually you will notice a slight drop in temperature — as well as breathtaking views in every direction on a clear day — and eventually you will come out on the Peak.

Old Peak Road is still a popular hiking trail for residents of the overbuilt Mid-Levels, but you'd better keep a watchful eye on the ground along here; like Bowen Road and elsewhere, the legions of housebound dogs from nearby apartment complexes that get 'exercised' around here are not often cleaned up after!

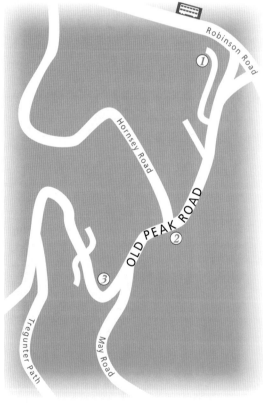

Bus stop
1 Canossa Hospital
2 Ladies Recreation Club
3 Dynasty Court and
   shuttle buses

1 *Canossa Hospital*

For many years the Canossa Hospital, one of Hong Kong's best private hospitals, was administered as part of the Canossian Mission, an Italian Roman Catholic order which first came to Hong Kong in 1860 and established themselves in substantial premises donated to the order on Caine Road, which became known as the Italian Convent.

In the 1920s, Mr M. E. J. Stephens, a local solicitor who acted as legal consultant to the Canossian Sisters, donated a house and a thatched hut located at the junction of Old Peak Road and Robinson Road to the Order. After some renovation, the old Canossa Hospital opened on the site and was equipped with sixteen beds and the very barest amenities.

During the Japanese invasion in 1941, the Canossa Hospital was destroyed by Japanese shelling; postwar reconstruction saw the new hospital building completed in 1960. On 1 June 1991, the management of the Canossa Hospital was transferred from the Canossian Order to Hong Kong Caritas, the Roman Catholic charitable organization.

2 *Ladies Recreation Club*

Originally established in 1883, the Ladies Recreation Club was extensively rebuilt in 1948 on the current Old Peak Road site and has since been further reconstructed. With tennis courts, swimming pools, restaurants, bars and other recreational facilities, the Ladies Recreation Club is one of Hong Kong's most popular clubs. In spite of the name membership is not restricted to ladies; couples and men are welcome as well.

Entrance fees to the club are currently $45,000 per single person or $90,000 per couple — a fairly hefty price tag which effectively keeps out the unwealthy *hoi polloi*; that fee carries the benefit of reciprocal memberships to such long-established institutions as the British Club in Bangkok and the Tanglin Club in Singapore.

3 *Dynasty Court and shuttle buses*

The 1980s property boom saw many mega-sized apartment complexes such as Dynasty Court burgeoning throughout the Mid-Levels, all of them offering tenants the 'luxury' and 'prestige' of on-site residents club houses, swimming pools, saunas, gyms and the rest. But for many Mid-Levels residents, probably the best thing about the 'extras' offered are the shuttle bus services that almost every major complex offers into Central. Frequent, clean, air-conditioned, residents-only minibuses chug up the hillside throughout the day and into the night. A pleasant alternative to taxis or, quite unthinkable for most, is actually *walking* up the hillside.

4 *Mid-Levels traffic*

Getting from here into downtown Central can take less than five minutes by car if the traffic conditions are favourable — and over half an hour if they're not! The sheer array of luxury cars pootling around these roads is staggering, and many, like the large numbers of Porsches, are simply not designed with the twists and gradients of Hong Kong roads in mind. But never matter — most of the people that buy a Porsche in Hong Kong don't make the purchase so they can enjoy the performance or purchase four-wheel drives for going on safari.

5 *Dogs in Hong Kong*

Pedigree breeds of canine are in evidence everywhere in Hong Kong and have become the *de rigueur* fashion accessory over the last few years. Never mind the complete inappropriateness of keeping a fully grown rottweiler in a small flat, or how a Siberian husky will cope in the Hong Kong summer — if a particular breed is the latest 'must-have' then there are plenty of Hong Kong people who simply *must have* one and will spend whatever it takes to get it. Mostly though, the owners can't be bothered exercising the poor animals and delegate the task to their maid, who often can't be bothered walking too far with it either.

How To Get There	
By Bus:	No. 12 from Central Ferry Piers, alight on Robinson Road at Bishop Lei International House. Walk along the road in the direction of the traffic and Canossa Hospital will be within sight around the bend. Or minibus No. 2 and No. 3 from terminus on the harbour side of Prince of Wales Building, alight at the Canossa Hospital.
By Taxi:	'Ga Nok Saat Yee Yuen' ('Canossa Hospital').

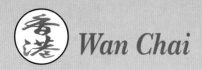

For many people, tourists especially, Wan Chai is a vital part of the 'real' Hong Kong, a colourful mélange of densely packed streets, intriguing back alleys, traditional crafts and vanishing trades.

Wan Chai, meaning 'small bay' in Cantonese, began in pre-British times as a small Chinese settlement grouped around the present Tai Wong Temple on Queen's Road East. Also known as Ha Wan (Lower Circuit), both names have long since become redundant as there is no longer a bay or a circuit there anymore.

The development of modern Wan Chai began in the 1840s with the intention of creating a high-class residential and commercial centre. The major foreign firms then based in Hong Kong all had substantial buildings, including extensive godowns and wharves, in the area known as Spring Gardens (centred around the present-day Spring Garden Lane).

Wan Chai did not develop further into a European residential quarter beyond this time, though a significant but steadily declining European presence remained a feature of the area for many years. The hillsides leading up from Queen's Road East to Wan Chai Gap had scattered groups of European-style houses, and in isolated corners a few examples remain.

Due to a sharp increase in population in the 1850s demand for land shot up, and the government responded by developing the area around Stone Nullah Lane and the southern side of Hospital Hill as an area principally for Chinese residence. This area is now Wan Chai Road and surrounding streets.

The Hongkong Tramways Limited opened for service in 1904 along that section of the waterfront — then known as the Praya East — that is now Johnston and Hennessy Roads; trams still pass through these roads today.

In the interwar period, Wan Chai had a number of medium-scale industries and other smaller enterprises employing quite significant numbers of workers. Industrial and commercial enterprises were also active from the mid-nineteenth century. Godowns were established and shipping-related businesses such as small dockyards, timber yards, coal merchants and metalworks were set up. One of the major factories set up in the area was the Oriental Sugar Refinery, established in 1876. Most of the raw sugar that it processed came from Java. By the 1930s, other

- Cross Street
- Johnston Road
- Kennedy Road
- Lee Tung Street
- Queen's Road East
- Ship Street
- Stone Nullah Lane

Wan Chai

large-scale factories were the Nanyang Brothers Tobacco Co. Ltd., established in 1905 near Canal Road and later expanded to the waterfront after the reclamation was completed, and the British-American Tobacco Co. Ltd. at Gloucester Road. Many of these businesses were very noisy, and a government ordinance, partly to control noise, was enacted in 1905.

An ambitious reclamation plan for the Wan Chai seafront was initially proposed in the early twentieth century by Sir Paul Chater, co-founder of Hong Kong Land. Due in part to sustained opposition from the military, who would have lost their seafrontage had the scheme gone ahead, the reclamation scheme, known as the Praya East Reclamation, did not commence until 1921. The modified scheme lacked the full sweep of Chater's early vision, and the barracks and the Royal Naval Dockyard remained firmly entrenched between Central and Wan Chai for another thirty years.

After the scheme was completed in 1930, modern Hennessy, Lockhart, Jaffe and Gloucester Roads were all built on reclaimed land. Part of the landfill used in the reclamation was obtained by quarrying down Morrison Hill, which took several years to remove. Closely packed, indifferently built tenements were built on the new land area. In time these came to accommodate some of the large numbers of Chinese who moved to Hong Kong in the late 1930s as a response to unsettled conditions on the mainland.

Gloucester Road, with its substantial and distinctive police station — still there today — remained the Wan Chai waterfront until further extensive reclamation

STREETS

work was started in the late 1960s. The newly created space was used for a time by the Hong Kong Products Exhibition, an annual trade fair for Hong Kong's industrial exports back in the days when manufacturing was the colony's lifeblood. The buildings further north were built in the early 1980s.

Spring Garden Lane was a red-light district in the late nineteenth century, and Ship Street in the early twentieth century; if a house had prostitutes within, then the houses were prominently numbered and known as *dai lum bah* (big number) houses. Before the Pacific War, there were a number of bars in the area, mainly owned by the Japanese and patronized by servicemen from the nearby dockyard and barracks. The international reputation of Wan Chai as a raunchy nightlife zone developed in the postwar period and became legendary during the Vietnam War, when large numbers of (mainly) American servicemen came to Hong Kong for R & R (Rest & Recreation) — also irreverently described by some observers as I & I (Intoxication and Intercourse).

Numerous popular novels have been written about the Wan Chai bar scene, most famously Richard Mason's *The World of Suzie Wong*. While bars and nightclubs with varying levels of sleaziness remain a prominent feature of parts of Wan Chai, there is a great deal more to the district than these aspects.

Wan Chai underwent considerable changes due to rapid redevelopment in the 1980s and 1990s. Large-scale developments, such as the Hopewell Centre, redeveloped entire areas of small lanes, completely altering the localized character of Wan Chai. Surprisingly though, large pockets of interest remain; many however, such as the lanes around Ship Street, are soon to be completely transformed by further redevelopment.

Wan Chai

STREETS

Much of Hong Kong's bustling, haggling-at-the-market atmosphere still thrives in the street market along Cross Street and Wan Chai Road. Cross Street was first laid out in 1855, though nothing now remains from that time. It was later extended to the lower slope of Hospital Hill, where the Ruttonjee Hospital now stands.

Gai see (street markets) are still commonplace all over Hong Kong although those in the heart of the older urban areas, like this one, often stock a greater diversity of goods, especially food products, than those found elsewhere in the city. Despite the increasing popularity of supermarket chains, it will be a long time yet — if indeed ever — that the movement, noise and colour of a Hong Kong street market finally becomes a thing of the past.

Permanently thronged with shoppers, browsers, stallholders and passers-by, Cross Street remains one of Wan Chai's most interesting back lanes and is well worth exploring — in addition to being a bargain place to shop. Many of the hawkers around the street have been here for many years, and in some cases several decades. Cross Street market's overall layout, and several of the stalls themselves, show interesting signs of recent cultural change (see below), if you know what to look for.

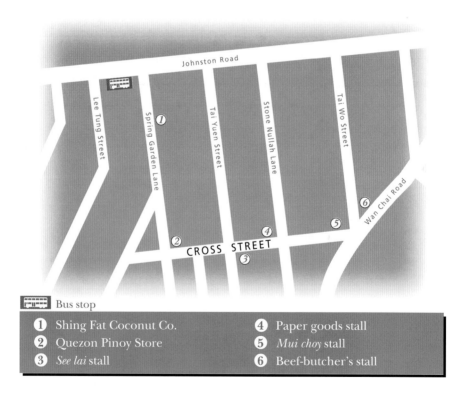

🚌 Bus stop

❶ Shing Fat Coconut Co.
❷ Quezon Pinoy Store
❸ *See lai* stall
❹ Paper goods stall
❺ *Mui choy* stall
❻ Beef-butcher's stall

1 Shing Fat Coconut Co.

Need some Penang *laksa* (sour fish noodle soup) seasoning, or red, green or yellow Thai spice pastes, or perhaps some fresh galangal, lemongrass or kaffir lime, or just a really fresh coconut to grind up for a curry lunch on the weekend? Despite the general Cantonese aversion to spicy food, there are growing numbers of shops like Shing Fat Coconut Co. springing up to satisfy changing culinary tastes. Shing Fat Coconut Co., just off Cross Street, has very reasonably priced spices, powders and other South-east Asian products. Stock is always very fresh because of the high turnover (they also supply restaurants), making this the place to come and stock up on supplies for the next curry lunch. Staff are very friendly and helpful, and prices a little bit lower than other South-east Asian products shops in the area.

Part of the reason for shops like this one opening is the increased numbers of domestic workers from South-east Asia, principally the Philippines but increasingly Indonesia and Thailand, who create demand for their national products. Another reason is that the average Hong Kong person now travels much more widely than before. Many people, for whom overseas travel even a generation ago would have been unthinkable, now regularly vacation in places like Thailand and Malaysia, and while there try different foods and want to eat them again on their return. And at the same time, previously difficult to obtain items such as curry pastes and spice mixtures have become more available for import.

2 Quezon Pinoy Store

All over Hong Kong numerous small *sari-sari* (sundry goods) stores have sprung up to cater to Hong Kong's legions of Filipinos when they want foodstuffs and other items to remind them of home.

Filipinos first started coming to Hong Kong as domestic workers in massive numbers in the early 1980s, and now number well over 150,000. Better-off families

STREETS

till then generally employed a Cantonese servant, known as a *mah je*. These women, known for their long braided hair and distinctive black-and-white outfits, had been a fixture of middle-class life for generations, both in Hong Kong and the Straits Settlements. By the early 1980s most were coming up to retirement age, and the younger generation of local Chinese women preferred to work in factories, as the pay was better and the job seemed less demeaning. Advances in education also meant that more local women were entering the workforce, and choosing to stay in their chosen careers after marriage.

This situation coincided with the beginnings of a large middle class in Hong Kong, who for the first time were in a position to employ servants. This emergent 'middle-class' usually had enough English to deal with domestic issues, and as most Filipinos spoke English there was no great language problem. Nevertheless, employer-employee relationships in Hong Kong are sometimes very fraught with real or imagined cultural misunderstandings on both sides. Many families who a generation before may have been servants themselves now employed a Filipino domestic worker.

Many Hong Kong families these days simply could not survive without their domestic helpers, for as they struggle under the crippling burden of sky-high mortgages, both partners in many cases simply *must* work, and thus cannot balance child care, elderly parents and domestic duties without assistance.

Aside from shops like this one, the massive numbers of Filipinos now living in Hong Kong have resulted in a wide variety of goods and services provided specifically to supply their needs.

There are even enough resident Filipinos to justify local Tagalog-language newspapers. Freight forwarders, remittance agents, and general shops that stock popular brands of canned *adobo*, face cream and headache remedy popular in the Philippines are both common and well patronized. Everything from Filipino-style tinned sardines, tiny bright-green *calamansi* (Philippine limes), phone cards and 'whitening' facial creams are on offer. A good example of a trend springing up all over Hong Kong, Quezon Pinoy Shop also has another branch at North Point, making it a successful and gradually expanding business according to its proprietors.

③ See lai stall

Beloved for years by legions of Hong Kong *see lai* (aunties) who are seldom seen in anything else, the brightly coloured jumpers and cardigans on offer here would raise the winter temperature just by looking at them.

Stock changes regularly at stalls like these, so come back in summer for rayon blouses and delicately patterned, lightweight *sam foo* (pyjama suit) outfits, or towards the end of winter for a store-away bargain outfit for next year — easy enough to do as the basic designs *never, ever* change. Fashion victims need not even pause here!

④ Paper goods stall

Small stalls like these sell joss-paper, *laap juk* (red candles), incense sticks and almost everything else required for the home altar. Thick wads of Hell Banknotes — essential for burning at funerals and to *baai jo sinn* (pray to ancestors) in the weeks after a death, go for a few dollars.

These *jee jaak po* are found all over Hong Kong; a sign of the persistence of traditional religion especially before big festivals, like Lunar New Year, *Gwai Jit* or *Yue Laan Jit* (Ghost Festival), *Ching Ming* (Grave-Sweeping), *Tuen Ng* (Dragon Boat), *Chung Yeung (Double Ninth)*, *Jo Chow Jit* (Mid-Autumn). The profit margin on goods sold on these stalls is very good, stall-holders' say, as the cost price is less than 10% for most items.

Bamboo-yellow incense-sticks go for as little as $6 a bundle, but as a general rule cheap sticks are very smoky and sometimes quite foul-smelling when lit. More fragrant ones, guaranteed to appeal to householder, neighbours and deity alike, sell for $20 or so a bunch.

5 Mui choy stall

Taking advantage of changing times, the canny owners of this dried goods stall mark their products in English. Time was when Cantonese servants knew exactly what to buy to prepare a particular dish, and in spite of many of them being completely illiterate no such signs were ever necessary.

Since the last of the professional amahs retired, their places have been taken by (mostly) Filipinos and Indonesians with very different dietary habits to Hong Kong Chinese, making more detailed explanations necessary to avoid confusion and resultant culinary disasters. And of course signs like these make very good business sense as well — the stall here always has a few foreign maids about buying things, at least here they know for sure what they're getting.

6 Beef-butcher's stall, corner of Tai Wo and Cross Streets

Don't look for pork at a beef-butcher's, or vice versa; market butchers only stock one type of meat. Places like this are great for getting stock-bones, stewing meat and offal, though what passes for steak is usually very tough, as it's actually **too** fresh. Meat on market stalls in Hong Kong isn't given time to hang and tenderize — the beast was likely mooing its last at Kennedy Town Abattoir in the early hours of the day you purchase its tongue, shanks or a few slices of liver for supper.

Some would criticize the hygiene aspects of having fresh meat hanging in the open air and exposed to flies and traffic fumes, but the majority of the local population don't seem to care, or suffer too many ill effects from eating it either.

Wan Chai

How To Get There

By Bus:	No. 90 from Exchange Square Bus Terminus, alight on Johnston Road at the bus stop outside Southorn Playground. Cross the road and walk up Spring Garden Lane.
By MTR:	Wan Chai MTR Station Exit B2. Walk through the covered walkway towards Johnston Road. Cross Johnston Road and walk up Spring Garden Lane.
By Taxi:	'Waan Tsai, Chun Yuen Gaai' ('Wan Chai, Spring Garden Lane').
By Tram:	From anywhere in Central, take any east-bound tram and alight on Johnston Road at Southorn Playground. Cross the road and walk up Spring Garden Lane.

Until the early 1920s Johnston Road was the Wan Chai waterfront, now located several hundred metres northwards due to reclamation. The Praya East Reclamation Scheme — first proposed in the late nineteenth century but due to military opposition only implemented

decades later — eventually extended from the Royal Naval Dockyard in Central across to Causeway Bay. When the reclamation was completed in 1930, it added several city blocks of new building land to Wan Chai, and extended the waterfront out as far north as modern Gloucester Road.

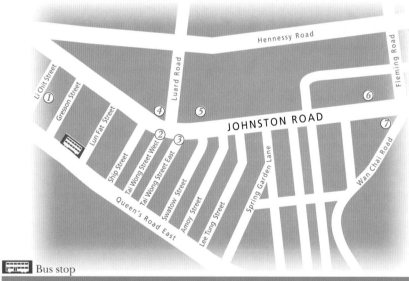

Bus stop

❶ Facades, Li Chit Street
❷ Kwan Kee Birdshop
❸ Woo Cheong Pawnshop
❹ Boston Restaurant
❺ Southorn Playground
❻ Yuen Ming Yuen
❼ Leung Kwok Ying Medicine Shop

Named after A. E. Johnston, the British Deputy Superintendent of Trade at the time of the First Opium War, who served as Hong Kong's first government administrator before Sir Henry Pottinger was appointed governor in 1842. Contrary to the urban myth, it has nothing to do with Sir Reginald Johnston, the talented Hong Kong Cadet who later became private tutor to the last Manchu Emperor of China Aisin-Goro Puyi. As late as the early 1930s, Johnston Road was still popularly known as Praya East (the former Praya Central and Praya West are now Des Voeux Road Central and Des Voeux West) and there are still a few reminders of those times if you know where to look for them.

1 Facades, Li Chit Street

Wan Chai

Wander off Johnston Road and you will see what appears to be a row of perfectly preserved old shop-houses, and more than a few credulous visitors have remarked at how wonderful it is to see at least *something* being preserved. Sorry to disappoint, but these facades are completely faux. Empty birdcages hang down from balconies, there are Chinese shop signs advertising pawnbrokers and goldsmiths, and it's all totally fake; a theatre setting designed to be a backdrop to a sitting-out area, in an otherwise dingy location. They do much to add colour and another dimension to an otherwise gritty corner, but remember they're not real!

2 Kwan Kee Birdshop

Established for many years now next door to Woo Cheong Pawnshop, Kwan Kee has some lovely songbirds for sale, mostly canaries, budgerigars and parrots — all sadly housed in quite dingy surroundings. Vivid green Amazon parrots and the aptly named African Greys are among the more expensive at $5,000 each; peach-face, pink and green lovebirds are much more inexpensive at $300 a pair. Glossily carved and varnished ornamental birdcages go for a couple of hundred dollars each.

③ *Woo Cheong Pawnshop*

The ochre-coloured old Chinese shop-house complex housing the Woo Cheong Pawnshop has been in existence for over eighty years. Once a common sight along most of urban Hong Kong's streets, three- and four-storey shop-houses like this one have mostly vanished elsewhere.

Many shops along the Praya East in the early 1920s were Japanese-owned, and included two Japanese hotels as well as a few coffee-shops and other businesses; Japanese- and foreign-owned bars such as the popular Nagasaki Joe's were located further north towards the harbour on Hennesssy and Lockhart Roads — still Hong Kong's major concentration of bars and 'nightclubs' today. All were very popular with servicemen from Victoria Barracks and the Royal Naval Dockyard nearby in Central, and their successors are still well patronized by visiting servicemen today.

4) *Boston Restaurant*

Places like the Boston Restaurant serve generous portions of what is perhaps best described as 'soy sauce Western' food; despite being commonplace all over Hong Kong and very good, what's on offer cannot be compared with, well, genuine Western food. To really enjoy restaurants like the Boston, think of them as being a bit like a Chinese take-away in the West but in reverse; *chop suey* isn't authentic Chinese food either, but when properly cooked it is a satisfying and tasty dish and the same principle applies here. Take it for what it is and enjoy, but food purists had better stay at home!

Black pepper steaks are the house specialty at the Boston, though don't expect anything to come much rarer than medium, however closely you specify your preference. *Sai laang* (the Cantonese transliteration of sirloin) and *T-gwat* (T-Bone) are the most popular cuts of *ngau pa* (beef-steak) and are tasty and excellent value at $73. *Gai pa* ('chicken chop' or Chicken Maryland to the rest of us) is another good bet at $52, and for an extra $10 you get a set menu including cream soup, bread and coffee or tea. What passes for salads here are probably best avoided: masses of potatoes and tinned pineapple glooped over with lashings of salad cream. And don't expect tiramisu or sticky toffee pudding either; the desserts run towards fruit salad and ice-cream parfait concoctions — fine if you like that kind of thing.

5) *Southorn Playground*

Hong Kong's tendency to fill in its greatest natural asset — Victoria Harbour — and replace it with new building land and the occasional public park has a long history. When the Praya East Scheme was being undertaken, a park was included to counterbalance the inevitable tenements.

Today's concrete and asphalt 'playground' surrounded by trees was named after Sir Thomas Southorn, Colonial Secretary in the early 1930s; his wife, Bella Woolf Southorn, wrote an interesting account of her life as the wife of a colonial civil servant in *Under the Mosquito Curtain*. Literary endeavour seems to have run in that family — Lady Bella was the sister of publisher Leonard Woolf, and sister-in-law of the famous Virginia Woolf.

Wan Chai

STREETS

As possibly befits a place that started life in the illicit drug trade, Hong Kong has a serious and steadily growing hard and soft drug problem; Wan Chai's Southorn Playground has a sordid and — it is said — completely justified reputation as something of a drugs supermarket, though the casual visitor to the area is unlikely to see much of that side of life.

6) Yuen Ming Yuen

Located in a surprisingly well-preserved 1930s' building, Yuen Ming Yuen is very popular for *shui gau* (dumplings). Mostly filled with minced pork, shredded black mushrooms, water chestnuts and garlic chives, they make a cheap and very filling snack. A generous bowl of freshly made *shui gau* washed down by a large glass of cold *dau cheung* (soya bean milk) will cost you less than $30.

7) *Leung Kwok Ying Medicine Shop*

Stocking a wide range of *fung yau* ('wind oil') from Southeast Asia, this intriguing shop has been around for many years. *Fung yau* are meant to help dispel wind in the body when rubbed on, and are held to be particularly effective with stomach-ache. Light-brown, heavily fragrant nutmeg oil-based rubs are a justly famed Penang specialty, and retail for around $18 a bottle depending on the brand; there is also an excellent nutmeg-based balm in various sized pots.

    Kayu manis (cinnamon) oils are also popular, but some say they are not as effective as the nutmeg ones; you'll smell like a rather highly spiced custard after rubbing it on, but don't let that put you off. Axe Brand, the ever-popular wintergreen-based embrocation oil from Singapore is another well-known item here, as well as various types of cough mixtures — possibly the best is Sea Coconut, at $17 a bottle; the black, yellow and red box comes complete with dosage instructions in Malay, Tamil, Chinese, Thai and English.

Wan Chai

How To Get There

By Bus:	No. 6 and No. 64 from Exchange Square Bus Terminus, alight on Queen's Road East at bus stop after Dominion Centre. Walk against the direction of the traffic towards Li Chit Street.
By MTR:	Wan Chai MTR Station Exit B2. Walk through the covered walkway towards Johnston Road. Turn right at the Southorn Playground and continue walking against the direction of the traffic until you reach the Chinese Methodist Church. Li Chit Street is directly across the road from the church.
By Taxi:	'Waan Tsai, Lei Tsit Gaai' ('Wan Chai, Li Chit Street').
By Tram:	From anywhere in Central, take any east-bound tram and alight on Johnston Road after passing the Chinese Methodist Church. Walk back towards the church and Li Chit Street is directly across the road from the church.

STREETS

Kennedy Road
堅尼地道

Named after Governor Sir Arthur Kennedy (1872–77), this long winding road connects Central and Wan Chai. Like Caine and Bonham Roads to the west, Kennedy Road marks a geographical — and to some extent social — boundary between the overcrowded city below and the relatively spacious Mid-Levels above.

By the time Kennedy arrived in Hong Kong, the Crown Colony — then just over thirty years old — had gradually taken on a steady, settled air, with established parks and gardens, numerous prosperous business houses, attractive public buildings, schools and churches and, most significantly, an air of settled permanence that was quite lacking even a decade or so earlier (see picture of No. 28 Kennedy Road).

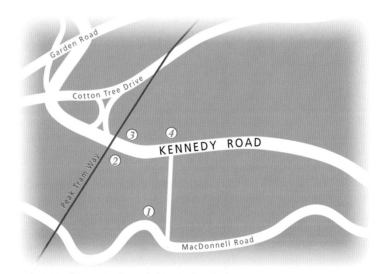

| ① St Paul's Co-Educational College | ③ Zetland Hall |
| ② Union Church | ④ St Joseph's College |

Something of this flavour of Sir Arthur Kennedy's time in Hong Kong — if not the original buildings themselves — still remains along here. Well-established churches and schools, a little-used Peak Tram stop, harbour views glimpsed among the trees and numerous older apartment buildings all make this an interesting road to wander along, with the vegetation-clad hillsides rising steeply above Kennedy Road along the Wan Chai section of the road.

1 St Paul's Co-Educational College

Established in March 1915 by the parishioners of St Paul's Church, St Paul's Girls' College, interestingly enough, was the first secondary school in Hong Kong to make school uniforms for students compulsory.

In 1927, the attractive verandahed campus extending between Kennedy and MacDonnell Roads was built at the then quite considerable cost of $180,000, which was underwritten almost entirely by donations from Hong Kong and American philanthropists.

After the war, St Paul's College turned co-ed, being the first school in Hong Kong to take the radical step of putting boys and girls in classes together. The once controversial experiment was a resounding success, and is now widespread elsewhere in Hong Kong. In 1950, the school was officially renamed St Paul's Co-Educational College; the Headmistress of St Paul's Co-Ed for many years was the late Dr Bobbie Kotewall, a noted educationalist and daughter of pre-war Executive Councillor Sir Robert Kotewall.

2 Union Church

A multi-denominational Christian church, the congregation at Kennedy Road's Union Church includes Presbyterians, Methodists, Baptists and — perhaps surprisingly — a few Roman Catholics as well.

Wan Chai

119

Union Church was established in 1844 by the famous British missionary Rev. Dr James Legge and originally stood on Elgin Street. During the Japanese occupation, the Union Church pastor Rev. K. Mackenzie Dow and many of the members of his flock were interned with the other European civilians at Stanley. Left unoccupied, it is alleged that timber salvaged from the roof of what was known in the late nineteenth century as 'the handsomest building in the colony' was used in the construction of the Japanese-style tower at Government House.

Union Church was completely rebuilt after the war ended and a number of annexes were added in subsequent decades. Numerous community-based activities also operate from the Union Church, including Weight-Watchers.

(3) *Zetland Hall*

Zetland Hall, the austere-looking building at No. 1 Kennedy Road, is Hong Kong's Masonic Temple, which was relocated to Kennedy Road after its original home on Central's Zetland Street dating from 1853, and was bombed out during American air raids near the end of the Pacific War.

For decades an entirely European preserve, the Masons started welcoming Chinese members from the 1890s; the first Chinese District Grand Master, Richard Charles (Dick) Lee, was installed in 1961. These days, over half the initiate membership are Chinese.

For generations membership of the Masonic Lodge has been a virtual roll-call of the great, the good and the influential in Hong Kong and includes — as with other Masonic Lodges elsewhere in the world — a fair sprinkling of policemen, lawyers, judges, government officials and prominent businessmen. Recently and extensively renovated, Zetland Hall's interior has some very beautiful stained glass windows which originally came from Bethany, the old French Mission chapel at Pok Fu Lam. There is also an interesting collection of Masonic jewels on display inside.

4 *St Joseph's College*

One of Hong Kong's most well-known boy's schools, St Joseph's College was originally established in 1875 in small premises on Caine Road. Under the supervision of the La Salle Brothers, who still run the school today, the institution moved to its present site on Kennedy Road in 1881.

Adjacent to St Joseph's College, the magnificent premises of Club Germania were a popular gathering place for Hong Kong's German community. Along with other German businesses, the Club Germania was expropriated by the Hong Kong government during the First World War and was not restored to the German community after the war ended. Built in 1902, the attractive main building was demolished and replaced by a new school building in 1962, but the college still retains another old building originally built in 1921–22 as an addition to the old Club Germania building, by that time taken over by the school. It is now protected from demolition as a monument.

For many years St Joseph's College was closely associated with the local Portuguese, and many members of that community were educated there from its inception up to the 1950s when many started attending the British schools instead. Prominent local Portuguese alumni included former Executive Councillors Leo d'Almada é Castro, Sir Albert Rodrigues and long-serving Club Lusitano President H. A. de Barros Botelho.

Wan Chai

How To Get There

By Bus:	No. 12A from Chater Road Statue Square bus stop, alight on MacDonnell Road in front of St Paul's Co-Educational College.
By Taxi:	'Mak Dong Loh Doh, Sing Bo Lor Nam Neui Chung Hok' (MacDonnell Road, St Paul's Co-Educational College').

STREETS

Lee Tung Street
利東街

This interesting, gritty Wan Chai backstreet connects Johnston Road and Queen's Road East and is also sometimes known as the 'Street of the Printing Shops' due to the large number of reprographic establishments found along here. Need to stock up on calendars or *lai see* (lucky money) packets? This is your place!

Lee Tung Street took its name from the Lee Tung Construction Co., managed at one time by the younger brother of Lee Hysan, one of the most prominent Chinese merchants in the early twentieth-century Hong Kong. Lee Hysan was a prominent opium merchant, later sensationally murdered; Lee Gardens

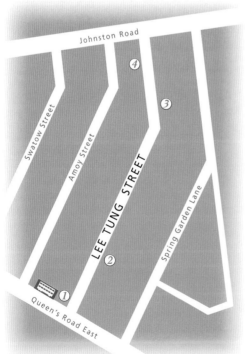

Bus stop
1. Wai Leung Mah Jong
2. Hanes Printer and Publisher Co.
3. Tat Ying Sewing Machine Co.
4. Parrot Shop

and Hysan Avenue in Causeway Bay recall his name. The entire property where Lee Tung Street was subsequently laid out was bought by the Lee family in 1918 — in the name of Lee Hysan's wife — from the prominent Mody family, Parsee businessmen who originally acquired the land back in 1867.

The entire street is composed of original 1950s buildings; plans have recently been mooted for its renovation for other uses, such as restaurants and bars.

1) *Wai Leung Mah Jong*

There can be few things more elemental to Hong Kong — or to Chinese life in general — than the game of mah-jong. At any time of the day or night, thousands of people in Hong Kong, somewhere, are busily clattering the tiles. The Cantonese expression for mah-jong playing — *dah pai* — literally means to hit the tiles, and the sound of several games being played in the same room can be almost deafening. And it is also highly addictive; epic overnight mah-jong sessions are quite common. Perhaps unsurprisingly, shops selling mah-jong tiles, tables, dice and the other items needed for the game are found all over Hong Kong.

Wai Leung Mah Jong has been on the corner of Queen's Road East and Lee Tung Street for over twenty years, says the cheery proprietress Lok Sau-hing, and according to her, business has always been brisk. A durable plastic mah-jong set will set you back about $200 here. Folding mah-jong tables with drawer inserts for keeping score cards and loose change are $200 or so upwards depending on quality, and brightly coloured dice and counters are less than $10 a set.

2) *Hanes Printer and Publisher Co.*

Little backstreet printing shops like this one are some of the best places to go in Hong Kong for customized printing of such items as menus, wedding invitations, personal stationery and so on. Prices are very reasonable and most individual requests for customized stationery can be entertained.

The ubiquitous *kaat pin* (name card), which no self-respecting Hong Kong person can *ever* be without, can be printed here for a couple of hundred dollars for a thousand; prices vary depending on the typeface and quality of paper.

STREETS

Name cards aside, do you perhaps fancy a brightly coloured calendar for the New Year? Hanes Printer and Publisher Co. stock a considerable range, with prices for a traditional Chinese almanac starting from as low as $15. Other calendars, with red-red covers and vivid pink, white and red *koi* fish swirling in a whirlpool-like formation, are just the thing to hang on the back of the pantry door. You will also find an inventive range of — um — *haam sup* (smutty) calendars, draped with wannabe Page Three girls who pout, sulk and show off what little allure Nature deigned to give them. Prices for these 'beauties' are a little more than for the *koi* fish calendars, though the colours are more or less the same.

③ Tat Ying Sewing Machine Co.

A legacy of Hong Kong's once massive garment industry which, over the last two decades, has almost completely relocated across the border, Tat Ying Sewing Machine Co. somehow manages to wholesale domestic and industrial sewing machines, along with their spare parts and needles and other paraphernalia, in spite of an empty-looking showroom and not a customer within a short range.

The ancient-looking treadle-model in the display window was 'just for display', said the grumpy old *baak* (uncle) behind the counter, declining to give his name and shooing me away with a universal gesture and a mutter aside. Similar models can be found in the China Products Department Stores for $800 or so — perfect for the novice home-sewing enthusiast.

4 *Parrot Shop*

Parrot Shop is probably *the* place to come in Hong Kong if you are a serious parrot fancier and stocks everything from vitamins to perches and shell-grit to high-quality imported bird foods. They stock a wide range of captive-bred birds, such as Blue and Gold Macaws, Lesser Sulphur-Crested cockatoos, African Greys, Galahs and Ambon parrots. Whilst they also have plenty of the more usual budgerigars, lovebirds and finches, Parrot Shop's specialty is, well, parrots.

Prices for these lovelies are very high, with few birds, especially the tame ones, going for less than $8,000 each and most are a *lot* more. Fancy sharing your home with a gentle friendly macaw? Then bring at least twenty of those elusive gold notes along when you come here.

Parrot Shop also have another branch at the Yuen Po Street Bird Market, near the Flower Market off Prince Edward Road West in Kowloon, with a wider range of birds, seeds and the rest.

How To Get There

By Bus:	No. 10 from Chater Road Statue Square bus stop, alight on Queen's Road East opposite Hopewell Centre.
By MTR:	Wan Chai MTR Station Exit B2. Walk through the covered walkway towards Johnston Road. Lee Tung Street is directly across the road from Southorn Playground.
By Taxi:	'Wong Hau Dai Doh Dung, Lei Dung Gaai' ('Queen's Road East, Lee Tung Street').
By Tram:	From anywhere in Central, take any east-bound tram and alight on Johnston Road at Southorn Playground. Lee Tung Street is directly across the road from Southorn Playground.

Early photographs of Queen's Road East show a quiet track with only an occasional rickshaw or pedestrian — a far cry from the thronged noisy thoroughfare of today. The road led from the old Victoria Cantonment (where Pacific Place and Hong Kong Park are today) through Wan Chai and into Happy Valley. Furniture shops and rattan weavers — still a specialty today along the western section today — were as much a part of Queen's Road East in the nineteenth century as they are today.

In pre-British times, the track that later became Queen's Road East ran along the coast a little above the high-water mark. Given how far inland the road is today, the extent of reclamation

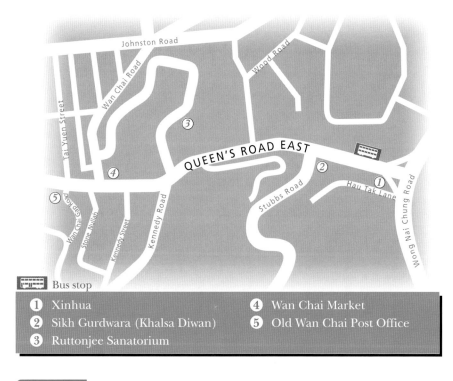

🚍 Bus stop

❶ Xinhua
❷ Sikh Gurdwara (Khalsa Diwan)
❸ Ruttonjee Sanatorium
❹ Wan Chai Market
❺ Old Wan Chai Post Office

over the decades is obvious. There is much of interest to explore along this stretch, with far more than just the furniture, curtain and rosewood shops that immediately catch the eye.

1 *Xinhua*

Now renamed the Liaison Office of the Central Government, for many years this fortress-like building on the easternmost corner of Queen's Road East was known as the New China News Agency, which functioned as China's de facto embassy in Hong Kong. A key focal point for demonstrations and rallies in years gone by, very few protests are held here these days. Either the political scene has changed dramatically or — perhaps more likely — the local population realizes there isn't much point to complaining anymore and doesn't even bother trying.

Wan Chai

2 *Sikh Gurdwara (Khalsa Diwan)*

The well-established Sikh community in Hong Kong are mostly the descendants of soldiers and policemen, or those such as tailors, storekeepers and other camp followers who came with them from India. The Hong Kong Police had two contingents of Indians serving pre-war, Sikhs and Punjabi Moslems. The Punjabi Moslems remained

STREETS

loyal to the British and were retained until the 1960s, while unfortunately the Sikh policemen — incited by their community leaders — worked enthusiastically with the Japanese. The internment camp for allied civilians at Stanley was partly guarded for a time by Sikh policemen, who were known for their spite and cruelty. Partly as a result of this behaviour, the Sikh police were cashiered after the war's end, and no more were ever recruited, either in Hong Kong or India, though many remained in Hong Kong, taking mainly low-paying jobs as watchmen, labourers and drivers. Some have branched out into business and the professions, but in general the Sikhs remain the poorer and less privileged members of the local Indian community.

At the height of Punjab separatism in the early 1990s, the Indian flag was burnt from time to time here, and worshippers often wore orange turbans as a sign of nationalism as well as religious devotion. From time to time devotees will stage a *langga* or feast, which is donated by a particular individual. The birthday of Guru Nanak, the founder of Sikhism, is celebrated with particular enthusiasm here. The Sikh Gurdwara is reached by taking a flight of steps down from Queen's Road East. Sikhs are generally very hospitable and friendly and visitors to the gurdwara are welcome. Though according to one elderly man there, this pertained as long as guests are 'decently dressed' and 'behave themselves' while on the premises.

③ *Ruttonjee Sanatorium*

Located on Hospital Hill, the Ruttonjee Sanatorium for tuberculosis patients was established in the late 1950s after the Royal Naval Hospital closed down following the reduction of the British naval presence in Hong Kong and endowed by the wealthy Ruttonjee family, Parsee businessmen long established in Hong Kong. J. H. Ruttonjee, who donated the original funds, was a prominent local businessman whose interests included the Hong Kong Brewery; his son Dhun Ruttonjee was a member of the Legislative Council. Both were badly tortured by the Japanese after they refused to encourage members of their community to work with them during the occupation.

Rampant tuberculosis, brought about by massive overcrowding and habits such as spitting in the streets encouraged the disease to spread rapidly, and was the endemic scourge of Hong Kong in the 1950s. The disease is making a frightening renaissance worldwide at present — including Hong Kong — where the combination of massive overcrowding and general public squalor are still major contributing factors.

4 Wan Chai Market

Built in the late 1930s, this attractive old building has recently been slated for preservation while the 'temporary' market across Wan Chai Road — built decades after the old market building — has recently been demolished for redevelopment.

Stalls inside sell fruit, vegetables and the usual market produce, but most shoppers tend to patronize the open-air Cross Street market a block or so down Wan Chai Road. *'Sun seen di lor* (fresher),*'* said one woman shopper to me as she groped and prodded her way towards the firmest, ripest papaya on the stall, much to the consternation of the watching stallholder. While the building itself is an interesting relic of the past, the general consensus of opinion among shoppers is that Wan Chai Market's fresh food stalls passed their best quite a while ago.

5 Old Wan Chai Post Office

Now an Environmental Resource Centre — something Hong Kong could certainly do with a few more of — this pleasant, low-key old building served as Wan Chai's post office until 1991. The Chinese roof tiles are the same as you'll find on any village house, and in the courtyard next to the building there is a massive old mango tree, unusual in Hong Kong as the climate is generally inappropriate for this type of tree to bear fruit; consequently it is seldom seen planted in gardens or on farms. Follow Wan Chai Gap Road which heads steeply uphill behind the old post office and eventually you'll come out up on the Peak near the Police Museum — a wonderfully scenic walk for the fit and energetic.

While serving a worthwhile purpose as an attractive reminder of the past, the heritage listing status of the old Wan Chai post office serves as a rather sad metaphor for the state of heritage preservation elsewhere in Hong Kong, as it really isn't anything that remarkable. What *is* remarkable is that a structure of its age is still there at all. Buildings such as this one were only saved from the wreckers' ball after it was realized that there was virtually nothing left from the past for future generations — and long after most of the best had been lost to redevelopment.

How To Get There

By Bus:	No. 6A, No. 6X and No. 64 from Exchange Square Bus Terminus, alight on Queen's Road Central East just outside Queen Elizabeth Stadium.
By Taxi:	'Wong Hau Dai Doh Dung, Chung Luen Baan' ('Queen's Road East, Central Liaison Office').

Ship Street extends up from the former waterfront almost to the Kennedy Road level.

In the early days of British settlement numerous sampans clustered in the harbour around the nearby Tai Wong Temple as a landmark seen from the water, which is one of the reasons advanced for the street being so

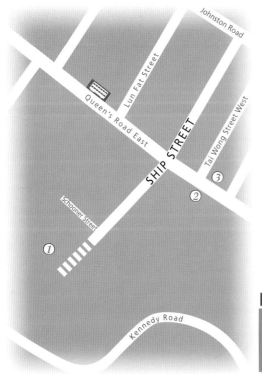

Bus stop

1. Nam Kwu Toi
2. Tai Wong Temple
3. Che Tsai Meen

named. The upper part of Ship Street has remained much the same for some decades, while the lower end, with new shops and buildings, reflects the constant changes that have taken place in Wan Chai in recent years. Ship Street now has a variety of shops, none of which are related to maritime trades.

The upper part of Ship Street housed a number of private dairies in the mid-nineteenth century, with several cowsheds located in the vicinity. In addition, there were also herds of goats reared by Indians which were allowed to forage freely on the hillside above Kennedy Road. This extremely damaging practice was finally stopped in 1877 as a result of agitation by the newly established Botanical Department after free-ranging goats ate all the trees that the Botanical Department had planted.

① Nam Kwu Toi

Built in the early twentieth century, these two-storey, red-brick dwellings at the top of Ship Street, just below Kennedy Road, are typical of more prosperous local residential architecture from that time. During the Japanese occupation, they were listed as being 'geisha houses' — most likely a euphemism for military brothels or comfort houses. Sadly decayed, one has been recently demolished, leaving only the massive stone foundations, enormous banyan and camphor trees and some old green-glazed balustrades.

The other house — Nam Kwu Toi (South Substantial Terrace) — has been seriously vandalized over the years, but is still in good structural condition and is, for the time being at least, one of Hong Kong's few remaining old middle-class houses. The view from its verandah, in the days when it overlooked the harbour and the Kowloon hills instead of the television aerials on nearby tenements, must once have been very attractive.

All these are slated to be demolished under an ambitious plan by Hopewell Holdings to build a megahotel complex on the site, a move that will completely transform the area over the coming few years, much the way the massive Hopewell Centre development did to nearby Spring Garden Lane in the late 1980s.

2) *Tai Wong Temple*

This small temple, nestled between Queen's Road East and the hillside, is more correctly known as the Hung Shing Temple. The principal deity worshipped there is originally from Nam Hoi, in the western part of the Pearl River Delta. In the nineteenth century, the temple stood close to the waterfront, a reminder of how far Victoria Harbour  has been reclaimed since the temple was first constructed. Renovated at various times since then, inscriptions on the columns record a substantial redecoration undertaken in 1860. The main hall was reconstructed in 1909 after the roof collapsed. Attractive and very lifelike figurines made from Shek Wan pottery were added to the ridge of the roof at this time, and can still be seen there today. The building nestles into the hillside, and has large banyan (*ficus netusa*) and camphor laurel (*cinnamomum camphora*) trees growing behind it. The temple also has a few savage dogs lurking behind, so take care when poking about the less frequented corners.

3) *Che Tsai Meen*

Until about a decade ago, it was still quite common to find rows of makeshift carts in the streets of Hong Kong selling all kinds of tasty tidbits (or barely edibles, depending on your taste) from fish balls on sticks to lurid orange-coloured squid, to a type of noodles particular to Hong Kong known as *che tsai meen*, literally 'cart noodles'. These days, most of the  erstwhile roving hawkers have moved into what pass for more hygienic premises.

The popularity of these establishments can be discerned by the fact that there are more tables *outside* the shop than inside. The main attraction of *che tsai meen*

Wan Chai

eateries for many customers is that the individual decides what goes into the noodles. On top of the basic noodle and broth, you can add *yu beng* (fish cake) and *yu daan* (fish balls), or *chu hong* or *huet* (pig's blood) and *fung jau* (chicken feet), or whatever it is you fancy. At Che Tsai Meen, you can mix and match two, three, four or even five different ingredients. With fifteen different things to choose from and five types of noodles, the permutations are almost endless.

How To Get There

By Bus:	No. 6 and No. 64 from Exchange Square Bus Terminus, alight on Queen's Road East after passing Dominion Centre.
By MTR:	Wan Chai MTR Station Exit B2. Walk through the covered walkway towards Johnston Road. Turn right at the Southorn Playground and continue walking against the direction of the traffic until you reach the junction with Luard Road. From there, cross Johnston Road and Ship Street will be within sight.
By Taxi:	'Waan Tsai, Suen Gaai' ('Wan Chai, Ship Street').
By Tram:	From anywhere in Central, take any east-bound tram and alight on Johnston Road at Southorn Playground. Cross the road and walk in the direction of the traffic until you reach Ship Street.

The name of Stone Nullah Lane comes from the stone-revetted 'nullah' — an Anglo-Indian word meaning a stone or concrete-lined water-channel — that once ran down the middle of the street. The small stream which flowed down the nullah ran down from the hillside above Kennedy Road and emptied into Victoria

Wan Chai

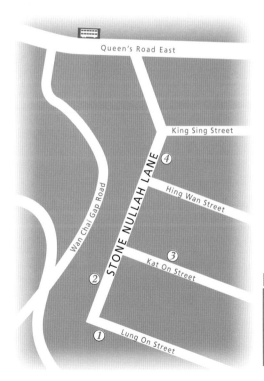

Queen's Road East

King Sing Street

STONE NULLAH LANE

④

Hing Wan Street

Wan Chai Gap Road

③

Kat On Street

②

Lung On Street

①

🚌 Bus stop

❶ Pak Tai Temple
❷ Stone Nullah
❸ Streetside barber shop
❹ Old tenement houses

STREETS

Harbour below Wan Chai Road. On its way it flowed alongside Hospital Hill (where the Ruttonjee Hospital now stands), and continue near the Cross Street Market, off Wan Chai Road. Still there today, the stream now flows underground and is channelled through drainpipes.

There was originally enough spare land between the stream (as it was before the nullah was constructed) and Hospital Hill for a variety of small landholdings to be surveyed, which were then sold for development to Chinese speculators in the 1850s. Nothing now remains, however, to remind us of these early days.

One of Wan Chai's more atmospheric backstreets and a photographer's delight, some corners of Stone Nullah Lane have barely changed for decades and offer a rare glimpse of what much of the district looked like until the past two decades.

① Pak Tai Temple

A quiet backstreet temple on the corner of Stone Nullah Lane and Lung On Street, the Pak Tai Temple is also known as Yuk Hui Kung. Principally devoted to the God of the North, the complex was built in the 1860s and has been renovated several times since then.

Heavy wooden supports now shore up the roof in places, which is in some urgent need of repair. Deep green and dark blue glazed Shek Wan pottery figurines of dragons and fish line the roof ridgeline. A well-known feature in many other temples as well, these decorations are particularly ornate.

A gigantic *ficus* tree overshadows one corner of the temple courtyard and seems like it may eventually claim possession of the outer fence as well.

The Pak Tai Temple is very popular for funeral rites. Paper offerings destined for incineration at funeral rituals can often be seen stacked in the adjoining courtyards; these sometimes include attractively made Mercedes, mobile phones, computers, perfume and designer gear — just what the ghostly recipient enjoyed, or at least coveted — during their time on earth.

② *Stone Nullah*

The creek which empties — now below the roadway — into Stone Nullah Lane rises on the Peak above Kennedy Road. Continue uphill on Wan Chai Gap Road and you will see the creek, now channelled into modern-day 'nullahs' (made of concrete); it enters storm water drains part-way down, and flows under Kennedy Road. The curve of Wan Chai Road below Hospital Hill, on the opposite side of Queen's Road East, formed the bank of this creek in the early 1840s.

At one time there were a number of laundries on the upper part of Stone Nullah Lane, with the laundry being washed in the waters of the nullah all long since vanished.

③ *Streetside barber shop*

One of Hong Kong's swiftly vanishing streetside trades, along with professional letter writers and scissor-grinders, alfresco barber shops such as this one just off Stone Nullah Lane provide an inexpensive service for those who don't require a 'salon experience'. They also provide gainful employment to people sometimes long past retirement age, such as the cheery old *ah baak* (uncle) who plies the clippers and brush here.

A quick trim and a detailed chat about backstreet life will set you back less than $30. Don't look *too* closely at the scissors, combs and razors being used — the thick encrustations of clotted dandruff and hairs would perhaps indicate that they've not been rinsed out for years! Wash your hair well afterwards.

STREETS

Wan Chai

4 Old tenement houses

Most old houses in the rest of Wan Chai have been demolished in recent years, but on Stone Nullah Lane and nearby streets a few still manage to survive. For how much longer though is anyone's guess. With narrow overhanging balconies packed with drying laundry, household overspill and the odd potted plant, these

decaying apartment buildings seem much more reminiscent of backstreet Macao than anything found elsewhere in contemporary Hong Kong; an often overlooked comparison, as both places were once so alike in many respects.

Buildings such as these have been the subject of heritage preservation efforts over the last few years; a worthwhile initiative but at the same time a reminder of how late in the day adequate conservation measures have been left. Almost all integrated precincts elsewhere in Hong Kong that once had attractive buildings and open space, such as Central's Statue Square, have long since been lost, and while a few heritage grade buildings still remain scattered about the territory, they are immediately noticeable by their very scarcity.

Old tenements in backstreet Wan Chai, such as these on Stone Nullah Lane, provide worthwhile examples of what life was like for the majority, and thus demonstrate how society has moved on. But that aside, they are little more than decaying slums and the interest shown in them in recent years shows — by default — how proactive heritage conservation in Hong Kong was largely ignored until it was far too late.

5 Bean curd manufacturies

In the early twentieth century, the area around Stone Nullah Lane was home to a particularly foul-smelling industry — soya bean processing. Vats of fermenting beans were a nose-curling nuisance to local residents who eventually complained enough about the stench to have the processing shops relocated elsewhere. These days more noxious industries are usually located in separate sections of modern industrial areas (there is a large soy sauce manufacturing plant at Tai Po), or have relocated altogether to the mainland.

The fact that these early bean curd factories were removed as a result of residents protests is, in itself, a compelling statement about just how foul-smelling they must have been; for the most part residents living in nearby tenements in those days had no interior sanitation whatsoever, only night-soil buckets that were placed on the landing to be collected by scavenger women in the dead of night. Living and working in cramped, basic conditions, they still found the nearby bean-works so unbearably offensive that they insisted on having them moved away to less populated areas.

How To Get There

By Bus:	No. 10 from Chater Road Statue Square bus stop, alight on Queen's Road East at Wan Chai Market.
By MTR:	Wan Chai MTR Station Exit A3. Cross Johnston Road and walk against the direction of the traffic. You will come across Stone Nullah Lane on your right. Ignore that and continue walking until you reach Tai Wo Street. Turn right and continue walking until you reach the junction of Tai Wo Street, Wan Chai Road and Cross Street. Walk along Wan Chai Road in the direction of the traffic until you reach Wan Chai Market at Queen's Road East. Cross Queen's Road East and Stone Nullah Lane is within sight.
By Taxi:	'Waan Tsai, Sek Shui Keui Gaai Fa Yuen' ('Wan Chai, Stone Nullah Lane Garden').
By Tram:	From anywhere in Central, take any east-bound tram and alight on Johnston Road at Southorn Playground. Walk on the Southorn Playground side in the direction of the traffic until you reach O'Brien Road. Cross Johnston Road and then walk against the direction of the traffic. You will come across Stone Nullah Lane on your right. Ignore that and continue walking until you reach Tai Wo Street. Turn right and continue walking until you reach the junction of Tai Wo Street, Wan Chai Road and Cross Street. Walk along Wan Chai Road in the direction of the traffic until you reach Wan Chai Market at Queen's Road East. Cross Queen's Road East and Stone Nullah Lane is within sight.

Causeway Bay

For centuries before Europeans first came to the China coast, the appropriately named Wong Nai Chung (Yellow Mud Creek) passed through the sparsely settled corner of Hong Kong Island which later became known as Causeway Bay.

For a few decades after the British established themselves in Hong Kong, Europeans called the area Bowrington, after the colony's fourth governor Sir John Bowring. But unlike Kennedy Town on the western end of Hong Kong Island, named after seventh governor Sir Arthur Kennedy, the name never really stuck and Bowrington has long since passed into the history books.

In the 1850s, the creek was channelled and became known as the Bowrington Canal. Early postcards show it, and a few elderly residents can

still remember fishing and swimming in its clean tidal waters in the early 1920s. Bowrington Canal was later covered over to make Canal Road, but the creek still empties into the sea through massive drainpipes. The canal itself was only finally covered over in the mid-1970s when the flyovers dealing with the Cross-Harbour Tunnel and Aberdeen Tunnel were built.

Until the 1930s the Causeway Bay area — more commonly known as East Point — housed numerous enterprises belonging to Jardine Matheson and Co., first established in the area after they moved to Hong Kong from Macao in 1841. Early engravings and photographs show East Point projecting into the harbour, with massive godowns on the waterfront and splendid residences on the bluff behind, including East Point House, the residence of Jardine Matheson's *taipan*. Jardine's original East Point residence was only demolished in the early 1950s, after standing for more than a century.

The Cantonese name for Causeway Bay, *Tung Lo Wan* (meaning Copper Gong Bay), is taken from the large gong found in the Tin Hau Temple which, in an earlier and much less magnificent form, pre-dated the British arrival in Hong Kong. Now several blocks inland due to successive reclamation projects, Causeway Bay's Tin Hau Temple, like all other Tin Hau Temples, was originally on the

- Blue Pool Road
- Causeway Road
- Leighton Road
- Shan Kwong Road
- Tai Hang Road
- Tung Lo Wan Road
- Wong Nai Chung Road
- Yee Wo Street

waterfront. Other sources suggest that the name was derived from the original shape, like a copper gong, of the coastline at Causeway Bay. The present Tung Lo Wan Road follows the original coastline.

Modern Causeway Bay still has numerous reminders of the early Jardine, Matheson & Co. conglomerate's presence: Jardine's Bazaar, Jardine's Crescent, Matheson Street, Yee Wo Street (Yee Wo, sometimes transliterated *Ewo*, is the Chinese name for Jardine's). Other thoroughfares, such as Paterson Street and Keswick Street, are named for long dead and otherwise long forgotten *taipans;* the whole area is overlooked by Jardine's Lookout in the hills behind.

In the early twentieth century, there were several hills in the Wan Chai/ Causeway Bay area. Of these, Morrison Hill and Caroline Hill were completely quarried down in the 1920s to provide landfill for the Praya East reclamation scheme. In 1923 a wealthy Chinese entrepreneur who held the opium monopoly for many years — Lee Hysan (murdered in mysterious circumstances a few years later on Central's Wellington Street) — bought East Point Hill, flattened it and built an amusement park on it. Lee Gardens now stands on this site, and Hysan Avenue recalls the name of this once prominent business figure. Lee's sons were extremely Anglophile; one, Richard Charles (Dick) Lee, eventually became District Grand Master of the local Masonic Lodge — the first Chinese to hold the appointment. Of the original hills only Leighton Hill still remains today.

Kellett Island, joined to Causeway Bay by reclamation work in the 1970s, was once several hundred metres out in the harbour. Known in Chinese as Tang Lung Chau (Lantern Island), a small fort was built on the island as early as 1841 to help defend the harbour area around East Point. The island was renamed in the 1860s after naval officer Sir Henry Kellett (Kellett Bay at Pok Fu Lam and Mount Kellett on the Peak are also named for him). The Royal Hong Kong Yacht Club has been located on Kellett Island for many years, and in the 1930s enjoyed keen competition with the rival Corinthian Yacht Club, now long since amalgamated with the Royal Hong Kong Yacht Club and its name all but forgotten.

Hong Kong's first properly constructed typhoon shelter was built at Causeway Bay in 1886, tellingly near

Jardine's East Point properties. The original typhoon shelter was reclaimed in 1950 and the land used for Victoria Park. Causeway Road situated along the Park's southern boundary was once, as the name suggests, a causeway across the shallows between East Point and North Point.

One of Hong Kong's more persistent myths is that the colony had no factories or industrial-scale enterprises *at all* before the arrival of wealthy Shanghainese entrepreneurs in the early 1950s. While large-scale industrialization in Hong Kong certainly dates from this time, Causeway Bay — and other parts of Hong Kong — had several substantial industries in the nineteenth century. Hong Kong's first full-scale sugar refinery, the Jardine-Matheson-owned

China Sugar Refining Company, was established at Causeway Bay in the early 1870s. The plant processed raw sugar imported from Java, the Philippines and the Straits Settlements, and had a distillery attached to it, which manufactured a popular local brand of rum. Unable to compete with cheaper Chinese competition, the mill eventually closed during the slump of 1906–08. Sugar Street recalls this early industry. Another sugar refinery, established by rival firm Butterfield and Swire around the coast at Taikoo, weathered the slump and was still operating when the Pacific War broke out.

A large-scale cotton mill, the Hong Kong Cotton-Spinning, Weaving and Dyeing Company, Ltd. (also a Jardine Matheson subsidiary) was established at Causeway Bay, but despite initial promise it too was not a great success and later closed down. Despite the cotton industry's failure in Hong Kong, Jardine's continued manufacturing cotton in Shanghai, where the Ewo Mills were famous. The mill buildings on Tung Lo Wan Road were subsequently given over to French nuns from the Order of St Paul de Chartres, who established a convent, orphanage, school and hospital there.

The Imperial Brewing Company was established on Wong Nai Chung Road in 1905 by the prominent local Portuguese firm of Messrs. Barretto and Company, manufactured beer and ale which was described in a contemporary report as being 'of excellent quality'. Jardine Matheson also had a successful brewery in Shanghai whose products were widely sold in Hong Kong; the now vanished Ewo Beer was one of the most popular brands in China before the war.

STREETS

Large-scale industry has long since moved elsewhere and Jardine Matheson have disappeared, at least visibly, from Causeway Bay. While its former name East Point has been almost completely forgotten, the area's overwhelmingly commercial character remains. Modern Causeway Bay is completely dedicated to money making with impossibly crowded streets, heavily polluted air and strikingly dirty appearance in places. Perhaps surprisingly, Causeway Bay is often better known these days as 'Hong Kong's Ginza' because of the numerous Japanese department stores located there, and steadily growing popular reputation among local people as *the* place to eat, shop, see and be seen. The name has survived even though with the economic downturn in recent years a number of the Japanese department stores have closed down.

Happy Valley

The name originated as a mordant British Army reference to the number of deaths caused by malaria in the early years of British settlement and the considerable number of cemeteries found in the vicinity.

Hong Kong's Happy Valley remained a sparsely settled area behind Causeway Bay for many decades, with little development beyond the racecourse, stables and a few scattered houses. Early writers refer to a coffee plantation that was planted there but failed in the 1840s, and the hills behind Wong Nai Chung village were popular with ramblers from the 1850s.

Now synonymous internationally with horse-racing, Happy Valley has had a racetrack since 1846. Quite primitive in the early days, it has been expanded and modified many times since it was first laid out. The most recent reconstruction was in the early 1990s. Despite the existence of the racetrack, the Hong Kong Jockey Club was not established until 1884; before then races were organized by various ad hoc groups.

By the 1920s, Happy Valley had expanded into a middle-class suburb of Victoria, conveniently linked by a tramline to the urban areas. The discreet presence of a few European-staffed brothels run by (mostly) American madams lent parts of the area a certain raffish local notoriety in the 1930s, but these had all disappeared by the late 1940s.

Spacious government quarters were built on Leighton Hill in the 1950s, and have recently been demolished to make way for a massive 'prestigious' residential complex. Clubs like the Craigengower Cricket Club, churches such as the attractive St Margaret's Church overlooking the racecourse on Broadwood Road, the long-established Parsee temple on Leighton Road, various schools, and the colony's principal non-Chinese cemeteries all helped add to the settled, community feeling of the area. Those who lived in Happy Valley during those years retain very pleasant memories of the place.

Blue Pool Road
藍塘道

Fairly quiet, like other roads in Happy Valley, Blue Pool Road has a few areas of interest, often overlooked even by those who live nearby. The long-since-disappeared Wong Nai Chung village, which predated British settlement on Hong Kong Island, was originally located part-way up the slope that Blue Pool Road follows today and under today's Village Road. Until Wong Nai Chung Gap Road was cut over the Gap to Repulse Bay in 1924, the only access to the southern side of Hong Kong Island was through a bridle-path above the village.

Once a well-known natural feature near old Wong Nai Chung, it was still possible to bathe in the 'Blue Pool' in the years around the First World War. It was fed from the Wong Nai Chung stream which flowed through the 'Blue Pool' and then down the valley and on into the harbour.

Once a well-known local landmark, the 'Blue Pool' is only remembered these days by a few very elderly residents, and of those, none seem to recall whether the name came from the sky's reflection in the pond, or was derived from some other now vanished natural feature, such as minerals present in the rocks or soil.

Along this stretch of Happy Valley hillside, there is an interesting and often-overlooked Tam Kung temple, and some quite amazing furniture shops, all waiting to be explored. Cyclists use Blue Pool Road for training rides — it's relatively traffic- and fume-free, they say, and yet steep enough to provide a solid workout on the way up.

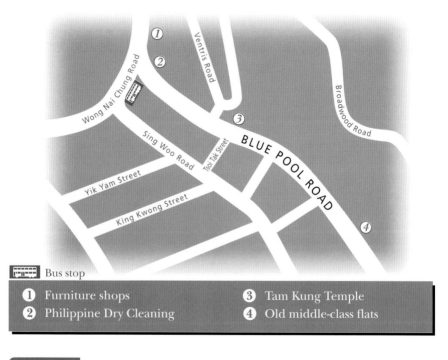

Bus stop

① Furniture shops　　　③ Tam Kung Temple
② Philippine Dry Cleaning　　④ Old middle-class flats

① Furniture shops

The lower end of Blue Pool Road, along with Wong Nai Chung Road further along towards Causeway Bay, is the place to go for 'designer' furniture and fittings. Italianesque labels are part of the manufacturing process, and some shops do indeed import their wares from Italy. But for many items, the only thing Italian about them is the design — and sometimes not even that!

That said, good deals can occasionally be had, especially during sale times. If swirling gilt and Versace-esque fabric patterns are to your taste, or a set of stylish-to-look-at, hard-to-be-comfortable-on chairs and sofas are what you've always wanted, then this part of Happy Valley is the place to come.

② Philippine Dry Cleaning

Operated — as the name unsurprisingly suggests — by Filipinos, Philippine Dry Cleaning charges $56 to dry-clean a men's wool or worsted suit, and $48 to dry-clean a long dress. As in most other laundries in Hong Kong, they have a minimum charge for other washing, of $30 for between one and seven pounds, and $4.50 for each additional pound.

Laundries are surprisingly popular in Hong Kong; though charging prices like these, it's surprising that more people don't just have washing machines of their own as the initial purchase price would be recovered in several months' time anyway.

STREETS

(3) Tam Kung Temple

Hong Kong's very own indigenous deity occupies this attractive small temple at the corner of Ventris and Blue Pool Roads.

According to the renowned local authority on Chinese gods, the late Colonel V. R. Burkhardt, Tam Kung was a Hakka boy from Wai Yeung, about eighty kilometres to the north-east of Hong Kong, who performed various marvellous feats after he moved to Hong Kong, drawing his strength and energy from the Nine Dragons that make up the Kowloon Hills.

The site for the present temple was chosen after Tam Kung appeared to a little boy in a dream, and told him to find a site for another temple. The lad was allowed to wander at will, followed by a steadily growing crowd of onlookers, until at last he found a spot he felt comfortable with and fell asleep there. That spot, at the corner of Blue Pool and Ventris Roads, was regarded as chosen by the deity himself, and is now the site of the Tam Kung Temple.

Tree-shaded, wreathed in incense smoke and generally very quiet, Happy Valley's Tam Kung Temple is one of the area's more unexpected hidden gems. Hong Kong has two other, rather larger, Tam Kung Temples, one at Ah Kung Ngam near Shau Kei Wan, and another at To Kwa Wan in Kowloon. Tam Kung also has a temple dedicated to him on the island of Coloane in Macao.

(4) Old middle-class flats

Happy Valley still has pockets of older middle-class housing, like these attractive, well-maintained flats — a legacy of life in less hectic, more spacious times when many of Hong Kong Island's once small middle class lived at Happy Valley. The driveway and stair balustrades seen here, lined with seasonal potted plants, are an attractive reminder of what much of Hong Kong — at least in the more affluent areas — used to look like in the days before the 'this-will-do-for-now' mentality became commonplace.

Until the 1950s, commercial nurseries would provide flat-dwellers all over the urban areas with flower-pots in bloom, which were changed with the seasons; heavily fragrant carnations in the spring, vivid scarlet salvias and orange marigolds in the summer, and chrysanthemums of all colours in the autumn. Included in the price of the pots were the services of a gardener, known as the *fa wong* (literally 'flower king'), who came every other day to tend them. While a few local nurseries still offer similar deals (though without the gardener!), few residents now bother to beautify their surroundings in this way anymore — a great pity.

Causeway Bay •
Happy Valley

How To Get There

By Bus:	No. 5A from Chater Road Statue Square bus stop, alight on Wong Nai Chung Road at the bus terminus at the junction of Wong Nai Chung Road and Blue Pool Road.
By Taxi:	'Pau Ma Dei, Laam Tong Doh' ('Happy Valley, Blue Pool Road').
By Tram:	From anywhere in Central, take the east-bound tram marked 'Happy Valley'. Alight at the tram terminus on Wong Nai Chung Road, and walk back towards Blue Pool Road.

STREETS

Seemingly a great distance from the sea, Causeway Road was, as the name indicates, originally just that; a breakwater-causeway connecting East Point (as Causeway Bay was generally known as until the 1930s) and North Point further across the Wong Nai Chung flood plain. Early photographs of Causeway Bay show the causeway stretching across the shallows, with little to the east beyond rocky hills and a few scattered houses, and Jardine Matheson's godowns and offices clustered around East Point.

Successive reclamations have placed modern Causeway Road several hundred metres inland. Permanently thronged with traffic, this stretch is one of the more convenient places to alight from the trams or buses, and is only a few minutes' walk from the consumerist nightmare — or paradise depending on your point of view — of downtown Causeway Bay. But wander a few blocks eastwards and the entire area's character changes, becoming much more workaday and very interesting for the casual ambler to wander around and explore, with numerous overlooked places of interest waiting to be discovered.

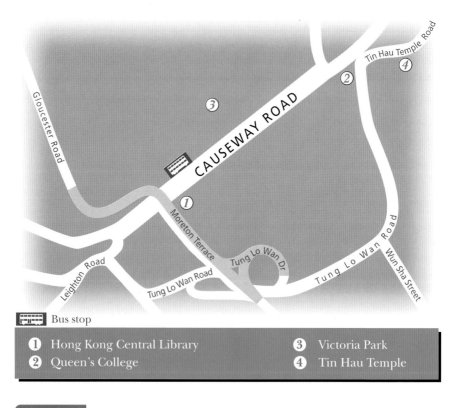

Bus stop

1 Hong Kong Central Library
2 Queen's College
3 Victoria Park
4 Tin Hau Temple

1 Hong Kong Central Library

Something of a misnomer for a book repository located in Causeway Bay, the new Central Library has magnificent holdings, state-of-the-art facilities and helpful staff, all housed in what must surely be one of Hong Kong's most hideous modern buildings. The interior isn't much better, however state-of-the-art it may be; imagine a recently built, 4-star(ish) Hotel Splendide lookalike anywhere on the mainland, all vast atrium, escalators to everywhere and lashings of blond wood fittings and you'll get the picture right away!

Hong Kong Central Library's somewhat eclectic design was approved by a committee of the now defunct Urban Council. One can only assume that the 'style' chosen somehow reflects the decorative tastes and preferences of its members themselves, and at least one prominent architect has remarked that if this building represented the very best that the councillors could achieve with the resources at their disposal, then on those grounds alone it was high time that the body was disbanded!

Ghastly exterior design aside, the Central Library has excellent resources and a superb range of books, and seems set to improve steadily when various holdings presently held in storage come into more open access.

2 Queen's College

For well over a century Queen's College was one of Hong Kong's most prestigious boys' schools and while it has since been eclipsed by the 'international' schools, like many once prestigious local institutions, it is still a very high-status school to attend. It started out as the Central School and eventually moved to magnificent premises on

Aberdeen Street (see Aberdeen Street section); renamed Queen's College in 1887, the institution remained on this site for almost a century before being relocated to Causeway Bay in 1950. The foundation stone for the extensive new building on Causeway Road was laid in 1950 by Governor Sir Alexander Grantham.

Ex-pupils of the Central School included Eurasian millionaire compradore Sir Robert Hotung and his brothers, and even revolutionary Sun Yat-sen attended the school for a time. Queen's College old boys are still prominent in business and government, but like graduates of most once prestigious local educational institutions, overwhelmingly the old boys now choose to educate their own children through the 'international' schools.

With playing fields and excellent amenities Queen's College still remains a highly desirable local school, with a history that closely reflects Hong Kong's own through to the present day.

(3) Victoria Park

The original typhoon shelter at Causeway Bay was built in 1886, near the Jardine, Matheson and Co. godowns and functioned for almost seventy years. The old typhoon shelter was reclaimed in 1950 and another typhoon shelter built further out to sea. Instead of being built upon, the government reserved the newly created land to become one of Hong Kong's largest and most popular open areas — Victoria Park.

Prior to the Pacific War, a bronze statue of Queen Victoria stood in Statue Square (the name is derived from this statue, and the Chinese characters still read Empress' Statue Square), but the Japanese removed it and took it away to Japan for scrap. Recovered and repaired after the war ended, Queen Victoria's statue was resited in Victoria Park and still stands there today. Vandalized a few years ago by a so-called 'performance artist', who hit the old lady on the nose with a hammer and poured red paint over both the statue and himself, Queen Victoria has since been repaired and stands there as doughty as ever. In spite of restoration work, the statue's nose is not quite the same as it appeared before.

Victoria Park is very popular with Hong Kong's Indonesian migrant domestic worker population on a Sunday — rather like Statue Square attracts a critical mass of off-duty Filipinos — and the signs erected around the park by the authorities in English, Chinese and Malay reflect an awareness of this situation on the part of the local administration.

4 *Tin Hau Temple*

Hard to believe today, this small but very atmospheric Tin Hau Temple on Tin Hau Temple Road, just past Causeway Road, was once located where all Tin Hau Temples are meant to be — very close to the seashore. However, the temple hasn't moved an inch — the shoreline has! And by several hundred metres.

A Tin Hau Temple, albeit rather smaller and less elaborate than this one, stood on the site several decades before the British arrived in Hong Kong; there is a seventeenth-century bell inside donated long ago as well. A local belief recalls in the early years of the Tao Kuang (Daoguang) reign in the mid-Ching (Qing) dynasty, this temple was used briefly as a barracks for troops on anti-piracy measures, but this has never been fully authenticated.

An 1893 guidebook described the temple as probably 'the most popular Chinese place of worship on the Island', and at festival times the description would still seem appropriate. Beautifully maintained and surrounded by venerable *yung shue* (banyan trees), Causeway Bay's Tin Hau Temple and courtyards are surprisingly quiet, though surrounded by modern buildings. The nearby MTR station, Tin Hau, derives its name from this temple, and this part of Causeway Bay is increasingly known as Tin Hau on account of it.

Causeway Bay • Happy Valley

How To Get There

By Bus:	No. 25 from Central Ferry Piers and No. 309 from Exchange Square Bus Terminus, alight on Causeway Road when you see the Central Library on your right and Victoria Park on your left.
By MTR:	Tin Hau MTR Station Exit B. Cross the road to Queen's College. From there, walk in the direction of the traffic for about 200 m until you reach the Central Library.
By Taxi:	'Tung Lo Waan, Goh See Wai Doh, Heung Kong Chung Yeung To Shue Goon' ('Causeway Bay, Causeway Road, Hong Kong Central Library').
By Tram:	From anywhere in Central, take the east-bound tram marked 'Shau Kei Wan' or 'North Point'. Alight on Causeway Road when you see the Central Library on your right and Victoria Park on your left.

Leighton Road

禮頓道

Leighton Road draws its name from the firm of Leighton and Co., early landholders in the Causeway Bay area who bought property shortly after the British settled in Hong Kong. Not long thereafter the firm vanished from view, and today their name is commemorated only by this busy Causeway Bay road and the low, once thickly wooded hill rising behind it.

Until the 1870s Jardine's maintained their stables on Leighton Road, on the site now occupied by the Po Leung Kuk. The stables have long since gone and been forgotten, but their gates are still in existence, removed decades ago to the Jockey Club at Beas River, near Fanling in the New Territories.

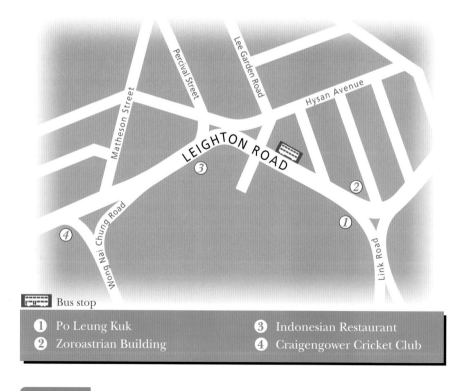

🚌 Bus stop

❶ Po Leung Kuk
❷ Zoroastrian Building
❸ Indonesian Restaurant
❹ Craigengower Cricket Club

Up to the 1940s Leighton Road was a relatively quiet, tree-lined thoroughfare, overlooked by Leighton Hill, the last surviving remnant of the hills that formerly stood in Wan Chai and Causeway Bay — a reminder that the area wasn't always as flat as it appears today.

Leighton Hill was riddled with air raid tunnels in the defensive preparations in 1940 and bitterly fought over in December 1941. For many years the hill was the site of spacious government flats built in the early 1950s. Designed with broad lobbies and extra-wide doors so that they could be converted to use as emergency hospitals if the need arose — it never did. These quarters were demolished a few years ago to make way for an enormous, closely packed luxury apartment complex, but whatever the new buildings might have in the way of glitz and snob appeal, they certainly won't be as open, breezy and pleasant, or as large and spacious, as the flats that they replaced.

1 Po Leung Kuk

Surrounded by banyan trees almost as old as the buildings themselves, the Po Leung Kuk (Society for the Protection of Virtue) has performed an extremely useful — and at times vital — social function ever since it was set up in Hong Kong in 1878.

Established to eliminate, or at least mitigate, abuses stemming from the then widespread trade in women and young girls for immoral purposes from China to burgeoning Chinese communities in Hong Kong, the Straits Settlements and elsewhere, the Po Leung Kuk was another very important form of parallel Chinese community leadership. Along with the District Watch and the Tung Wah Hospital Committee, membership of the Po Leung Kuk's management committee was a coveted badge of social arrival among the Chinese community.

Widely criticized in the 1890s as being little more than a cheap and easy source of domestic servants and concubines for the Po Leung Kuk's administrative hierarchy, the organization was the subject of an official enquiry at that time which proved the allegations largely false. Nevertheless, it did much to stem female

155

trafficking and curb other social abuses prevalent among the Chinese community at that time, such as the buying and selling of young girls (known as *mui tsai*) as virtual slaves.

Another branch of the Po Leung Kuk was established in the Straits Settlements and performed a similar role within Overseas Chinese communities there. The organization also took into protective custody small boys known as *mai jai* 'bought sons' who had been kidnapped and sold to meet the need for heirs, principally for the needs of ancestor worship.

These days, the society's function is more orphanage than protective institute, and many abandoned children live in this and other institutions elsewhere in Hong Kong organized by the Po Leung Kuk.

The Po Leung Kuk buildings behind their imposing entrance gates remain one of the rare attractive reminders of past days in downtown Causeway Bay. The meeting hall can be visited without prior arrangement, and the Po Leung Kuk provides an interesting information pamphlet to visitors free of charge.

② *Zoroastrian Building*

These days, one could search in vain for any reference to the once prominent local Parsee community; a visible exception is this unremarkable building on Leighton Road, where the remaining members of Hong Kong's Parsee community maintain their temple on one of the upper floors. Followers of the Zoroastrian religion, the Parsees fled religious  persecution in their native Persia (modern Iran) and settled in India before moving on to other trading settlements further east, such as Canton (now Guangzhou), Macao and later Hong Kong. Prominent early Hong Kong Parsees included Sir H. N. Mody, who endowed the University of Hong Kong.

The Parsee community has a beautifully maintained cemetery in Happy Valley, and another one — rather more decrepit — over in Macao that predates British settlement in Hong Kong. Even the existence of a Parsee cemetery is in many ways a contradiction, as Zoroastrianism prohibits them from polluting the four elements (earth, fire, water and air) by burial in any of them. That is why, in Bombay, home of the international Parsee community, the dead are exposed on the famous Towers of Silence to be picked apart by vultures. There being a distinct shortage of these creatures in southern China, at least of the avian variety, burial in lead-sealed coffins was adopted as the next best alternative.

③ Indonesian Restaurant

A little more expensive than other Indonesian restaurants around Hong Kong — but then in Causeway Bay you're paying for the rent rather than the food — Leighton Road's appropriately named Indonesian Restaurant is about as authentic as you're likely to get in chili-shy Hong Kong. A plate of *daging rendang* (looking more like a beefy stew

than the fiery, oily, chilli-coconut-flavoured hunk of meat you'd find in Sumatra) goes for $50, a dish of wan-looking chicken or beef satays floating in a tepid dish of somewhat flavourless satay sauce are $45 or so. *Tjendol* (the distinctive, super-sweet Straits dessert made of shaved ice, sweetened beans, grass-jelly cubes and violently coloured sugar-syrup) is a better bet at $35 a bowl.

④ Craigengower Cricket Club

Cricket never really caught on among the Chinese population in Hong Kong, unlike other British territories such as Australia, the West Indies and the Indian subcontinent where the game became — and has remained — something of a national mania. These days about the only people you'll see thwacking the ball and willow

about in Hong Kong are Indians, Pakistanis or Europeans.

Craigengower Cricket Club was founded in 1894. Membership at first was confined to Old Boys of Victoria English School, and the clubhouse was named after the school buildings; later in 1901 it admitted others as members. Like the Kowloon Cricket Club across the harbour, this club originally had a marked local Eurasian membership, but has been completely 'international' for many years now. It has now occupied the same site for well over a century.

Causeway Bay • Happy Valley

157

Popularly known as *saam C wui* (Three C's Club), the Craigengower has a number of racehorses, and has a cup presented at the Jockey Club every year. They no longer have a cricket-pitch on the premises, and lawn bowls is rather more popular these days, as well as tennis on a number of courts.

How To Get There

By Bus:	No. 10 from Chater Road Statue Square bus stop, alight on Leighton Road, just in front of Bonaventure House. Walk in the direction of the traffic until you see a Chinese gateway.
By MTR:	Causeway Bay MTR Station Exit A. Go to the corner of Sharp Street East and Matheson Street, cross Matheson Street and walk along Sharp Street East towards the junction of Leighton Road, Percival Street and Hysan Avenue. Cross the junction and walk down Leighton Road until you reach a Chinese gateway on your right.
By Taxi:	'Tung Lo Wan, Lai Dun Doh, Po Leung Kuk' ('Causeway Bay, Leighton Road, Po Leung Kuk').
By Tram:	From anywhere in Central, take the east-bound tram marked 'Happy Valley' and alight on Leighton Road at the Craigengower Cricket Club.

Close to the site of Happy Valley's long-vanished Wong Nai Chung village lies Shan Kwong Road, meaning 'Sun Beam Behind the Hill' or 'Mountain View'. One of Happy Valley's numerous, relatively quiet 'roads to nowhere', it extends steeply uphill from the southern end of the racecourse and terminates at the Hong Kong Jockey Club clubhouse.

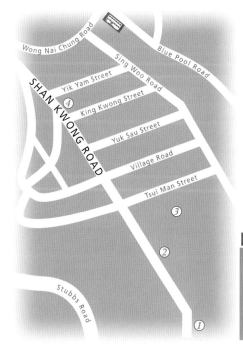

Causeway Bay • Happy Valley

🚌 Bus stop

1. Jockey Clubhouse
2. Tung Lin Kok Yuen (Hotung and Lin Kok's Garden)
3. Jewish Cemetery
4. Flower shop

From the 1920s onwards sleek racehorses, mostly China ponies or 'Walers' imported from New South Wales, were a common sight along here and remained a distinctive local feature for decades. As the animals used to be brought down from the stables to the racecourse as early as 3 a.m. for training and practice, the sound of racehorses clattering along here in the small hours meant that the side-streets off Shan Kwong Road were very noisy; eventually the road was resurfaced to help muffle the sound.

Shan Kwong Road was also a popular place for people to collect horseshoes (to be made into good-luck symbols and then resold) and for amateur and professional horticulturists to shovel up a few sacks of completely free — and *very* fresh — horse manure from the road to fertilize their gardens.

1 Jockey Clubhouse

Now the site of the Hong Kong Jockey Club's massive clubhouse, the land at the top of Shan Kwong Road was used as stables from the 1920s and 1930s right up to the early 1990s, when the last of the Jockey Club's stables were moved to Sha Tin. The stables were then demolished and the clubhouse opened in mid-1990s.

The expansive green-roofed building contains several excellent restaurants and all the usual 'clubhouse' facilities such as swimming pools, tennis and squash courts, reading rooms and so on.

2 Tung Lin Kok Yuen (Hotung and Lin Kok's Garden)

Tung Lin Kok Yuen, the extravagantly Chinese series of buildings along Shan Kwong Road, was built and endowed by prominent multimillionaire Sir Robert Hotung and his devoutly Buddhist *ping chai* (equal status wife) Lady Clara (Cheung Lin-kok), the mother of well-known Nationalist General Ho Shai-lai. Lady Clara was one of Hotung's two principal wives (the other Christian one, Lady Margaret, also known as Mak Sau-ying, is buried with him in Happy Valley's Colonial Cemetery). Both of these ladies were Eurasian and cousins.

Built in the 1930s, Tung Lin Kok Yuen has a big hall with a large Buddha image and shrines for worshipping family members of the Hotung family. The complex includes primary and secondary schools and as it was a Buddhist school, schoolgirls were not allowed to bring lunch-boxes containing meat onto the premises. The primary school, Po Kok Siu Hok, was established to commemorate the name of Lady Clara Hotung. In the past Po Kok's secondary section was partly a vocational girl's school, which taught needlework, domestic management and other useful skills, but which

now teaches conventional school subjects.

Staff here were very devoted to their place of work, and some were as old as seventy when they finally retired. Both schools provided a heavily subsidized education for the children of poorer families, and costs were entirely paid for by the Hotung family themselves. The Hotung family hall is open to the public every year on *Yuk Fat Jit* (Buddha's Birthday), which falls on the eighth day of the fourth Lunar month.

The Tung Lin Kok Yuen buildings unintentionally emphasize some of the cultural contradictions of the early Eurasian families, as Sir Robert Hotung and Lady Clara, like many of the early Eurasians, wished to be emphatically and unmistakably Chinese, and the somewhat over-the-top Chinese-Buddhist style of these buildings attests to this fact.

③ *Jewish Cemetery*

Hong Kong's small but historically significant Jewish cemetery, now completely hidden from easy public view by high-rise apartment buildings, is located just off Shan Kwong Road, and numerous prominent Jews — mostly Sephardic immigrants

from Baghdad — from Hong Kong's early days lie buried here. An interesting place to wander, full of history and atmosphere, the Jewish cemetery is generally kept firmly locked up for security reasons, and visitors must arrange access well in advance.

Happy Valley's Jewish Cemetery was described in an 1893 guidebook to Hong Kong as 'neglected' and 'by following a stone pathway on the western side of the

Causeway Bay • Happy Valley

'village' one reached the graveyard. Nearby was a secluded site known as 'the haunted house', popular in the late nineteenth century for romantic picnics — a world away from the densely packed area that surrounds the cemetery today.

4 Flower shop

Selling elegant flower arrangements and bunches of reasonably priced roses, carnations, lilies and other popular florist-blooms, this Happy Valley flower shop, like many others elsewhere in Hong Kong, caters to the floral needs of those in the immediate vicinity.

The increasing prevalence of flower shops all over Hong Kong is an interesting marker of both increased general prosperity in the last two decades — previously few had money to spare for such frivolities as fresh flowers — as well as ongoing cultural change. Many older Chinese still won't have flowers in the home (other than yellow or white *kook fa* (chrysanthemums) on the family altar) believing them to be bad luck. Increasing Westernization and 'romantic' advertising images means that many younger people now give flowers to each other for graduations and other occasions — most notably the grossly commercialized blossom-giving orgy on St Valentine's Day, when a single rose can sell for the same price as six or even ten dozen do the week before or after!

How To Get There	
By Bus:	No. 5A from Chater Road Statue Square bus stop, alight on Wong Nai Chung Road at the bus terminus at the junction of Wong Nai Chung Road and Blue Pool Road. Walk further along Wong Nai Ching Road until you come to Shan Kwong Road on the left.
By Taxi:	'Saan Kwong Doh, Choi Ma Wui Wui Sor' ('Shan Kwong Road, Jockey Club Clubhouse').
By Tram:	From anywhere in Central, take the east-bound tram marked 'Happy Valley'. Alight at the tram terminus on Wong Nai Chung Road and walk along Wong Nai Chung Road in the direction of the traffic until you reach the junction with Shan Kwong Road.

One of the more appealing of Causeway Bay's generally overcrowded backstreets, Tai Hang Road is leafy and almost quiet in parts, and seems light-years away from the densely packed shopping streets that lie just a few blocks away to the west. Beyond the St John's Ambulance headquarters, the road becomes a very busy thoroughfare heading up the hillside towards the expensive residential area at Jardine's Lookout.

Tai Hang takes its name from the *tai hang* (big stream) that formerly flowed down the hillside near here and out into the harbour between East Point and North Point. Tai Hang village, further up the hillside, is also home to a popular Fire Dragon Festival

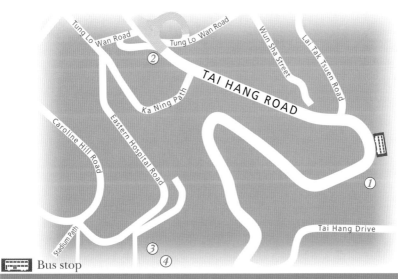

▦ Bus stop

❶ Tiger Balm Gardens   ❸ Tai Hang squatter settlements
❷ St John's Ambulance Building   ❹ Tai Hang Racecourse Fire Memorial

(see Tung Lo Wan Road) and until the early 1970s these hillsides were covered in some of Hong Kong Island's most ramshackle and overcrowded squatter settlements, teeming with refugees from the mainland, its upper slopes covered in scabrous accretions of sheet-tin huts and wooden shanties, now long since resettled and demolished.

1 Tiger Balm Gardens

Part Chinese theme park, part magnificent private villa, Haw Par Villa and the adjoining Tiger Balm Gardens now stand rather forlorn and forgotten overlooking Causeway Bay. Depicting scenes from Chinese mythology and folklore, the gardens are a fascinating place to wander around.

Built in 1935 at a cost of $16 million by Aw Boon Haw and Aw Boon Par with part of the proceeds of the Tiger Balm cure-all, the gardens were for decades one of the sights of Hong Kong; numerous movies were made using the villa and grounds as a set.

Part of the reason for the Tiger Balm Gardens popularity was its well-marketed connection with the cure-all embrocation which, while still extremely popular, is rather looked down on these days by the younger generation who tend to see it as an 'old folks' thing.

Another was its accessibility. In the 1950s and 1960s, a visit to the Tiger Balm Gardens was a popular family outing, especially for people who couldn't afford lavish entertainments in the years before widespread affluence. Admission was free, and every Sunday afternoon saw throngs of families wandering the terraces overlooking the villa, snapping photographs of each other if they happened to have a camera, and frightening their children with gruesome tales of what would happen to them if they were naughty, all illustrated by the statuary and murals. An ice-cream and some soft drinks were the usual treat enjoyed to round off the afternoon.

Capitalizing on the popularity of the Tiger Balm Gardens, other 'Chinese-themed' theme parks such as the Sung Dynasty Village at Lai Chi Kok and the varied attractions at Ocean Park sprang up elsewhere in Hong Kong. Kitsch, vulgar and unabashedly existing for no other purpose than to extract the tourist dollar, these places have all rather lost their lustre in recent years in the wake of rising local expectations and changing tourist tastes.

Perhaps the most well-known sight in the entire Tiger Balm Gardens, and a prominent landmark seen from the road below, is the Tiger Pagoda. Elegantly proportioned like most such towers, the Tiger Pagoda was nevertheless cramped up against the proliferation of ornate, garishly painted statues and grottoes that made up Tiger Balm Gardens.

Haw Par Villa hasn't been lived in since Sally Aw Sian, daughter of Aw Boon Haw, sold it to property developers after her mother's death and moved elsewhere, and the Tiger Balm Gardens stand locked-up, neglected and uncared for. This wonderful relic of Hong Kong's past, full of meaning and memories for many local families, has been repeatedly threatened with demolition and while at least part of the complex — Haw Par Villa itself — has been slated for preservation, the rest is, at the time of writing, being obliterated to make way for another apartment complex.

2 *St John's Ambulance Building*

The three-storey, whitewashed St John's Ambulance Headquarters building, situated on a low rise at the very bottom of Tai Hang Road, was built in 1935 and is still used by the organization today. The top floor has a very spacious apartment, very much in the old style, alas seldom seen anywhere now in Hong Kong as most buildings that had them have long since been demolished, while the lower floors are used for offices and a staff club.

The upper apartment was lived in for many years by the former commissioner of St John's Ambulance, prominent local Portuguese solicitor H. A. de Barros Botelho, until his death in 1999. The St John's Ambulance Headquarters building is one of the few remaining pre-war buildings in the area, along with some of the buildings within St Paul's Hospital and Haw Par Villa further up Tai Hang Road.

③ Tai Hang squatter settlements

A large squatter settlement rapidly grew on the hills above Tai Hang Road after the civil war in China drove thousands of refugees into Hong Kong in the late 1940s.

The communist victory further increased the number of people who came, and in the absence of anything better, many ended up in settlements such as this, and others like it on the Kowloon side.

Perched on hillsides and other marginal areas numerous fires swept through squatter settlements, prompting the development of public housing, one of Hong Kong's greatest — and least recognized — postwar success stories.

Most who came to the colony in those years did not expect to remain long. The Hong Kong government assumed that they would eventually return to the mainland, as previous refugee influxes fleeing flood, famine and civil war over the previous century had done; this time, however, most had strong political objections to the new government, and remained in Hong Kong, as their descendants still do today.

④ Tai Hang Racecourse Fire Memorial

Tucked away up a flight of steps behind the Hong Kong Stadium is one of Hong Kong's most interesting, lesser-known sights — the magnificent Chinese-style memorial to those who died in a catastrophic fire at the Happy Valley racecourse.

On 26 February 1918, on the second day of the racing season, a fire broke out in the temporary matshed stands at the Happy Valley racecourse. Charcoal-burning chatties from the food stalls situated under the matshed were held responsible for the outbreak, and even though the fire lasted for only twenty minutes, 614 people lost their lives. Fire services were unable to get in and extinguish the flames, as when the building collapsed the waterproof roof ensured that those within were crushed, suffocated or else burnt to death before help could reach them. According to the list of those who perished, most of the victims were Chinese, though there were also a dozen or so Indians and a few Portuguese who lost their lives as well.

The Fire Memorial on the hillside at Tai Hang was built in the early 1920s, and has been well maintained ever since; recently the Tung Wah Group of Hospitals assumed responsibility for its upkeep. Unsurprisingly in Hong Kong for a place which harbours the ghosts of so many people who died violent premature deaths, the monument gets very few visitors.

An interesting and often overlooked feature here is that the *heung ha* (home villages) of those who perished in the blaze are recorded as well as their names; a reminder that at this point in its history most of Hong Kong's inhabitants considered towns elsewhere in the Pearl River delta, such as Shun Tak, San Wui, Hoi Ping, or Nam Hoi as their real and permanent homes, and not the British colony where they actually lived, worked and spent most of their lives.

How To Get There

By Bus:	No. 11 from Central Ferry Piers, alight on Tai Hang Road near Lai Sing Court apartments. Walk about 150 m in the direction of the traffic until you reach Tiger Balm Gardens.
By Taxi:	'Dai Haang Doh, Fu Pau Beet Shui' ('Tai Hang Road, Tiger Balm Gardens').

Causeway Bay • Happy Valley

Tung Lo Wan Road
銅鑼灣道

Tung Lo Wan, or Copper Gong Bay, was the original Cantonese name for the Causeway Bay area, and among the Hong Kong Chinese, the name has persisted to the present day. The area's Chinese name takes its inspiration from — depending on the source — an old copper gong housed within Causeway Bay's Tin Hau Temple, or the original shape of the bay itself, which was shaped somewhat like the outline of a copper gong.

Tung Lo Wan Road closely follows the original shoreline on this section of Hong Kong Island. Early photographs show this stretch of coast looking rocky, wild and almost remote, with the unusually shaped Lin Fa Kung

Bus stop

1 Tai Hang Fire Dragon   **3** St Paul's Hospital and French Convent
2 St Mary's Church   **4** Shing Hing Loong Fruits Compradore

Temple being almost the only building in the area. Times have changed, and today the former waterfront track is almost as crowded and noisy as the rest of Causeway Bay; nevertheless there are numerous elements of interest along here and some, like St Paul's Church, secluded behind the walls of the French Convent, are little-known and pleasantly unexpected.

1 *Tai Hang Fire Dragon*

Each year at Mid-Autumn festival, the villagers have a fire dragon festival which lasts for three days. The popular festival starts in front of the Tin Hau Temple on nearby Tin Hau Temple Road, and winds its way around the entire Tai Hang area.

Two versions exist as to why this custom originated. One has it that there was a pirate band who attempted to land at Tai Hang village and rob the inhabitants. However, when they saw a shimmering dragon flying towards them and heard drum-beats and shouts, they took fright and decamped. Another version recounts that, during a plague outbreak at Tai Hang, Tin Hau appeared to a villager in a dream and instructed him to perform a dragon dance to cleanse the village of the disease. While these stories are appealing, the custom of performing dragon dances was once very common throughout Kwangtung (Guangdong) Province at the time of the Mid-Autumn festival.

Fo Lung (Fire Dragons) are unique to the people of Kwangtung (Guangdong) and are the most primitive form of dragon dance. Originally, the dragons were made from a special type of wild grass, and when that was unavailable, from *wo cho* (rice plant stalks). Incense sticks are lighted and affixed to the dragon to represent the dragon's scales. From a distance they shimmer and smoke, adding to the sense of movement.

The Fire Dragon procession starting at the Lin Fa Kung (Lotus Flower Palace) Temple on Tung Lo Wan Road winds its way throughout the Tai Hang area. Dedicated to Kuan Yin, the Boddhisatva Goddess of Mercy, the attractive Lin Fa Kung temple was built in 1864 and is architecturally unique, following no traditional Chinese design. The rocky hillside behind the temple is known as Lin Fa Shan (Lotus Flower Mountain).

Causeway Bay • Happy Valley

169

STREETS

② St Mary's Church

This Anglican church was built in the early 1930s and designed by the Franco-Belgian consortium Credit Foncierre d'Extreme Orient. This firm was responsible for a number of other religious buildings constructed elsewhere in Hong Kong at this time as part of an expansion programme by the Roman

Catholic Bishop Valtorta, including St Teresa's Church in Kowloon Tong, the Carmelite Convent at Stanley and the Little Sisters of the Poor at Ngau Chi Wan.

Designed to look as Chinese as possible, so lessening the cultural gap between the Christian religion and the everyday Chinese, St Mary's Church is one of Hong Kong's most eclectically styled buildings — religious or secular — tucked away on an obscure backstreet corner in Causeway Bay, the ornate facade is lovingly maintained.

Another prominent religious building designed in this syncretic religious style was the Methodist Church and Mission at the corner of Johnston Road in Wan Chai, sadly demolished in the mid-1990s. Another similar example, the Chinese Young Men's Christian Association (YMCA) building on Central's Bridges Street, is still in existence and well maintained.

③ St Paul's Hospital and French Convent

Established by the French order of St Paul de Chartres in disused cotton mills, St Paul's Hospital has been known to generations of Hong Kong residents as *Faat Kwok Yee Yuen* (French Hospital)

The beautiful old church situated within grounds of St Paul's Hospital is one of Hong Kong's little-

known treasures, and almost completely obscured these days by taller buildings all around. A world away from the noise, crowds and squalor only metres away on the streets of Causeway Bay, St Paul's Church is immaculately maintained and still regularly used for services.

The convent is also home to one of Hong Kong's best-known girl's schools. Old girls from 'the French Convent' have filled a number of senior government positions over the years. Perhaps the most well-known old girl is the former Executive Councillor Dame Lydia Dunn, now retired from public life.

4 *Shing Hing Loong Fruits Compradore*

One seldom sees a shop sign like this anymore.

In times past a 'compradore' was a Chinese middleman-manager employed in a European firm; the word comes from the Portuguese word 'compra' meaning 'to buy'. Compradores were leading figures in treaty port life and many became spectacularly wealthy, as well as figures of contempt for the more nationalistic, who saw them as opportunistic collaborators with foreign imperialism in China and parasites upon their own people. Others have viewed them as agents of social change. Whatever the polemics of their historical role, the continuing wealth and position of more than a few long-established Hong Kong families owes its start to a nineteenth- or early twentieth-century compradore's position in Hong Kong,

Shanghai, Tientsin (Tianjin), Amoy (Xiamen) or elsewhere on the China coast.

A 'compradore's shop', on the other hand, was a general merchandise store, which usually — but not always — catered principally to European clients. Foreigners in those days relied almost entirely on imported foodstuffs, which for the most part the Chinese community either knew nothing about, didn't like or couldn't have afforded anyway.

Payment in these shops was almost always by the 'chit' system, where one would sign for goods purchased on an account payable at the end of the month.

Causeway Bay • Happy Valley

Tung Lo Wan Road

This small but interesting shop, one of the few anywhere in Hong Kong to still have the term 'compradore' incorporated on the signboard, has been located here, under the same management, for many years now.

How To Get There

By Bus:	No. 25 from Central Ferry Piers and No. 309 from Exchange Square Bus Terminus, alight on Causeway Road when you see the Central Library on your right and Victoria Park on your left. Walk along the traffic until you reach Tin Hau MTR Station. Cross the road to Tung Lo Wan Road and walk along this road for about 200 m until you reach Lin Fa Kung Street West.
By MTR:	Tin Hau MTR Station Exit B. Tung Lo Wan Road is directly across the road. Cross the road (King's Road) and walk along Tung Lo Wan Road for about 200 m until you reach Lin Fa Kung Street West.
By Taxi:	'Tung Lo Waan Doh, Leen Fa Gung' ('Tung Lo Wan Road, Lin Fa Kung Temple').
By Tram:	From anywhere in Central, take the east-bound tram marked 'Shau Kei Wan' or 'North Point'. Alight at Queen's College and turn right into Tung Lo Wan Road. Walk along this road for about 200 m until you reach Lin Fa Kung Street West.

The section of Wong Nai Chung Road at the lower end of Happy Valley is an apparent contradiction, especially so when one considers the symbolism. On one side is the racetrack thronged by punters who look for favourable signs and portents everywhere around, and on the other a string of cemeteries, Moslem, Catholic, Parsee, Hindu and Protestant. Further up in Happy Valley, near the Jockey Club's palatial clubhouse, there is a small but very interesting Jewish cemetery. (See Shan Kwong Road.)

In pre-British times, the Wong Nai Chung valley had a number of paddy-fields cultivated by the villagers who made their homes in the village above. The water lying about, and the mosquitoes that bred there, encouraged the rapid spread of virulent strains of malarial and dengue fever, then known generally as 'Hong Kong Fever'. In the first few years of British rule mortality from these and other endemic diseases remained very high in Hong Kong, especially among the

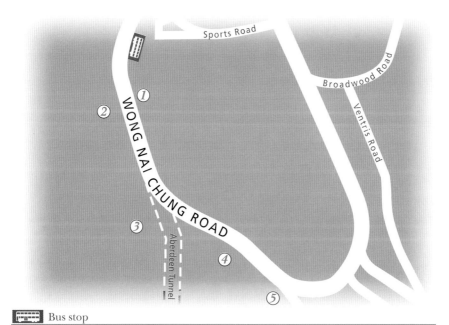

Causeway Bay •
Happy Valley

📟 Bus stop

① Hong Kong Jockey Club   ④ Parsee Cemetery
② St Michael's Catholic Cemetery   ⑤ Hong Kong Sanatorium
③ Hong Kong Cemetery

STREETS

military encamped in the valley. In 1846 the indigenous cultivators were resettled, the paddy-fields cleared and drained and a ring-road put around the valley for recreational purposes — precursor of today's modern racetrack.

Due to its fever-prone reputation, the picturesque area around the racecourse remained sparsely settled, with only a few isolated houses situated here and there and the cemeteries strung out around the lower ridges. Proper drainage works eventually ensured that fever became less of a problem and a few houses were built on the surrounding hillsides. As the city gradually grew in the 1910s and expanded into hitherto marginal areas, the tramway was extended into Happy Valley. The area gradually became a popular middle-class suburb in the years before the Second World War, and has remained so to this day.

(1) Hong Kong Jockey Club

The Hong Kong Jockey Club, until 1996 known as the Royal Hong Kong Jockey Club, has been Happy Valley's most prominent feature ever since the first race meeting opened in December 1846. The first grandstand was a matshed — a far cry from today's magnificent premises — and was used for the next twenty-five years. For decades many jockeys were 'gentlemen amateurs', who worked as stockbrokers and the like in their spare time. Many of these were Eurasian, and a number of the best trainers were White Russian. Until the Pacific War, these days many jockeys and trainers from Shanghai and elsewhere in China came to Hong Kong for what were known as Interport meets; now many jockeys, as well as horses, come from as far afield as New Zealand and Ireland to race at Happy Valley.

For generations the Jockey Club and its executive committee members have wielded an element of power and influence in Hong Kong quite beyond what many would expect from a 'mere' racecourse; by arrangement with government the profits generated from horse-races are put back into the local community and are used to endow schools, clinics and many other charitable activities.

In 1994 the Happy Valley racecourse was expanded and new headquarters built, in the process completely swallowing up Sports Road; the century-old banyan trees that lined it were spared and have been transplanted near the side of Wong Nai Chung Road.

2 St Michael's Catholic Cemetery

Extremely overcrowded these days, like so much of Hong Kong, St Michael's Roman Catholic Cemetery is where many of Hong Kong's first true locals lie buried.

Most of the graves here bear Portuguese names, a reminder of the once significant local Portuguese community that has gradually dwindled over the past four decades. One of the earliest is of Leonardo d'Almada e Castro, who came across to Hong Kong from Macao in 1842 with Sir Henry Pottinger, Hong Kong's first governor. With his younger brother José Maria, d'Almada served in the local administration until his death in 1875. Members of their extended family still remain living in Hong Kong today.

Also buried here is Sister Aloysia Emily Bowring, the daughter of Sir John Bowring, Hong Kong's third

governor. Under the influence of the d'Almada family, she became a Canossian nun, and is interred with her fellow religious in the Canossian Ossuary. There are numerous burial plots and ossuaries for other religious orders elsewhere in the cemetery.

Another grave is of Dr Pedro José Lobo, well-known Macao businessman and the model of a rather cruel caricature by novelist Ian Fleming in his James Bond thriller *Goldfinger,* later made into a popular film.

Built of pink marble with a pair of angels, the tomb of 1960s' film goddess Lin Dai, Hong Kong's answer to Marilyn Monroe, is on the southern side of the cemetery. When she died her funeral was mobbed by hundreds of grief-stricken fans, and from time to time aging admirers still leave flowers on her grave. Lin Dai won four best actress awards in a career spanning a decade.

Sitting outside the cemetery gates on Wong Nai Chung Road, there is usually an old woman with a bucket of flowers to sell, generally white or yellow *kook fa* (chrysanthemun) — most commonly used by Chinese for remembering the dead — and sometimes a few pink or red roses and carnations. In telling contrast to the adjacent Colonial Cemetery, the graves in the Roman Catholic Cemetery are visited quite frequently and are generally much better maintained — a reminder that for some of their descendants at least, Hong Kong remains home. Family plots

Causeway Bay • Happy Valley

are also still used for burials, and some contain the remains of several family members, as the inscriptions on the gravestones attest.

(3) Hong Kong Cemetery (formerly the Colonial Cemetery)

The earliest graves in this very extensive cemetery date from the mid-1840s. One of the oldest is that of Reverend Karl Gutzlaff, whose name is also commemorated by a backstreet in Central. Gutzlaff was the first Lutheran missionary in China; in addition to handing out religious tracts, his knowledge of several Chinese dialects made Gutzlaff a valued interpreter from time to time on opium vessels during smuggling runs up and down the coast. His wife organized a small school in Macao, which they reopened in Hong Kong in 1843.

Many graves here are military, a reminder of the fact that from the very earliest years of British rule Hong Kong was very much a garrison town; for many servicemen and their families, especially in the disease-ridden nineteenth century, Hong Kong proved to be their last posting. Several massive obelisks are dedicated to the dead from entire ships or regiments, some dating back to the Second Opium War (1857–60) and earlier.

Other prominent graves include those of compradore Sir Robert Hotung, Armenian businessman Sir Paul Chater, White Russian artist George Vitalievich Smirnoff, and early American missionary and educator Henrietta Shuck. Perhaps the most poignant graves are of young children, dead of a scratch, disease or animal bite that these days wouldn't even warrant hospitalization.

Part of the cemetery grounds were resumed by the Hong Kong government in the 1970s when the Aberdeen Tunnel was built, but for the most part, it remains tranquil and overgrown. An interesting and not at all creepy place to wander, there are many large old flowering trees and a great deal of open space, remarkable in itself so close to the heart of the teeming city. The many thousands of mosquitoes that rise up from the marshy ground still found in some parts of the cemetery are a modern reminder of Happy Valley's fever-plagued past, which saw so many early settlers in Hong Kong consigned to an early grave. For the most part the families of those buried here have long since moved away from Hong Kong and very few graves are tended or even visited from decade to decade.

4 Parsee Cemetery

Probably the first merchants from the Indian subcontinent to recognize the potential offered by the China trade, the Parsees are largely forgotten today. Indistinguishable to most Hong Kong people from the wider Indian community, the numerically small Parsee community has nevertheless included some of Hong Kong's most prominent and influential residents.

While 1852 is the date given on the gates of their cemetery in Happy Valley, there were Parsees in Hong Kong from a much earlier period. Macao also has a small and these days rather neglected Parsee cemetery which long predates that in Happy Valley, a reminder of the fact that most early Parsee merchants came on to Hong Kong from their earlier trading bases at Macao and Canton.

Some of Hong Kong's early founders who lie buried here include Dorabjee Naorojee, whose most notable contribution to Hong Kong was starting the cross-harbour passenger ferry services, the Star Ferry, that still run today.

Another is Sir Hormusjee Naorojee Mody, an opium trader and early property developer (Mody Road in Kowloon is named after him) who towards the end of his life played a key role in the establishment of the University of Hong Kong. The attractive old Main Building on Bonham Road — which he largely paid for — is his most permanent memorial, and bears a plaque just inside the entrance describing Mody as 'a Parsee gentleman 50 years resident in Hong Kong'.

Causeway Bay • Happy Valley

5 Hong Kong Sanatorium

The Hong Kong Sanatorium was originally 80 percent owned by Dr Li Shu-fan, a prominent Hong Kong surgeon and philanthropist, and is now administered by the Foundation that bears his name. A graduate of the Hong Kong College of Medicine, forerunner of the University of

STREETS

Hong Kong, Dr Li was a member of the Legislative Council from 1937–41, and remained active in public life till his death.

A big game hunter and friend of Ernest Hemingway as well as a keen gardener, Dr Li was one of the very few to successfully grow roses in Hong Kong's humid climate, at his now demolished home — 'White Jade' — high on the hillside overlooking Happy Valley. His autobiography, *Hong Kong Surgeon*, is a fascinating record of a richly lived Chinese life in Hong Kong, spread over sixty very eventful years.

How To Get There

By Bus:	No. 97 from Exchange Square bus terminus, alight at Happy Valley Racecourse.
By MTR:	Causeway Bay MTR Station Exit A. Walk to the Shell Tower end of Times Square and then turn left into Canal Road. Walk in the direction of the traffic. After crossing Leighton Road and walking about 50 m past the Craigengower Cricket Club, you will reach the Hong Kong Jockey Club Headquarters on Sports Road.
By Taxi:	'Ma Cheong' ('Jockey Club Headquarters').
By Tram:	From anywhere in Central, take the east-bound tram marked 'Happy Valley'. Alight on Wong Nai Chung Road at Craigengower Cricket Club and walk along Sports Road for about 150 m to reach the Hong Kong Jockey Club Headquarters.

This busy thoroughfare recalls the Chinese name of Hong Kong's oldest conglomerate, Jardine Matheson and Co. Hong Kong Island was ceded to Great Britain in 1842 after the First Opium War ended which, to their lasting notoriety, Jardine's had helped to incite. Shortly thereafter the company established themselves at Causeway Bay, then known as East Point, which remained their Hong Kong nerve-centre for well over a century. As well as wharves and godowns, Jardine's also established a cotton mill and a sugar refinery, both early and not terribly successful forerunners of Hong Kong's later industrialization.

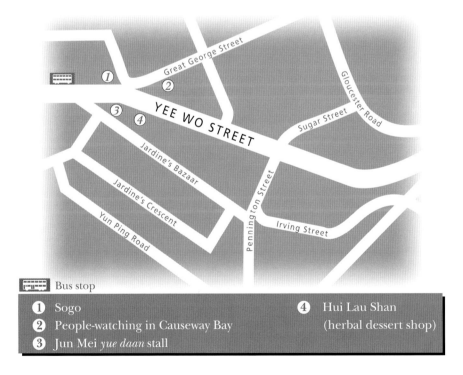

Causeway Bay • Happy Valley

🚌 Bus stop

① Sogo
② People-watching in Causeway Bay
③ Jun Mei *yue daan* stall
④ Hui Lau Shan (herbal dessert shop)

STREETS

Jardine, Matheson and Co. are more widely known as *Yee Wo* (also sometimes transliterated as Ewo) which means, 'Harmony'; the firm's Chinese name was first used at Canton in the 1820s. The name 'Yee Wo' was much more commonly used in Shanghai, where the firm also had very extensive business interests. In Hong Kong it was better known until the early twentieth century by the Anglicized term 'Jar Deen'. Numerous other street names in the area recall Jardine Matheson and Co. connections, but none perhaps is more prominent than Yee Wo Street.

Permanently thronged with people, buses and trams, Yee Wo Street is right at the very heart of Causeway Bay. Pollution is always extremely bad along here, made worse by the endlessly idling engines of minibuses lined up along nearby Jardine's Bazaar. Wear a gas mask if at all possible! Probably at it's most bearable in the early afternoon mid-week, Yee Wo Street is definitely **not** the place to go on a Sunday afternoon if you can't stand crowds.

1 Sogo

Opened in the mid-1980s, this Japanese department store has been a name to reckon with ever since. Although there are members of the wartime generation who still won't willingly buy anything Japanese, manufactured goods from Japan started becoming popular in Hong Kong in the 1960s. Prior to that time Japanese goods, while cheap, were not renowned for either durability or status.

For cheap-and-cheerful these days, people go to the China Products Department Stores, but for high-end items discerning shoppers head for Japanese stores like Sogo and Mitsukoshi which stock everything from shoes and handbags to dinner services and stationery.

The building itself on the corner of Hennessy Road and East Point Road, just before Yee Wo Street, is a well-known landmark in Causeway Bay, and the store's entrance is usually surrounded by people who've made arrangements to meet up in front. Recently, all the other Sogo Department Stores elsewhere in Asia have been closed down but for now, the Causeway Bay branch still hangs on.

2) People-watching in Causeway Bay

One of the most interesting things to do in this corner of Hong Kong is just to stand back and watch what comes past. Sooner or later everything that passes for the cool and interesting around town — and whoever fancies themselves as such — comes parading down Yee Wo Street and the nearby thoroughfares. People-watching aficionados aver that the constantly moving scenery is better along here than almost anywhere else in Hong Kong — only parts of Mong Kok can compare for the sheer volume and variety.

Bored-looking wannabe *tai tai* types wander in and out of the little boutiques, giggly teenage couples out for a good time sit and share a plate of dessert at Hui Lau Shan, the occasional muscle-boy couple wander along hand-in-hand, bewildered-looking Japanese tourists poke about on street-stalls looking for bargains, tiny withered old women decades past retirement age sift through rubbish bins looking for empty soft drink cans to recycle, baggy-trousered, in-your-face expat teenagers burn up their father's credit cards, and the traffic noise never abates. But don't stand and watch the world go by here for too long at any one stretch — your lungs will never forgive you for it!

3) Jun Mei yue daan stall

Ever wondered which shops have the highest rents in all of Hong Kong? High-end boutiques in Prince's Building or the Landmark or tourist-trap electronics shops along Tsim Sha Tsui's Golden Mile would seem the obvious contenders, but no. Instead, this grubby-looking little fast food stall at the corner of Yee Wo Street is one of the prizewinners in that dubious contest, and has a daily turnover that would turn most other businesses quite green with envy.

Perpetually thronged with people at all hours of the day and night, and in just the right location to block pedestrian traffic for metres in every direction, Jun

Causeway Bay • Happy Valley

Mei *yue daan* (fish ball) stall has been on the same location for over twenty years. Fifteen dollars will get you a satay stick like skewer of fish or squid balls dipped in curry-like sauce, or you could always have a few lumps of battered *heung cheung* (red-skinned sausage). Or perhaps some deep-fried capsicum slices stuffed with fish paste will do to fill the gap  till dinner-time? Or maybe some pig's intestines would be more to your liking?

Those who like this sort of thing won't eat anything else, but for others the smell of the fish ball sauce alone is almost enough to make them ill. This type of snack is Hong Kong's quintessential street-food, and love it or hate it, Jun Mei's perennially popular offerings are about as local as it comes! Try it at least once.

(4) *Hui Lau Shan (herbal dessert shop)*

What started out as a humble herbal shop in Yuen Long has become an extremely popular franchised outlet with branches all over Hong Kong. Hui Lau Shan has apparently been around since the 1950s, but only mushroomed in the 1990s. There can be few local residents who haven't tried their *leung cha* (herbal tea) at least once, and the ever-  changing, bewildering variety of cold desserts attract a devoted following, especially in the summer months.

Ever-popular *gwai ling go*, black jelly made from stewed tortoise abdominal shells is probably the most popular item. Slightly bitter with a wonderful smooth texture, *gwai ling go* is definitely an acquired taste. Other items are made from *hoi dai yeh* (sea coconut), while *shuet garp goh*, meant to be a good restorative tonic for pregnant women, is made from frogs' fallopian tubes; it really is. Recently Hui Lau Shan has been inventing new and different mango-based desserts, some involving tapioca, ice-cream and grass jelly — all very delicious and just the thing on a hot day.

The Yee Wo Street branch is *always* thronged with people, and late at night the queue outside can be five deep waiting for a seat — but it's worth it! Prices for various items vary from $15 to $35 (*gwai ling go* is one of the most expensive items) and are often slightly cheaper for take-away.

Causeway Bay •
Happy Valley

How To Get There

By Bus:	No. 5 from Chater Road Statue Square, No. 2 from Connaught Road Central City Hall bus stop, alight on Yee Wo Street at Sogo Department Store.
By MTR:	Causeway Bay MTR Station Exits D3 and D4, which open directly into Sogo Department Store.
By Taxi:	'Yee Wo Gaai, Sung Kwong' ('Yee Wo Street, Sogo').
By Tram:	From anywhere in Central, take the east-bound tram marked 'Causeway Bay', 'Shau Kei Wan' or 'North Point'. Alight on Yee Wo Street just after Sogo Department Store.

North Point

Until just before the Pacific War, the area extending beyond Causeway Bay towards North Point was relatively open country, and the name itself is the last generally used reference to any of the 'points' that once jutted out into the harbour along the northern coast of Hong Kong Island: East Point at Causeway Bay and West Point near Sai Ying Pun have all long since been subsumed by waves of reclamation, and the names themselves have vanished from everyday usage.

In the 1920s bathers would alight from the tram at North Point, cross King's Road and be able to swim in clean clear water. This bucolic situation rapidly changed over the next decade, and by 1941 North Point had a power station, a refugee camp built to house Nationalist soldiers (later used for a time to intern Canadian prisoners-of-war after the Japanese capture of Hong Kong), some small factory buildings and not much else. Beyond to the east were the godowns, docks, shipyard and sugar refinery at Taikoo.

North Point became much more built up in the years immediately after the Pacific War, and in the process developed a distinctly separate flavour to the rest of Hong Kong. This transformation owed its genesis to brash new arrivals from the north — the Shanghainese. The term 'Shanghainese' in those days did not only denote natives of that city; it was also used by people from Hong Kong to refer to places in Eastern China such as Ningpo (Ningbo), Nanking (Nanjing), Soochow (Suzhou), Wuxi and points further north.

Immigrants always tend to settle in areas where there are people who come from the same place, speak the same language and have similar food habits, attitudes and customs. The Shanghainese newcomers to Hong Kong, whilst still being ethnically Chinese, were nevertheless in many other respects quite foreign to the Cantonese who made up the bulk of the local population, and so congregated in one particular area — North Point.

The arrival of this community and North Point's transformation began in 1947–48, with the arrival of increasing numbers of people seeking a safe haven from the civil war then raging in earnest in China. None expected to remain for very long, either in North Point or Hong Kong itself, and expected to remain in the safe haven afforded by the British colony only until the dust settled and they could return home again, as refugees from internal disorder in China had always done.

This time though things were not to work out that way. Most of these 'temporary' residents from Shanghai never went back. The surrender of the city to the Communists in 1949 brought a fresh wave of migrants from Shanghai that continued until the late 1950s; the flow slowed from then on, as most of those with the means and ability to leave had already done so. By the 1950s, North Point was known all over Hong Kong as *Siu Sheung Hoi*, or Little Shanghai.

Buildings erected at North Point around this period, some still standing today, reflected this underlying sense of impermanence. Known as *tong lau* (Chinese buildings), these three- to six-storey high apartment blocks were quickly and often very shoddily built with an eye to a fast return, a pattern later repeated endlessly in the rest of Hong Kong.

These days, Japan and its fashion trends symbolize the modern and the smart to Hong Kong's young people and are slavishly copied, but until the 1950s, however, it was Shanghai styles that were emulated; aging signboards in North Point today still advertise beauty parlours, restaurants and barbershops, first established and popularized over fifty years ago.

Shanghai barbershops, especially, were the rage for many years, and to this day, one can still find these establishments all over Hong Kong. Staffed by dapper elderly barbers, their windows screened by lace-net curtains and emblazoned with

185

STREETS

the word 'Shanghai', the interior décor — and the choice of hairstyles offered — haven't changed much in forty years. Now chiefly patronized by old men in search of a cheap trim, these barber-shops are an enduring reminder of the time when Shanghai represented all that was smart, fashionable and modern in China.

With increasing affluence, many of the early generation of Shanghai immigrants moved from North Point to other areas, leading to a decline in the formerly visible and obvious Shanghainese presence. The younger generation of Shanghainese brought up in Hong Kong learned Cantonese, intermarried with other dialect groups and are now largely indistinguishable from the bulk of Hong Kong's population. Thus the regional differences that divided the first

generation of newcomers have been subsumed into a common Hong Kong identity.

The Shanghainese have forged a very distinct role in Hong Kong's public life. Chief Executive Tung Chee-hwa, President of the Legislative Council Rita Fan Hsu Lai-tai, former Chief Justice Sir T. L. Yang, former Chief Secretary Anson Chan and numerous prominent business figures are all Shanghainese (by the definition above), much as they may choose at times to publicly downplay their regional origins.

As the Shanghainese moved away, North Point was gradually taken over by another immigrant group, the Fujianese. Many were *wah kiu* (overseas Chinese) from Indonesia who, displaced by political events in South-east Asia, had moved to China and, finding conditions there uncongenial, gradually made their way to Hong Kong. The preponderance of small Indonesian *tokos* (specialist grocery shops) found in this area selling coffee, coconuts and *bumbu* (spices) reflect their origins. *Siu Sheung Hoi*, Little Shanghai, is today much more widely known as *Siu Fook Kin* (Little Fukien or Fujian). A few elements of the not-so-distant past still linger around North Point, however, and recall a time when this part of Hong Kong Island felt more like a transplanted suburb of Shanghai.

Quarry Bay/Taikoo

Older residents — both Chinese and European — still refer to the area as Tsat Tsz Mui, but for most people these days, it's just Quarry Bay. In Cantonese the area is known as Juk Yue Chung (arrow fish creek), which recalls a stream near the old Taikoo Docks, now long since vanished and forgotten, along with the carp-like fish that gave the stream its name.

According to some Chinese scholars, there was a pirate encampment here in the early years of the nineteenth century named Tung Ying Pun (Eastern Soldier's Camp), a counterpart to Sai Ying Pun (Western Soldier's Camp in Western) but this has been widely disputed. Hakka stonemasons began settling in the area shortly after the British arrival, and opened quarries in the hillsides nearby, hence the English name for the area — Quarry Bay.

Tsat Tsz Mui: The 'Seven Sisters'

Back in the days when Victoria Harbour still had an extensive rocky shoreline — now largely vanished through successive waves of reclamation — there were once seven distinctive tall granite boulders on the beach, on the seaward side of King's Road. Local legend had it that seven beautiful village maidens, all sisters, known as the *Tsat Tsz Mui* (seven sisters), had once lived in the hamlet nearby. When one of them suddenly died, the others made a pact and all killed themselves to be reunited with her. Always together in life, they remained linked in death; a wandering goddess who happened to be passing by took pity and turned their dead bodies to granite stones on the seashore. Now long since vanished, both from sight and the local memory, the Tsat Tsz Mui could still be seen near here in the early 1920s.

Shau Kei Wan: Rice Basket Bay

Shau Kei Wan means 'Rice Basket Bay', and in old photographs and on old maps it closely resembles the shape of a rice basket, though successive waves of reclamation in the area have dramatically altered the coastline. The original small settlement predates the British arrival in Hong Kong by centuries. It was a quietly prosperous small fishing town, and in the first Hong Kong Census in May 1841 there were 1,200 people living there.

After 1841 the bay at Shau Kei Wan was known in English as Aldrich Bay, after Major R. E. Aldrich, a Royal Engineers officer stationed in Hong Kong in the

STREETS

early years. For a time Shau Kei Wan was also known as Ngo Yan Wan (Hungry People's Bay) — the name had been in use for decades before the British arrived — and for a time in the 1850s Ngo Yan Wan was even used officially.

A little further around from Shau Kei Wan is the settlement of Ah Kung Ngam (Grandfather's, or Ancestor's, Rocky Cave) which in 1913 had a population of 213, of whom 159 were males. Scarred hillsides around Ah Kung Ngam indicate a number of abandoned quarry sites, like similar areas immediately opposite the Lye Mun Strait.

Official reports in the late nineteenth century indicate that the Shau Kei Wan quarries were more significant than anywhere else on either Hong Kong Island or British Kowloon; their importance gradually declined however; in 1872 there were only 72 quarries operating and 51 in 1891 — down from over an estimated hundred or so in the mid-1850s.

Missionaries began operating in the Shau Kei Wan area in the early 1860s, with the German Protestant Basel Mission operating among the Hakkas; Basel Road near Ah Kung Ngam is named after these early missionaries.

Shek O

The Peak is usually thought of as Hong Kong's most desirable residential area, but for scenic beauty, as well as that rarest of Hong Kong commodities — space — Shek O wins out every time. First developed as a residential alternative to the

Peak, unpopular with some because of its fogs, dank mists and walls streaming damp most of the year, Shek O has retained an air of exclusivity, as it is still relatively remote and undeveloped. The bungalows are still there scattered among the ridges of the golf-course and overlooking the cliffs on the way up to Big Wave Bay, and the expansive views over islands and sea haven't changed much in over half a century.

Shek O village has developed considerably in recent years and can get very crowded on weekends and public holidays. Fairly clean relative to the others elsewhere on the island, the attractive beach remains one of Hong Kong's more popular bathing spots. It is quite busy in the summer months, but on weekdays at least the open sandy beach remains much as it appears in photographs from the 1920s, surrounded by cliffs and mostly empty.

Until the late 1940s there was very little at Chai Wan beyond a few scattered villages. These were for the most part occupied by Hakka people mostly stonecutters from the nearby quarries. One remaining Hakka village house is Law Uk which has been turned into a popular and well-curated folk museum.

Nearby Shau Kei Wan had been a quietly prosperous local fishing port since pre-British times. It expanded considerably after the British settled on Hong Kong Island as the growing city created a greatly expanded market for their catch. Chai Wan is sometimes also known as Sai Wan — very confusing for some as Kennedy Town is known as Sai Wan as well.

Postwar refugee influx had many families living in precarious squatter settlements on the then marginal hillsides around Shau Kei Wan. The area was a desirable place for the poor to live as it was relatively open country in those days and the tramlines ended nearby, making travel to other parts of Hong Kong Island for work cheap and relatively easy. Gradually these ramshackle areas were cleared, making way for the massive public housing estates and factories that are a feature of the Chai Wan area today.

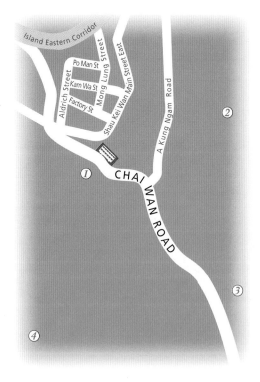

Bus stop

1 Salesian Mission
2 Lyemun Barracks
3 Sai Wan Battery
4 Little Sai Wan and Cold War 'listening'

The inauguration of the MTR Island Line with Chai Wan as its eastern terminus has made the area much more accessible, but rentals around here remain some of the lowest on Hong Kong Island.

1 *Salesian Mission*

Built in 1939, for many years this Roman Catholic Mission House was one of the very few substantial buildings in the area apart from the nearby Lyemun Barracks. A massacre of medical personnel by the invading Japanese forces took place here in December 1941 when the nearby gun battery on Sai Wan hill was overwhelmed. Two men survived the atrocity after being grievously wounded on the hillside above the mission and lived to tell the tale. One of them, Dr Osler Thomas, became a well-known medical practitioner in Hong Kong after the war; he now lives in Sydney.

The Salesian Mission is still used by the Roman Catholic Church as a mission house and printing press, and also has a school attached to it; some of the buildings were donated by Aw Boon Haw, the Tiger Balm millionaire.

2 *Lyemun Barracks*

Overlooking the Lyemun Strait, the eastern approach to Victoria Harbour, Lyemun Barracks has had an interesting history stretching back to the early years of the British colony. Barracks were first built on the cliffs overlooking the Lyemun Strait in the early 1860s, but this early military cantonment was later abandoned due to high malarial fatalities suffered by troops stationed in the area. Some of the remaining old buildings here date from the 1880s when the barracks were re-established, with substantial additions from the late 1930s.

Lyemun Barracks reverted to the Hong Kong government in 1987; the 2/7 Duke of Edinburgh's Own Gurkha Rifles were the last regular battalion to be stationed there. Part of the complex has since been renovated and transformed into a government-operated leave centre known as Lei Yue Mun Park, which members of the general public can use.

Two gun batteries and a redoubt were built here in the 1880s, as well as housing for the recently developed Brennan torpedo, an early form of guided torpedo, all of which can be visited on the cliffs below the nearby Museum of Coastal Defence, built into the old Lyemun Redoubt.

③ Sai Wan Battery

This gun battery was built in 1936–37 as part of increased defence preparations in Hong Kong. Manned by the local Hong Kong Volunteer Defence Corps when the Japanese invaded in 1941, Sai Wan Battery was swiftly overrun and the men caught here where massacred. Two however managed to  survive, and subsequently gave evidence at postwar war crimes trials.

Sai Wan Battery is a quiet reflective place with spectacular views of Victoria Harbour, Lyemun Strait and the Tathong Channel on a clear day. Unlike many other easily accessible wartime sites, it is not overrun by war gamers — at least most of the time. The steep winding path up the hill through dense vegetation is very popular with early morning walkers from the nearby housing estates, and a number of them have established flower beds and ad hoc sitting-out areas along the way.

4) *Little Sai Wan and Cold War 'listening'*

There were a number of advanced 'listening' posts in Hong Kong that provided an ear to mainland China, when more conventional means of observation were not possible. The most substantial of these until the 1940s — and in its time one of the most advanced in the world — was located at Stonecutter's Island; before the Pacific War this was home of the Far East Combined Bureau, Britain's principal intelligence gathering facility in the Far East.

Other high-powered listening posts were built elsewhere in Hong Kong after the Pacific War, at Little Sai Wan (above Chai Wan Road), Chung Hom Kok and at the very top of Tai Mo Shan, Hong Kong's highest mountain. In advance of the handover these were all closed, and the Chung Hom Kok facility moved to Geraldton, Western Australia, in 1995.

How To Get There

By Bus:	No. 780 from Connaught Road Central City Hall bus stop, alight on Chai Wan Road at the bus stop across from Salesian School.
By MTR:	Shau Kei Wan MTR Station Exit A2. Walk along Aldrich Street until you reach the junction of Aldrich Street, Shau Kei Wan Road, Shau Kei Wan Main Street East and Chai Wan Road. Walk up Chai Wan Road for about 150 m until you reach Salesian School.
By Taxi:	'Chai Waan Doh, Tsz Yau Chung Hok' ('Chai Wan Road, Salesian School').
By Tram:	From anywhere in Central, take the east-bound tram marked 'Shau Kei Wan' and alight at terminus station on Shau Kei Wan Main Street East. Walk up to the Ming Wa Housing Estate and walk along a shaded path below the apartment blocks until you reach Chai Wan Road.

King's Road
英皇道

King's Road was once almost on the waterfront, and until the 1920s North Point was a pleasantly remote part of town, with attractive bathing beaches on the harbour side — a long way in every sense from the overcrowded, rather workaday part of Hong Kong that North Point and Quarry Bay look like today.

An interesting area to wander about, King's Road and the surrounding streets have much to offer the casual ambler, and while still very crowded, North Point — being a relatively newer part of town — somehow feels rather different to the more historic western end of the island. And as an interesting aside, King's Road in Chinese reads 'English King's Road' — not as neutral a moniker as it may at first appear!

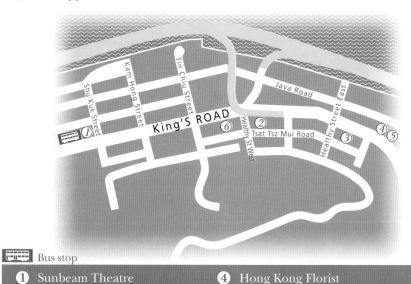

🚌 Bus stop

❶ Sunbeam Theatre
❷ Tong Lau and Yeung Lau
❸ Choi Heong Yuen cake shop
❹ Hong Kong Florist
❺ Hong Kong Funeral Home
❻ North Point and 'Little Shanghai'

1 Sunbeam Theatre

Back in the 1950s and 1960s, there were many mainland-owned or leftist-supported businesses in Hong Kong; the most well-known being the China Products Department Stores. The Sunbeam Theatre was another leftist-owned business, which in addition to screening popular movies also showed films produced by leftist film companies: those

with 'patriotic' themes were generally given priority. Other cinemas with political overtones were the Chu Kong (Pearl River) in Ma Tau Wai and the Nam Yeung (South Pacific) in Wan Chai; these have long since closed and the sites been redeveloped, but for now at least, this one in North Point continues to operate.

Sunbeam Theatre has long had another popular entertainment function, as it is the only theatre of its type in Hong Kong which is also suitable for staging Chinese opera; Peking, Shanghai and Chiu Chow styles have all been presented here regularly for over thirty years and performances are generally very well attended.

2 Tong Lau and Yeung Lau

Mainly built in the postwar period, *tong lau* (Chinese residential building) proliferated in the densely overcrowded, accommodation-scarce 1950s and 1960s.

Generally five- or six-storey high, they sometimes have quite spacious apartments within; most however are quite dilapidated now and these have been subdivided into much smaller flats and rented out to *sun yee mun* (new mainland immigrants) unable to afford anything better. While they look almost identical, the main distinction between *tong lau* and *yeung lau* (Western building) was that the former was a walk-up while the latter was usually, but not always, several storeys higher and had lifts; a *yeung lau* also commanded a higher rental.

For the most part *tong lau* and *yeung lau* are found in older residential areas ; places like Yau Ma Tei, To Kwa Wan and North Point have many examples. While some would question their architectural merit, perhaps the Urban Renewal Authority will keep at least a few of them as a reminder of what life was once like for most Hong Kong people before today's widespread affluence, as most of Hong Kong's older buildings have long since been lost to redevelopment.

(3) *Choi Heong Yuen cake shop*

With the rapid proliferation of modern cake shops in recent years offering Hong Kong-style Japanese interpretations of Western cakes, shops like Choi Heong Yuen are almost a dying breed, which is a great pity as their products are excellent and very reasonably priced.

The friendly staff in Choi Heong Yuen — so unlike many other shops — make you want to stock up on these goodies, which isn't difficult to do! Perennial favourites, *daan gwoon* (egg rolls) are light and crumbly — so crumbly that they can easily disintegrate if not handled gently while getting them home, and a snap at $10 a packet. Delicious *hang yun beng* (almond biscuits) contained in a brightly papered handmade box that looks like something from the 1940s and go for $34 for a big box.

(4) *Hong Kong Florist*

Conveniently located next to the funeral home, Hong Kong Florist makes a wide variety of wreaths and funereal floral arrangements, both to conventional patterns and by individual design, to suit all budgets. A basic but attractive, bright yellow or creamy-white wreath made of *kook fa* (chrysanthemum) will set you back $300 or so, while arrangements involving more expensive lilies, carnations and roses go from about $800 upwards. The bamboo stands used for funeral wreathes are generally collected after a funeral service and reused for subsequent ceremonies.

⑤ *Hong Kong Funeral Home*

Painted white, for millennia the traditional colour used by the Chinese for funerals, and trimmed with the pale blue known by the Cantonese as *sei yun laam* (dead man's blue), the Hong Kong Funeral Home on King's Road sees an average of a dozen services a day in several parlours.

The funeral home can arrange traditional Chinese-style funerals, complete with bands and officiating Taoist and Buddhist priests, as well as Christian services of various denominations, embalming and the like. Pre-paid funeral packages can also be arranged. Coffins on offer range in price from a couple of thousand dollars for a simple wooden one to tens of thousands and more for a silk-lined bronze casket.

6 North Point and 'Little Shanghai'

In the late 1940s, large numbers of wealthy and middle-class Shanghainese moved to Hong Kong, fleeing the Chinese civil war and the resultant communist takeover of their city. While almost all came to the British colony intending to eventually return in more settled times to Shanghai, most never went back. By the early 1950s North Point became a favoured place of residence for these émigrés.

Speaking a different dialect and eating very different foods, as well as coming from a modern, genuinely cosmopolitan city, the new arrivals rather looked down on both Hong Kong and the local Cantonese, regarding them as — at best — rather unsophisticated and provincial. Not finding what they found here in Hong Kong to their taste, the Shanghainese created a home away from home, and by the late 1950s North Point had become the Hong Kong outpost of a Shanghai that had already largely vanished, with branches of well-known restaurants, popular nightclubs, long-established Shanghai businesses that had relocated to the British colony and a glittering air of glamorous prosperity, well-reflected in local movies from that time.

How To Get There

By Bus:	No. 2 from Connaught Road Central City Hall bus stop, alight on King's Road at bus stop after passing Tong Shui Road and the Chinese Goods Centre.
By MTR:	North Point MTR Station Exit B1. Sunbeam Theatre is just across the road.
By Taxi:	'Ying Wong Doh, Sun Kwong Hei Yuen' ('King's Road, Sunbeam Theatre').
By Tram:	From anywhere in Central, take the east-bound tram marked 'North Point' and alight at the tram terminus at Tong Shui Road. Get onto King's Road and walk in the direction of the traffic until you reach the Sunbeam Theatre at the junction of King's Road and Shu Kuk Street.

Shau Kei Wan Main Street East was first laid out between the 1850s and 1870s, and traces of those buildings still remained in the early 1970s, though all have now been demolished. There were originally 5 rice shops, 9 Chinese herbalist's, 7 joss-paper shops, 5 goldsmiths and 7 fishing suppliers along the street, all of which existed to cater to the seafaring population who based themselves at Aldrich Bay.

According to an interior plaque, Shau Kei Wan's Tin Hau Temple was built in the twelfth year of the Tung Chih (Tongzhi) Emperor's reign (1873) by the seafaring people of Shau Kei Wan, though another plaque (above the door) indicates that a smaller temple had stood on the site for many years before then. The Tin Hau Temple has been managed by the Chinese Temples Committee since 1928.

Numerous squatter settlements grew up near here in the 1950s and as they were gradually cleared, private and public housing estates took their place. The MTR Island Line made Shau Kei Wan much more accessible from the business district, but for many people, unless they happen to live or work there, Shau Kei Wan is one of those 'remote' places, seldom visited without a definite reason to go there.

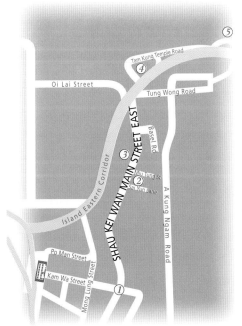

▦ Bus stop

❶ Hongkong Tramways Terminus
❷ Tin Hau Temple
❸ Rope-spinning
❹ Tam Kung Temple
❺ Shau Kei Wan Wholesale Fish Market

While the typhoon shelter has shrunk greatly due to large-scale reclamation in recent years, there is still quite a strong flavour — and odour — of Shau Kei Wan's seafaring past to be found in these backstreets.

(1) Hongkong Tramways Terminus

The eastern terminus of the Hongkong Tramways line is at Shau Kei Wan, just at the end of Shau Kei Wan Main Street East. One of Hong Kong's few remaining bargains of *any* description, one can go all the way to Kennedy Town from here by creaking, clanging *deen che* (electric tram) for $2. Along the way, bear in mind that for decades the original coastline of northern Hong Kong Island was, more or less, where the tramlines now run.

This is sometimes very hard to believe when one is stuck in traffic on Johnston Road, Wan Chai, or along Des Voeux Road, Central, that these streets were once right on the sea, instead of, as now, being several blocks away. The same applies in Shau Kei Wan, once little more than a quiet fishing port, now another of Hong Kong's high-rise agglomerations.

(2) Tin Hau Temple

Tin Hau, Queen of Heaven, was originally a maiden surnamed Lin who lived in Foochow (Fuzhou) in the early Song dynasty. Born with supernatural endowments, she performed numerous miracles to save vessels and their crews from storms and other disasters. She is now venerated as the patron deity of the boat people in Hong Kong, and is also extremely popular in Macao. The most active period of worship at the temple is during the Tin Hau Festival, which celebrates the goddess's birthday, held on the twenty-third day of the third lunar month.

The goddess's image in this temple at Shau Kei Wan is reputed to be the most beautiful Tin Hau image in Hong Kong. A sculptor was specially hired from Fat Shan (Foshan) in Kwangtung (Guangdong) in 1874 to mould it. There are three types of Tin Hau image: images with gold faces are worshipped by officials; those with painted faces are for the common people, while black-faced Tin Hau images are only for fishermen. The Tin Hau image in this temple at Shau Kei Wan is a black-faced one.

A stele in the temple recalls prominent merchants, members of the once powerful *yu laan* (fish wholesaler's cartel), guilds, shipyards and chandlers who donated funds for the temple's construction. The original temple was destroyed in the great typhoon of 1874 — just a year after being built — and subsequently rebuilt two years later. Commercial activities in the area during this time were obviously quite prosperous, as residents could afford to rebuild the temple within two years of its destruction. Many of the donors were from other areas elsewhere in Hong Kong with business or personal connections to Shau Kei Wan.

3 *Rope-spinning*

As perhaps befits a city founded on the maritime trade, one of Hong Kong's earlier industries was rope-spinning and marine cable manufacture. The Hong Kong Rope Manufacturing Co. was established in 1885 at Kennedy Town by prominent early conglomerate Shewan, Tomes and Co. The Kennedy Town factory made ropes from a plant fibre known as Manila help (a species of banana) specially imported from the Philippines. Along with a number of other smaller enterprises, the Hong Kong Rope Manufacturing Co. supplied large quantities of ropes and cables to the many shipping companies that were based in Hong Kong or whose vessels passed through the port. Locally made rope and marine cables were also exported to other parts of China and South-east Asia as well.

STREETS

Commercial rope-spinning is still undertaken elsewhere in Hong Kong, with some smaller-scale enterprises operating in locations such as this one at Shau Kei Wan, close to the typhoon shelters and boat anchorages frequented by commercial fishermen and their vessels.

4 Tam Kung Temple

This well-maintained temple at Ah Kung Ngam (Grandfather's Cave) was built by the fishing people of Shau Kei Wan in the thirty-first year of Emperor Kuang Hsu's (Guangxu's) reign (1905) and, like the Tin Hau Temple further up the street, it has been managed by the Chinese Temples Committee since 1928. The gradual growth of the Tam

Kung Temple tracks the evolution of Shau Kei Wan from a tiny fishing village to the large area found today. However, the largest Tam Kung Temple in Hong Kong is not this one at Ah Kung Ngam, but another at To Kwa Wan in Kowloon.

Tam Kung was originally a native from Waichow (Huizhou) in Kwangtung (Guangdong) Province. Gifted with supernatural powers, he had the ability to prophesy the future — always a useful skill for a deity — as well as a knack for healing people of their sickness. After his death, Tam Kung was deified and gradually become a patron deity of the boat people, along with Tin Hau.

Tam Kung is also very popular with stonecutters, a legacy of the days when Shau Kei Wan had a number of small-scale quarries at Ah Kung Ngam, just around the cliffs from the Tam Kung Temple. The temple's busiest period — and one of the best times to visit — is during the Tam Kung Festival, held on the eighth day of the fourth moon. There is another Tam Kung Temple elsewhere on Hong Kong Island (see Happy Valley section).

5 Shau Kei Wan Wholesale Fish Market

Shau Kei Wan has long been a major fishing port, with numerous deep sea trawlers based within the typhoon shelter here. Many are very large and stay at sea for a week or two at a time. Fishing grounds around Hong Kong have been decimated

by massive, uncontrolled overfishing and not helped further by increasingly bad water pollution in recent years. Many fishermen now need to go as far afield as the coastal waters of Hainan Island and northern Vietnam in search of a worthwhile catch. Few fisher-families live on their boats when in port these days, as most have flats on land.

Until after the Pacific War, fishermen in Hong Kong were permanently indebted to a powerful *laan* or wholesaler's combine that controlled their credit and the sale of fresh fish. This kept prices artificially high and in the process ensured that fresh fish was beyond the means of most working-class people, who had to make do with a little salted fish instead. The power of this group was eventually broken and fresh fish, rather than *haam yu* (salted fish), is now much more readily available. Like other wholesale markets, most goods here are sold and the vendors packed and gone by mid-morning.

How To Get There

By Bus:	No. 720 from Connaught Road Central City Hall bus stop, alight at Shau Kei Wan bus terminus. Walk up Aldrich Street until you reach the junction of Aldrich Street and Kam Wah Street. Walk straight through the street market until you reach the tram terminus.
By MTR:	Shau Kei Wan MTR Station Exit A2. Walk up Aldrich Street until you reach the junction of Aldrich Street and Kam Wah Street. Walk straight through the street market until you reach the tram terminus.
By Taxi:	'Sau Gei Waan Dung Dai Gaai, Deen Che Chung Tsam' ('Shau Kei Wan Main Street East, tram terminus').
By Tram:	From anywhere in Central, take the tram marked 'Shau Kei Wan' and alight at the Shau Kei Wan Main Street East tram terminus.

Shek O Road
石 澳 道

The dramatically scenic road out to Shek O around the coast from Tai Tam — the recent blight of shotcreted slopes aside — is one of the few areas of Hong Kong Island that has not changed much in recent years.

Shek O's attractive beach remains one of Hong Kong's more popular bathing spots. Clean relative to the others elsewhere on the island, it is nevertheless quite busy in the summer months, while one of the best ways of seeing all of Shek O is from high on the Dragon's Back, a scenic ridge walk over the crest of Pottinger Peak which is deservedly one of Hong Kong Island's most popular hiking routes.

First developed as a residential alternative to the Peak, Shek O has retained an air of exclusivity, as it is still remote and relatively underdeveloped. The old bungalows are still there and the expansive views over islands and sea haven't changed much in over half a century. In the past the purchase of land for new bungalows had to be approved by a resident's committee, which effectively kept out 'undesirables'.

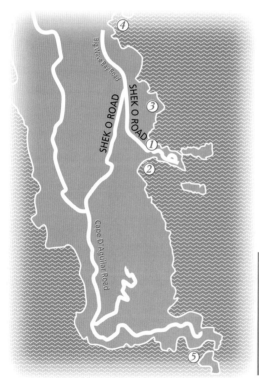

❶ Shek O Bus Terminus
❷ Shek O Beach
❸ Shek O Golf Club
❹ Rock Carving, Big Wave Bay
❺ Cape D'Aguilar, Gun Batteries and Lighthouses

Bungalows are scattered among the ridges of the golf-course and overlooking the cliffs on the way up to Big Wave Bay.

Shek O village has developed considerably in recent years and can get very crowded on weekends and public holidays, but on weekdays at least the clean sandy beach remains pleasantly uncrowded.

1 *Shek O Bus Terminus*

This little old bus terminus may be one of Hong Kong Island's smallest, dealing as it does with what must be one of the island's last remaining 'rural' bus routes. In about forty minutes one winds up from the tower blocks at Shau Kei Wan and across the hills to Shek O. The hillside slopes along this route across from Shau Kei Wan have been extensively shotcreted all the way from Tai Tam Gap to Shek O, plastering once scenic roadside vistas in a shell of dismal grey concrete. At the aptly named Windy Gap, Shek O Road makes a sharp bend and

STREETS

descends into Shek O. One can go straight ahead and end up at Cape D'Aguilar, dramatically beautiful, wave-swept and still very wild. Stop along the way and walk up along the Dragon's Back for stunning views, and then continue down into Shek O for lunch or dinner.

② Shek O Beach

The sandy beach at Shek O is popular at weekends, but seldom will you find it overcrowded, unlike Repulse Bay or Deep Water Bay which can feel very much like Causeway Bay's crowded streets on a hot Sunday afternoon. The water quality here is a bonus as  well, usually being categorized as far cleaner than other Hong Kong Island beaches. That does *not* however mean that the water there is what most of us would usually consider *clean*. The water grading mean that it is generally *cleaner* than the others — a small difference as far as the health authorities are concerned perhaps, but a major one for the rest of us. The vistas from here though are one of the best reasons for coming, as the cliffs reach right down to the sea; the views of distant islands rising sheer from the sea are quite stunning and the water looks cool and very inviting in the warmer months.

③ Shek O Golf Club

Situated in one of Hong Kong's most beautiful locations, on a rocky headland overlooking the Tathong Channel, with Beaufort Island and other more distant islands beyond, the golf-course at Shek O is one of Hong Kong Island's loveliest surprises. Houses are dotted along its length and breadth, their gardens opening onto the fairways in an extension of greenery.

The Shek O Development Company was established in the early 1920s by Lennox Godfrey Bird, a partner in the architectural firm of Bird and Palmer (later renamed Palmer and Turner and still in existence today). Lots were quickly taken up and an active out-of-town social life developed through the 1930s, mostly centred around the golf-course and club buildings.

The Shek O Country Club was built by the same firm in 1925, with purchasers of the development company's sites automatically becoming club members — an early forerunner of the condominium-with-clubhouse concept so popular elsewhere in Hong Kong today.

Early bungalows at Shek O — mostly still there today — were designed with low, sweeping Chinese-style rooflines, the better to withstand summer typhoons and strong sea winds. Residents in the 1920s were attracted by the outdoor life, fresh sea air and sense of space that life at Shek O offered. Then quite remote from the city, the area still manages to maintain much of that feeling today. Attractive and highly sought after, these stunningly located bungalows seldom come on the market. And what was once said about Rolls Royces applies just as well to these villas — if you have to ask the price, then you probably can't afford one.

4 *Rock Carving, Big Wave Bay*

Big Wave Bay, further up the road from Shek O, still retains a distinct village feel, with old village houses, semi-wild dogs and lots of trees. It is also very popular with surfers. As the name suggests, the waves there can be quite high, particularly during the monsoon season.

Located on the eastern coast of Big Wave Bay, the rock carving was discovered by a policeman in 1970 and listed as a heritage monument in 1978. Measuring nine by eight metres, there are geometric patterns of birds and beasts on the carving. According to experts, the main figure depicts a Chinese mythical beast called Tao Tien which intended to bring good fortune; Tao Tien is shaped rather like 'ET' in the popular American film of the same name, with big eyes and a flat head. The carvings are estimated to be at least three thousand years old, but no

STREETS

clues have yet been revealed as to who carved it or why they did so. A few possible explanations of their purpose are as totems of prehistoric people or protective deities for now vanished indigenous people. They might also be deities for expelling evil or for protecting fishermen, or as beacons for ancient mariners.

Obtrusive yet protective, bars and wire mesh make the carvings a little difficult to appreciate, but ensure that 'Ah Loong and Mavis' and pals can't record their names for posterity all over it in white correcting fluid, a common enough sight in so many other more accessible places.

Big Wave Bay's prehistoric rock carving, along with other similar examples found further around Hong Kong Island's southern coast near Wong Chuk Hang, and at the islands of Cheung Chau and Po Toi off Stanley all provide interesting proof of Hong Kong's earliest pre-Chinese inhabitants.

⑤ *Cape D'Aguilar, Gun Batteries and Lighthouses*

Named for Major-General G. C. D'Aguilar, first general officer commanding in Hong Kong (Central's D'Aguilar Street is also named after him), Cape D'Aguilar is one of Hong Kong Island's more remote locations, and home to Hong Kong's first marine reserve. A manned lighthouse opened at Cape D'Aguilar in 1875 but closed in 1896 when the lighthouse on Waglan Island was completed.

Another lighthouse here, unmanned and automatic, commenced operations in 1975. Hok Tsui (Crane's Beak), one of Hong Kong Island's few remaining original villages, lies part way between Windy Gap and the marine reserve.

In the late 1930s two massive gun batteries were built at Cape D'Aguilar, just below Shek O, as part of Hong Kong's defensive preparations. Known as the D'Aguilar and Bokhara Batteries, they were manned by men of No. 1 Battery

Hong Kong Volunteer Defence Corps. The Cape D'Aguilar guns saw little action during the Japanese invasion in 1941, and were eventually destroyed by their own men shortly before the British surrender.

How To Get There

By Bus:	No. 309 from Exchange Square bus terminus, alight at Shek O bus terminus.
By MTR and Bus:	Shau Kei Wan MTR Station Exit A3. Take No. 9 from Shau Kei Wan bus terminus.
By Taxi:	'Sek O Ba See Chung Tsam' ('Shek O bus terminus').

Tong Chong Street
糖廠街

Back in the days when the local economy actually produced things, the commercial dockyard at Taikoo — along with others at Hung Hom, Aberdeen and Tai Kok Tsui — was one of Hong Kong's major industries. Construction work here started in 1902 and was completed in 1907.

Taikoo (Great and Ancient) was the Chinese name for shipping and trading firm Butterfield and Swire (now subsumed into the massive Swire Group conglomerate which has among other interests a major share in Cathay Pacific, Hong Kong's airline). As well as dockyards and wharves Butterfield and Swire operated a sugar refinery here for many years, processing raw sugar brought from as far afield as Java. Ever wonder why one of Hong Kong's most popular brands of sugar is named Taikoo?

Taikoo Docks had slipways and dry docks, model company housing (including the attractive old Woodside, on the slopes of Mount Butler), a sugar refinery (hence Taikoo Sugar and Tong Chong, meaning Sugar Factory), electric generating plants

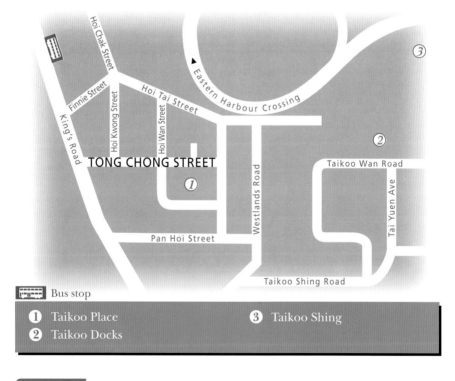

Bus stop

1 Taikoo Place
2 Taikoo Docks
3 Taikoo Shing

and extensive wharves and warehousing. A specially-laid-on Taikoo company launch took European children daily across the harbour to the Central British School on Nathan Road before the war; one of the more vivid memories of a childhood spent at Quarry Bay for ex-Taikoo residents. All this has vanished, and the name is recalled by Taikoo Shing — Taikoo City — the massive residential complex built on the old dockyard site.

With new developments all around, Quarry Bay is now in every way reminiscent of the more modern parts of Central — indeed it is sometimes referred to as 'Central East'. Trend-setting popular restaurants opened along Tong Chong Street, after the completion of Taikoo Place, offering everything from authentic Thai and north Indian curries to what must be some of the best hamburgers in all of Hong Kong.

1 Taikoo Place

Reinforcing the development of Quarry Bay as an alternative business address, some of Hong Kong's more prominent corporate giants such as telecommunications giant Cable and Wireless (since taken over and renamed Pacific Century CyberWorks), and the English-language newspaper *South China Morning Post* maintain their offices here. Business-suited office types are not as out of place along here as one might at first expect in an otherwise rather gritty part of Hong Kong Island. Office buildings along Taikoo Place are named after some of England's more picturesque counties: Devon, Dorset, Somerset, Cornwall. Spacious and well-designed, office space along here is highly sought after and rents are correspondingly very expensive.

② *Taikoo Docks*

Owned and operated by the trading firm Butterfield and Swire, Taikoo Dockyard was one of Hong Kong's principal industries and built numerous ocean-going vessels. In the early twentieth century, Taikoo had a 750-foot-long dry dock fully equipped for all building and ship repair work; the underground car park at Taikoo Shing now utilizes this space.

Along with the sugar refinery, the dockyard was a model employer, with clubs, shops and subsidized company housing on the hillsides above Quarry Bay, all linked to the workplace by cable car. Vestiges of these buildings still survive, including the well-preserved old company house 'Woodside' on nearby Mount Butler Road.

3) *Taikoo Shing*

One of Hong Kong's more popular middle-class residential areas, Taikoo Shing (Great and Ancient City) may be somewhat short on the antiquities, but as far as its residents are concerned, it is a fairly great place to live. As well as every conceivable variety of shop, Taikoo Shing also has an indoor ice-skating rink that has proven extremely popular.

Whilst it was built on the site of what for nearly a century had been one of Hong Kong's foremost enterprises, nothing whatsoever in the entire Taikoo development — not a statue, plaque or even a street name — indicates that the area used to be home to two of Hong Kong's most important industries.

How To Get There	
By Bus:	No. 2 from Connaught Road Central City Hall bus stop. Alight on King's Road after the Hong Kong Funeral Home at the bus stop just before Finnie Street. Tong Chong Street is about 100 m in the direction of the traffic.
By MTR:	Quarry Bay MTR Station Exit A. Tong Chong Street is across the road.
By Taxi:	'Tsut Yue Chong, Tong Chong Gaai' ('Quarry Bay, Tong Chong Street') or 'Tsut Yue Chong, Tai Goo Fong' ('Quarry Bay, Taikoo Place').
By Tram:	From anywhere in Central, take the east-bound tram marked 'Shau Kei Wan' and alight on King's Road after the Hong Kong Funeral Home at the bus stop just before Finnie Street. Tong Chong Street is about 100 m in the direction of the traffic.

 *Southside*

Stanley

Relatively few visitors to Stanley venture much beyond the famous market, and leave again without realizing that beyond the market bustle is a quiet, interesting place with a history stretching back beyond the foundation of Hong Kong as a British colony.

On the scenic, ruggedly attractive Stanley peninsula, prior to the British arrival in 1841, there was a small and relatively insignificant settlement of fisherfolk. The original Stanley village was located roughly where the parade ground at Stanley Fort is now and the villagers were moved to make way for the military, and subsequently resettled on the site of the present-day Stanley market. The area was named after Lord Stanley, Secretary of State for the Colonies when Hong Kong Island was ceded to Great Britain, but the older Chinese name *Chek Chue*, meaning Red Pillar, still persists to the present day.

One of Stanley's most fascinating locations is the old cemetery above St Stephen's Beach; remote and little-frequented — at least during weekdays — the cemetery is one of Hong Kong's most interesting places to wander among pleasant lawns and tree-shaded corners, and is surprisingly popular as a sitting-out area on weekend afternoons.

- Stanley Main Street
- Tung Tau Wan Road/Wong Ma Kok Road
- Repulse Bay Road
- Deep Water Bay Road

STREETS

Southside

For many years after the war ended, Stanley remained somewhat out-of-the-way and seemingly remote from the city, a tranquil place of schools, religious buildings and secluded private villas. Some of the exterior scenes from the popular 1955 film *Love Is a Many Splendoured Thing* were shot at Stanley but they are almost unrecognizable today; such has been the pace of development. Stanley's beaches have always been very popular; the further one goes towards Stanley Fort, they become quite secluded and both sand and water are very clean. These days, however, all of Stanley's beaches are thronged with bathers on hot weekend afternoons.

Repulse Bay

Tsin Shui Wan (Shallow Water Bay) acquired its English name in commemoration of the HMS *Repulse*, a Royal Navy vessel that visited Hong Kong waters in the mid-nineteenth century. Repulse Bay was described by one early twentieth-century writer as 'remote and unravished' — words that, sadly, could not possibly be used in connection with the area today.

Despite considerable development, the superb natural setting of Repulse Bay Beach, Middle Bay and South Bay beyond remains spectacular to this day, with magnificent views of near and distant islands and the seemingly endless sea. One of Hong Kong's most popular swimming beaches, on a hot Sunday afternoon Repulse Bay is completely packed. Middle Bay and South Bay, a short distance along the coast, are much less crowded as people have to walk to get there.

With towering hillsides, sandy beaches and an almost Hawaiian setting, Repulse Bay has long been one of Hong Kong's more sought-after places to live. In the 1950s the cliffsides were dotted with secluded villas set in lovely gardens, which over the last two decades have gradually given way to high-rise apartment blocks of ever-increasing ostentation. Few original bungalows now remain, and while Repulse Bay's massive overdevelopment over the last twenty years has damaged some of the area's charm, it nevertheless remains a very beautiful part of Hong Kong Island.

Deep Water Bay

Shum Shui Wan (Deep Water Bay), located just around the rocky headland from Repulse Bay, has long been one of Hong Kong's most popular beaches. Deep Water Bay is also a very exclusive residential area, with a number of attractive villas scattered around the hillside overlooking the golf-course and the sea, though gradually these are giving way to obtrusive apartment blocks.

Surrounded by towering jungle-clad hillsides, with sharply pointed Mount Nicholson rising steeply behind and fronted by a casuarina-lined beach, is one of Hong Kong Island's two golf-courses (the other is at Shek O). Being jostled along the pavements of hopelessly overcrowded places like Causeway Bay, it is often easy to forget just how much of Hong Kong Island is actually open space — something that is very apparent along this stretch of coast.

Southside

Stanley Market with its eclectic collection of shops and stalls has been firmly part of the local tourist itinerary for many years, with more traditional street market items such as homewares and foodstuffs giving way to sand-washed silk garments, cut-price garment factory outlets, scroll paintings, chops, seals, carvings and every possible variety of Chinese-flavoured tourist tat. For decades Stanley Market was indeed a functioning market, with all the usual shops and stalls, but gradually these have given way to numerous tourist shops and eateries, where the quality varies as greatly as the prices.

In the late eighteenth century, during the reign of the Chia Ching (Jiaqing) Emperor, the notorious local pirate Cheung Po-tsai had a headquarters at Chek Chue, and traces of Cheung's presence still remain in the Tin Hau Temple at nearby Ma Hang. Among other locations associated with Cheung in Hong Kong is Cheung Chau where according to legend he had a storehouse-cave for his loot, and lookout posts high on the side of the mountain later renamed Victoria Peak.

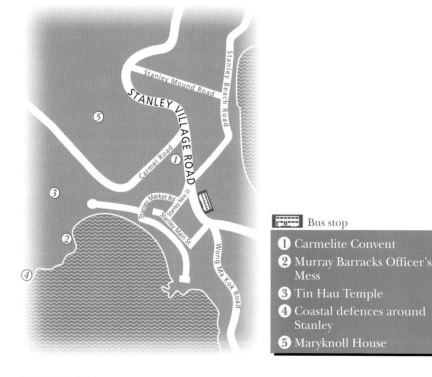

Bus stop

1. Carmelite Convent
2. Murray Barracks Officer's Mess
3. Tin Hau Temple
4. Coastal defences around Stanley
5. Maryknoll House

1 Carmelite Convent

Just up the road from the bus terminus, the Carmelite Convent was built in 1934 by the Franco-Belgian firm Credit Foncirre de Extreme Orient. This once prominent firm was responsible for other ecclesiastical architectural work in Hong Kong, including the Little Sisters of the Poor at Ngau Chi Wan. Credit Foncierre was also heavily involved in construction work in the Treaty Ports such as Tientsin (Tianjin) and Hankow (Hankou), and was also responsible for large areas of Kowloon Tong in the late 1920s.

Work on the Carmelite Convent was authorized in the early 1930s by Bishop Valtorta, an Italian who was then Roman Catholic Bishop of Hong Kong. A number of other Catholic buildings date from the 1930s and were initiated by him. On completion the nuns moved there from their previous premises in the Mid-Levels. During the Japanese occupation, the nuns remained unmolested in their convent. The Carmelites are a closed order of contemplative nuns who devote their lives to prayer and meditation. The chapel is open to the public for services, but the rest of the convent is completely closed to outsiders. There is a small graveyard behind in the garden, where some of the nuns lie buried.

The high walls and iron fences emphasize the separateness of the Carmelite nuns from the world outside and ensure that they have minimum distraction from their life of prayer. Every day the nuns have an hour for reading and then after lunch and dinner they gather together for discussion. Each nun has an individual cell where she can meditate, pray or work.

According to Carmelite tradition, the nuns engage in cottage industries and the Stanley sisters make a particularly good type of honey candy, which they sometimes sell to visitors to the convent.

2 Murray Barracks Officer's Mess (formerly in Central)

Incongruously situated on a new artificial headland abutting the old Ma Hang squatter settlement (now cleared), Murray Barracks Officer's Mess formerly stood in the Central district, on the site now occupied by the Bank of China Tower. The original, elegantly proportioned building in Central was designed by Major Edward Aldrich RE, along with the formerly adjacent Headquarter House (now known as Flagstaff House and used as a Museum of Tea Ware).

Murray Barracks Officers Mess was carefully demolished in the early 1980s, with the ultimate intention of eventually reconstructing it elsewhere. The stones and other materials were kept in storage until 1998, when work was started at Stanley. Despite earlier plans however, the building was *not* reconstructed; a concrete shell was built on this site at Stanley and the old exterior fittings such as verandahs were attached to it.

③ Tin Hau Temple

The Tin Hau Temple at Stanley dates back to the late 1700s. Tin Hau is the goddess of seafarers and fishermen. Her cult is originally of Fujianese origin but has spread along the southern Chinese coast over the years. Tin Hau temples are always located near the sea; some of them, such as the one at Causeway Bay, have been gradually marooned inland by successive reclamation works.

Inside Stanley's Tin Hau Temple is a bronze bell from the reign of the Ch'ien Lung (Qianlong) Emperor, which once belonged to the notorious pirate Cheung Po-tsai. On the wall of the temple is a somewhat decayed-looking tiger skin; the animal, an escapee from a circus along with several apes and other animals, was caught and killed at Stanley during the Japanese occupation.

4 *Coastal defences around Stanley*

British troops were stationed in Stanley from shortly after Hong Kong Island was ceded to Great Britain until 1994, except during the Japanese occupation of 1941–45 when Imperial Japanese Army troops used Stanley Fort as accommodation for their own garrison. Up until the early 1930s, defence policy had always given priority to defences around Victoria Harbour and no large-scale military installations were constructed on the southern side of Hong Kong Island, including Stanley.

Defence policy towards Hong Kong changed in the mid-1930s and most of the newer installations at Stanley, as well as those at Chung Hom Kok, Cape D'Aguilar and elsewhere date from this time. Construction on the gun batteries at Stanley started in 1936 and was completed in July 1937. Calibration trails commenced in November 1937, after which Eastern Fire Command Headquarters was relocated to Stanley from Devil's Peak. In late 1941 another new, improvised battery was built at Bluff Head.

At around the same time as Stanley Battery was constructed, another slightly smaller gun battery was built just around the coast at Chung Hom Kok. The remains of one can still be seen there today; the other was demolished when the Cheshire Home was built. In the late 1930s, an extensive network of pillboxes was built along the coastline of Hong Kong Island, and a number of examples can still be seen today.

5 *Maryknoll House*

Attractively situated at the top of the hill, the red-brick Maryknoll House was built in 1935 as a language school and leave centre for the Maryknoll Mission, then very active in Kwangtung (Guangdong) and Kwangsi (Guangxi). Missionaries based on the mainland had to deal with bandits and quite primitive living conditions, and as a result, missionaries who had been several months in China could come down to Hong Kong for a fortnight's break, collect mail and enjoy more modern conveniences.

Maryknoll had four mission areas in southern China: Jiangmen, Meixian (famous as a place for Hakkas), Huzhou and Guilin, and language training offered included Cantonese, Hakka and Mandarin.

During the Japanese occupation, the Maryknoll House was taken over by the Japanese and all staff interned with other Allied nationals at Stanley. Valuables such as altar items and the library were sent for safe keeping to the nearby Carmelite Convent. The building itself was damaged during the occupation; part of the floor was damaged by fire and the ceilings were taken apart. Within a year of the war's end, Maryknoll House was fully restored, becoming again the centre of activity for regional Maryknoll missions.

After 1949 Maryknoll missionaries — like most other religious organizations — were expelled from China and the Maryknoll House became a refuge and sanatorium for these and other displaced missionaries. In the 1950s and 1960s, the House became a very popular leave destination for Maryknoll staff members based elsewhere in Asia due to its beautiful location and convenient facilities.

Many Maryknoll missionaries assisted with refugee work during those years and the language school reopened. In 1968 the Hong Kong Maryknoll mission broke its ties with the mission in Taiwan and became a separate organization. Fewer people came in the 1970s as more missionaries returned to the United States and other locations for furlough due to more convenient air travel and part of the grounds were sold and the proceeds used to restore the building, which was completed in 1974. A section of the building has become a convention centre accessible to the general public, with the mission still retaining part of the premises for its own use.

How To Get There

By Bus:	No. 6 and No. 6X from Exchange Square bus terminus, alight at Stanley Market bus stop.
By Taxi:	'Chek Chue Sun Gaai' ('Stanley New Street').

The southern end of Stanley peninsula is somewhat different in atmosphere from the crowded areas around the market and main beach. A more spacious institutional flavour prevails, with the pleasant open spaces and playing fields of St Stephen's College, the tranquil, historically interesting Stanley Cemetery with its numerous wartime graves and a number of quiet, almost secluded beaches and coves. Stanley Prison dominates the eastern side of the peninsula while Stanley Fort takes up what remains of the scenic rocky headland.

1) *Kaifong Association*

Also known as the Seen On Kung Sor, the Stanley Kaifong was set up principally as a mutual aid association and to settle disputes arising between local residents. It is one of the oldest such associations in Hong Kong. The name was changed in 1947 to Mutual Affection Association of Land and Sea Residents. It changed again two years later in 1949 to Stanley Kaifong Association when more sea-dwellers moved onto land.

Southside

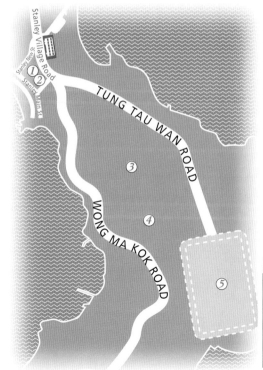

🚌 Bus stop

❶ Kaifong Association
❷ Old Stanley Police Station
❸ St Stephen's College
❹ Stanley Military Cemetery
❺ Stanley Prison

Annual Cantonese opera shows used to be held to celebrate Tin Hau's birthday, but unfortunately these popular performances were not held after 1995 when the land on which they were staged was resumed by the government.

② Old Stanley Police Station

This old building was constructed in 1859, and replaced the earlier original Stanley Police Station built in 1844. This is the oldest remaining building in Hong Kong originally built for police purposes; one of six built around the same time, the other five have long been demolished. It also remains one of the oldest British-built buildings in Hong Kong. A police station was established at Stanley partly to combat piracy; more troops were stationed at Stanley and a jail was built around the same time.

During the Japanese occupation, Stanley Police Station was used as a Japanese military police headquarters. The building was gazetted a monument in 1983, but despite this it was leased to private enterprise in 1991 and renovated as a restaurant, which has recently closed down.

3 *St Stephen's College*

St Stephen's College was founded by a number of prominent Chinese who wanted to 'save China' by means of education. In 1923 the college moved to Bonham Road where they used classrooms in the University of Hong Kong for a time. Finally in 1930, when the Stanley campus at Tung Tau Wan was completed,

the college moved there. In terms of ground area, St Stephen's College is the largest on Hong Kong Island.

The older buildings at St Stephen's College date from the late 1920s. Known at that time as 'the Eton of the East', the college received many students from South-east Asia. One of the few local schools with extensive grounds and playing fields, it is still one of Hong Kong's premier local educational establishments. The present-day school library was used at that time as a Field Ambulance hospital, and witnessed a massacre of doctors, nurses and wounded patients on Christmas Morning, 1941.

St Stephen's College was used as part of an internment camp for Allied civilians during the Japanese occupation. On 16 January 1945 one of the bungalows on the grounds was destroyed during an American bombing raid and a number of internees killed. Repaired and renovated after the war, St Stephen's College reopened in 1947, became co-educational in 1968 and started receiving government subsidies in 1970.

St Stephen's College has a small chapel which can be visited on Sundays when it is open to the general public for religious services, and recently celebrated its fiftieth anniversary. Inside the chapel is a very attractive stained glass window commemorating those who suffered and died at Stanley designed by the late Lady May Ride, a former Stanley internee.

Southside

4 Stanley Military Cemetery

The tranquil old Stanley cemetery dates from two separate periods, and has three very distinct types of gravestones marking some 691 graves. Victorian-style chest-tombs recall the first twenty years or so of British rule, when many of those who died from the garrison stationed nearby were buried here. After the 1860s those who died at Stanley Fort were buried at Happy Valley, and Stanley Cemetery fell into disuse.

It was reopened in early 1942 to deal with war dead. The roughly hewn granite markers, originally destined to be road milestones, were carved as gravestones for the internees who died when part of Stanley was the internment camp during the Japanese occupation. The standard pattern markers found in all Commonwealth War Graves Cemeteries are mostly of those who died in fierce fighting around Stanley in the closing stages of the Japanese invasion in 1941.

The cemetery is a popular sitting-out area for weekend visitors to Stanley who — perhaps surprisingly given strongly held Chinese taboos concerning death and graveyards — hold family picnics and take snapshots on the lawns among the gravestones. During the week the spot is mostly deserted, a quiet and contemplative spot just up the road from the noise and bustle of Stanley Market.

5 Stanley Prison

Located at the far end of the peninsula, Stanley Prison was built in 1938 and can house 1,604 prisoners. Intended at that time to be remote from settled areas, and largely surrounded by sea which made escape much more difficult, the prison surroundings have gradually become more built up.

Many of the prison buildings are from this time, including the attractive Prison Officer's Club. This is located just past the main gates and has a private lawn bowling green. Prison officers in previous years were mainly Indian, though now most are Chinese. Until the death penalty in Hong Kong was effectively abolished in 1966, Stanley Prison housed the gallows; the death penalty formally remained on the statutes until shortly before the handover.

Before the war, the Indian warders had separate married accommodation within the grounds of the prison, as did European prison officers. These married quarters formed part of the wartime internment camp at Stanley, along with St Stephen's College and the

cemetery. The prison is now one of many in Hong Kong, and houses mainly maximum security inmates.

Southside

How To Get There

By Bus:	No. 6 and No. 6X from Exchange Square bus terminus, alight at Stanley Market bus stop. Walk down Stanley Village Road until you reach the junction of Stanley Village Road, Tung Tau Wan Road and Wong Ma Kok Road.
By Taxi:	'Chek Chue, Dung Tau Waan Doh' ('Stanley, Tung Tau Wan Road').

Venturing into the swimmer-thronged waters at Repulse Bay beach in mid-summer is rather like being basted in suntan oil — and heaven knows what other waterborne nastiness as well. Water quality is consistently rated good or above at Repulse Bay beach by the government — a standard which, compared to the rest of the world, is really pretty yucky; but don't let that put you off, as most bathers don't seem to mind either that or the crowds.

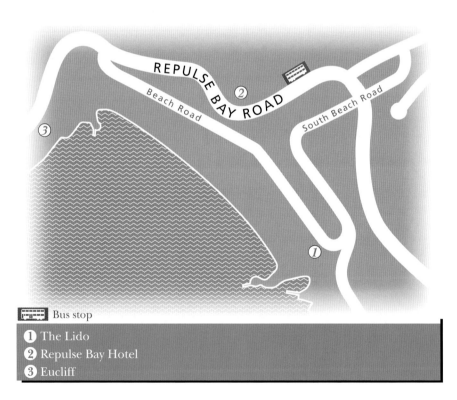

Bus stop

❶ The Lido
❷ Repulse Bay Hotel
❸ Eucliff

1) The Lido

The very popular art-moderne-style Repulse Bay Lido was opened in 1937, and was well patronized for tea dances on Sunday afternoons; still standing today, it houses, among other things, a giant-sized McDonald's and a KFC — a far cry from the pre-war fare. The former name of Lido is largely forgotten, though if you look closely enough among the peeling paintwork you can still just make it out.

The Lido's interior staircase — now darkened, decayed and grotty with mould — remains a 1930s' marvel, even though it smells of rats, mustiness and neglect. The old guards posted outside will chase you away if you show too much interest in the place — for who, they reason, would want to see the inside of a decrepit old building like this one unless they had dubious intentions?

2) Repulse Bay Hotel

The Repulse Bay Hotel first opened its doors in 1919 and rapidly became a favoured out-of-town resort, popular with honeymooners and round-the-world tourists. Hong Kong's answer to similar hotels in South-east Asia such as Penang's Eastern and Oriental, or Colombo's Mount Lavinia, the Repulse Bay Hotel became world-famous, as much for its magnificent setting and superb views as the quality of the rooms and service.

The road leading up to the hotel was lined with Flame of the Forest trees (*Delonix regia*), which have magnificent scarlet flowers in the heat of summer, and the grounds were full of other flowering trees and plants. The Repulse Bay Hotel was also popular with

STREETS

honeymooners, both from Hong Kong and further afield, as Marjorie Bird Angus recalls in her memoirs, *Bamboo Wireless:* 'We had a huge room and bath, all for $9 each a day, and our own special table for two on the front verandah. We had ten lovely days there.'

In December 1941 the hotel was besieged by the Japanese for three days, with dozens of refugees from the city taking shelter there. During the subsequent Japanese occupation, the Repulse Bay Hotel, renamed the *Midori hama* (Green Bay), remained as popular as ever. Dances were still held and life went on, more or less as normal, for those who had both money to spend and the confidence of the Japanese.

The Repulse Bay Hotel was demolished in 1981 — a black period for heritage conservation in Hong Kong — and blocks of luxury flats now occupy the site. Locally famous as the blue-and-white 'flats-with-a-hole-in-the-middle' and pointed out eagerly by tour bus guides, the reasons for the hole being there in the first place are variously ascribed to the *fung shui* demands of a mythical dragon living on the hill behind — this is the most commonly held urban myth and all new arrivals get told it. Another story, perhaps more likely, recounts that the owner saw a similar building in Miami, liked it hugely and told the architects to include the feature in the new building. But whichever direction you come from, it's impossible to miss this one, curved in front of the mountainside like a makeup-clogged gash.

The front section of the apartment complex which replaced the Repulse Bay Hotel looks quite old, but is in fact a different replica built after the original had been destroyed. In much the same style as the original hotel verandah overlooking the beach, though rather smaller, a faux antique complex of restaurants and shops was built in front of it as well. Known as The Repulse Bay, it manages to trade very successfully on 'the elegance of a bygone era' to customers who, for the most part, are completely unaware that the building they're admiring is actually a well-made fake.

The sad fate of the Repulse Bay Hotel graphically points up the fact that it is almost impossible under existing heritage legislation to adequately protect privately owned buildings such as hotels, theatres, clubs and offices. While strictly speaking such buildings are private property, they have also had a public role for generations, and are a fondly remembered part of the collective memory for many.

③ Eucliff

On the cliff leading down into Repulse Bay there used to be a fabulous mock-Gothic castle, built in the 1920s by the Straits Chinese millionaire Eu Tong Sen. Demolished in the early 1980s, the present Royal Cliff apartment block was built on the site, with its pointed windows strangely echoing the Anglophile folly that stood there before.

The Eu family made part of their fortune from the manufacture of Chinese medicines, with popular brand Eu Yan Sang — still around today — being their trademark. In addition to Eucliff, the family owned another Hong Kong castle, Euston on Bonham Road with famous hanging gardens, and Sirmio, a Schloss-like country  house overlooking the Tolo Harbour near Tai Po; they also had palatial residences at Kuala Lumpur and Singapore. According to a popular myth — and it may well be true — Eu Tong Sen was told by a soothsayer that as long as he continued to build, he would not die. Accordingly, carpenters were kept busy at one or another of his homes all the time; he died anyway in 1940 and was buried at Sirmio.

One of Eu Tong Sen's favourite collections was of statuary, and one of these pieces formerly displayed at Eucliff can still be seen elsewhere in Hong Kong, but with a frequently mistaken identity. This is a statue of a soldier from the First World War, donated to the British Garrison by the Eu family when Eucliff was demolished. After standing for almost twenty years in Osborn Barracks in Kowloon Tong, it was relocated to Hong Kong Park where it stands today. Popularly thought of as a statue of Company Sergeant-Major John Osborn, the Canadian soldier who posthumously won the Victoria Cross during the battle for Hong Kong, the statue at Hong Kong Park was originally one of the Eu family's garden ornaments, and is not, in reality, of John Osborn at all.

How To Get There

By Bus:	No. 6, No. 6A and No. 6X from Exchange Square bus terminus, alight on Repulse Bay Road at the bus stop in front of steps leading up to The Repulse Bay apartments. Cross over to Beach Road and walk the direction of the traffic until you reach the Lido.
By Taxi:	'Tseen Shui Waan, Hoi Taan Doh, Lai Doh' ('Repulse Bay, Beach Road, the Lido').

STREETS

Deep Water Bay Road
深水灣道

Perennially popular for swimming due to its calm sheltered waters and convenient location, Deep Water Bay, like the other beautiful beaches along Hong Kong Island's southern coast, is thronged with bathers on every sunny weekend afternoon. The main road between Repulse Bay and Aberdeen runs just beside the beach, making Deep Water Bay — depending on your point of view and tolerance to traffic — either a very noisy or very convenient place to come for a swim.

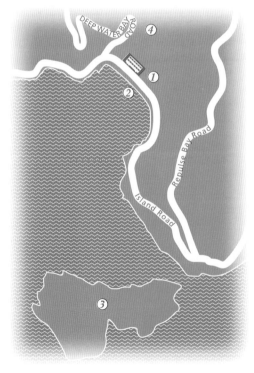

 Bus stop

1 Hong Kong Golf Club
2 Beaches and sea-bathing
3 Middle Island
4 Telegraph links

1 Hong Kong Golf Club

Deep Water Bay's splendidly situated golf-course is one of two that can be found on 'overcrowded' Hong Kong Island — the other is at Shek O. Enclosed on three sides by jungle-clad mountainside with a popular sandy bathing beach in front, the golf-course has been a

popular feature of Hong Kong Island life ever since it opened in 1889. Deep Water Bay has nine holes, and membership is affiliated to the much more extensive Hong Kong Golf Club at Fanling in the New Territories. Prior to the 1997 transfer of sovereignty, both Fanling and Deep Water Bay were known as the Royal Hong Kong Golf Club; the Hong Kong Jockey Club also had a royal prefix.

For reasons best known to their executives — second-guessing the Chinese authorities' wishes is probably a reasonable surmise — these long-established institutions chose to part with some of their own history and relinquished their royal patronage in 1996, a year prior to the handover. The Royal Hong Kong Yacht Club, based at Kellett Island in Causeway Bay, elected to retain its former title at this time and has not, at least yet, suffered any adverse effects from the decision.

2 Beaches and sea-bathing

Until the 1950s sea-bathing at the numerous picturesque beaches around Hong Kong was, for the most part, only popular with Europeans. Wealthy Chinese still wanted to preserve fair complexions, as a suntanned face was generally associated with the need to work manually. As a result, they tended not to go to the beaches, or if they did, sat in the shade and wore plenty of clothes. And Hong Kong's working classes were so taken up with the grind of daily living that many never ventured much beyond their place of residence and work in an entire lifetime.

Popular taste changed with growing Westernization, and the release of numerous films that emphasized the fun and glamour of a day at the beach. The cosmetics industry also played its part in this and continues to do so. 'Bleaching' creams and 'whitening' lotions are widely sold all over Asia; advertising campaigns continue to associate fairness with feminine beauty, and as a result many Hong Kong Chinese women still don't like to go to the beach — however hot it is — for fear of making them look *haak mung mung* (very dark).

③ Middle Island

During the fighting for Hong Kong in December 1941 the colony's sole remaining destroyer, the aged HMS *Thracian*, along with two superannuated river-gunboats, HMS *Cicala* and HMS *Robin*, lay off Hong Kong Island's southern coast bombarding Japanese positions. After being badly damaged by

Japanese air attacks, the decision was made to beach HMS *Thracian* on Middle Island. The vessel remained there for some years afterwards, but long since cut up for scrap, no trace now remains at all.

For many years rocky, sugar-loaf-shaped Middle Island has been a prized 'out of town' location for the Royal Hong Kong Yacht Club and many club members, especially those who live on the south side of Hong Kong Island, keep their pleasure craft moored here semi-permanently.

④ Telegraph links

Direct telegraphic communications between Hong Kong and the outside world were established in 1870 by the Great Northern Telegraph Company, a Danish-owned concern registered in Copenhagen. Prior to that, messages had first to be taken by ship to Galle, a port city on the southern coast of Ceylon (now Sri Lanka) and only telegraphed on from there — a time-consuming process that ensured many pressing commercial and administrative decisions were made entirely by 'the man on the spot', without reference to London offices.

Hong Kong became linked northwards by cable with Amoy (Xiamen) and Shanghai, and southwards with Singapore via Labuan, an island off the coast of Borneo, by means of telegraphic cables brought ashore at Deep Water Bay. Later, additional submarine cables were laid at the appropriately named Telegraph Bay on the Pok Fu Lam coast, all now being completely subsumed by the massive Cyberport development.

How To Get There

By Bus:	No. 6A and No. 6X from Exchange Square bus terminus, alight on Island Road at the bus stop next to the Hong Kong Golf Course.
By Taxi:	'Sum Shui Waan, goh yee foo kau cheung' ('Island Road, golf course').

Aberdeen

The fishing port of Aberdeen was given its English name to commemorate Lord Aberdeen, Foreign Secretary when the British took possession of Hong Kong in 1841. In Cantonese it is known as Shek Pai Wan, meaning Stone Sign Bay. It was an early manufactory of incense sticks and became known as Heung Kong (Fragrant Harbour), because the scent of sandalwood crushing carries for a great distance. Gradually the name came to refer to the entire island — hitherto remote and relatively insignificant enough to have no formal name — until it was designated Tai Ping Shan (Great Peace Mountain), according to local legend so named after notorious pirate Cheung Po-tsai's band was pacified in 1806. Shek Pai Wan then acquired the colloquial name Heung Kong Jai (little Hong Kong), a reference to the small sheltered harbour that mirrored the function of the much larger Victoria Harbour further around the coast.

The first recorded link between European navigators and the then remote Hong Kong Island took place at Aberdeen in the 1740s, when 'to a great banyan tree on a small island in the harbour (possibly modern Ap Lei Chau) Commodore George Anson fastened his ship to haul her over for repair'. Often quoted, nevertheless a number of sources have disputed this somewhat tenuous early link.

Heung Kong Wai, the flat area of terraced fields above the fishing village of Aberdeen, was shown on early maps as Staunton's Valley below which flowed Staunton's Creek, a stream whose mouth in Aberdeen harbour is found near the present Ap Lei Chau bridge. Staunton's Creek was a frequent resort of small craft owing to its relatively sheltered position, but the lower reaches have since been reclaimed. Both creek and valley were named after Sir George Staunton, who accompanied the Amherst mission to China in 1817 — Staunton Street in Central is also named after him.

After the British took possession of Hong Kong Island in 1841, town lots were granted at certain parts of Hong Kong Island, including Aberdeen. In that year a narrow bridle path was opened across the hills towards Aberdeen from the developing urban area on the northern shore of Hong Kong Island. Other town areas outside the city of Victoria were Wong Nai Chung (Happy Valley) and Chek Chue (Stanley); the rest of the island was classified suburban and remained so for almost a century.

Early on in British times, troops were stationed at Aberdeen, in addition to those garrisoned at Stanley and near the Central area. Eventually, the Aberdeen detachment was withdrawn and the principal military cantonments outside the urban areas thereafter were at Sai Wan (Shau Kei Wan) and Chek Chue (Stanley).

A substantial dockyard was built at Aberdeen by businessman John Lamont in 1855, with the Admiralty contributing to the capital costs of the docks. The Lamont dockyard was eventually acquired by the newly formed Hong Kong and Whampoa Dock Company in 1866.

- Aberdeen Main Road
- Pok Fu Lam Road
- Victoria Road
- Wong Chuk Hang Road

An additional Royal Naval Dockyard was planned for Aberdeen in the mid-1930s as a complement to the other in Central. Construction began in 1938 but works had not advanced beyond a small graving dock facility when war broke out.

Although by 1911 Aberdeen had a substantial police station (rebuilt from the one first constructed in the early 1840s) and an imposing harbour office, it still remained remote enough from the urban area not to have many houses.

The fishing population remained substantial and continued to grow. The population of Aberdeen recorded in the 1865 census including Ap Lei Chau, numbered 1,664 Chinese in 1865 (no non-Chinese) with a further floating population of 1,712 living on 205 boats. In the same census, the land-dwelling population of nearby Heung Kong Wai village stood at 263.

Although very close to the sea, Tin Wan, or Farm Bay, was — as the name implies — a predominantly agricultural area until the 1950s, with numerous vegetable fields, pig and poultry farms and, perhaps remarkably given the appearance of the area today, even some rice fields. While the name persists, the fields and farms have all long vanished.

Ap Lei Chau

Ap Lei Chau — Duck Tongue Island — is so named as its shape somewhat resembles a duck's tongue. There were people living on the island over three hundred years ago, but these were, as in other peripheral areas of coastal China, in a few scattered villages that had little contact beyond their own world. No population figures for the island were recorded in the first population census in 1841. According to oral tradition, a group of Hokkiens (Fukienese) from Amoy (Xiamen) colonized the island, followed by other settlers from Swatow (Shantou), Tung Koon (Dongguan) and Waichow (Huizhou). By the 1940s, the Ap Lei Chau villages were quite prosperous.

The two small islands that now make up Ap Lei Chau — Aplichau and

STREETS

Aplipai — were joined by reclamation before 1937 while another small island, Fo Yeuk Chau (Magazine Island), remains separate. For many years Ap Lei Chau was known as Aberdeen Island, a name that persisted until after the Pacific War but which is now extinct.

As part of the planned defence of the Aberdeen Naval Dockyard, the Aberdeen Battery was built here (near the present Lee Nam Road). This gun battery had two 4-inch naval guns and was manned by men of the No. 3 Battery Hong Kong Volunteer Defence Corps when the Pacific War broke out. The only reported action was on the morning of 11 December 1941 when, with the Jubilee Battery, it fired on a Japanese party attempting to land on Lamma Island. The guns were finally destroyed on either 24 or 25 December 1941.

In the 1960s the southernmost part of the island was extensively colonized by refugees from the mainland who established large squatter settlements; a situation Ap Lei Chau shared with many other areas elsewhere in Hong Kong during those overcrowded, underprivileged years.

In 1964 Hong Kong Electric acquired a site on the north-west corner of the island for a power station, which became fully operational in November 1968. Eventually, the facility was decommissioned and the modern South Horizons residential complex was built on the site in the early 1990s.

By the late 1980s urban development at Aberdeen began to spill over the recently completed Ap Lei Chau bridge, and the small, once isolated island has become one of Hong Kong Island's more popular dormitory communities.

Pok Fu Lam coast

Among the first places that European explorers visited on Hong Kong Island was near Waterfall Bay. It is probable that ships approaching the mouth of the Pearl River en route to Canton (Guangzhou) habitually stopped to take on water here as the site was already well-known as a reliable source of clean fresh water by the early years of the nineteenth century.

The first mention of this specific locality was made at the time of the Amherst diplomatic mission to China in 1816–17. The Amherst mission to China in 1816–17 was an attempt to regularize British diplomatic relations with Peking. Three ships, the *Alceste*, *Lyra* and *General Hewitt* comprised the mission, with the Ambassador, Lord Amherst, travelling in the frigate *Alceste*. The mission separated off the coast of Java, with *Lyra* travelling ahead to bring Sir George Staunton, a member of the East India Company Select Committee at Canton who was also a Chinese linguist, to the rendezvous point at Malihoy Bay, a corruption of Ma Liu Ho (literally Horse Urine Creek in Cantonese, more elegantly also known as Waterfall Creek). The mission took on water from the falls, as the supplies previously obtained for the expedition in Java was inferior. Following the departure of the Amherst mission from local waters on its journey north, there was no further mention in British sources of either Waterfall Bay or Hong Kong itself for the next thirteen years.

The Eastern Extension of the Australasia and China Telegraph Company's cable came ashore at Telegraph Bay just up the coast from Waterfall Bay. As several cables from different directions came ashore here, it was suggested that the matshed bathing club that used the bay should take their premises further around the coast, as dragging of anchors by launches inshore might cause damage to the cables. A government report stated that this would not happen if launches only tied up at their piers, but that this could hardly be insisted upon or enforced. The bathing club were recommended to find another beach suitable for their purposes in the vicinity; they did so, and so vanished from history.

The village and settlement at Telegraph Bay had been in existence since approximately 1896, as the earliest squatter permits date from this time. Villagers resident there were also engaged in fishing and some pig-rearing at this time. By 1909 the squatter village at Telegraph Bay was reported to be in a very insanitary condition, with most of the buildings in areas set aside for settlement being little more than unimproved matsheds. Reports indicate that the villagers were informed that their present dwellings must be removed and proper houses constructed on sites which would be set aside by government for the purpose, or else they must vacate the area and forfeit their leases. Despite repeated warnings, a straggling squatter settlement persisted here till the early 1950s.

Little further happened in the vicinity until the years immediately preceding the outbreak of war with Japan. The international situation in the Far East had changed significantly for the worse since the Japanese invasion of China in July 1937. A series of fixed defensive positions ringing the coast of Hong Kong Island were built in the late 1930s as more extensive preparations for Hong Kong's defence were put in place.

Until the massive Cyberport development commenced, there were still several pillboxes, searchlight positions, bunkers and fixed emplacements to be seen in the vicinity of Telegraph Bay. Some showed signs of having been used illegally at various times since the end of the war, either occupied by squatters or used as storage by the villagers. Many were still in quite good condition until all were recently cleared away for the Cyberport development. None were fought over during the Japanese invasion in December 1941 and the emplacements along this stretch of coast remained unused by the Japanese during their occupation in 1941–45.

By 1911, between Pok Fu Lam Road and the sea there were only two buildings, Bisney Villa and Villa Miramar. The Chinese Christian Cemetery was already in existence; originally pressed into service in the 1890s as a burial place for bubonic plague victims, it has since extended greatly in size. The entire area was very sparsely populated and only serviced by the main Pok Fu Lam–Aberdeen Road. After Queen Mary Hospital opened in 1937, the area gradually developed and more private houses were built, including a large villa on Sassoon Road owned by Madame Kung Soong Ai-ling, the eldest of China's famous Soong Sisters; it too has long been demolished.

Sandy Bay was named for the small sandy cove — now lost to reclamation — that made the area a popular resort for bathers and launch picnics early in the twentieth century. With clean and relatively shallow water the beach was a convenient distance just below Victoria Road. The Duchess of Kent's Home for Disabled Children was built in 1956, and still stands on the same site, though it has been further extended since the original construction. Donated by local philanthropist Noel Croucher, Sandy Bay was the largest such home in the world and the first of its kind in South-east Asia when it was built. The University of Hong Kong built staff quarters in the area in the 1970s, which have been added to since that time, along with a number of popular sports fields built on reclaimed land.

Kennedy Town

The narrow but scenic passage that lies between Kennedy Town and Green Island was named Sulphur Channel after the Royal Navy survey ship HMS *Sulphur;* this vessel was commanded by Captain Edward Belcher, RN, after whom Belcher's Street, Belcher's Bay (since reclaimed) and the former Belcher Battery at Kennedy Town were named. HMS *Sulphur* was present at the raising of the British flag on Hong Kong Island on 26 January 1841.

Kennedy Town, located in the extreme west of the city, was first developed as a planned suburban area to absorb some of the population in rapidly expanding Sai Ying Pun, which had seen a marked increase in population in the 1860s and gradually become overcrowded. Named after Sir Arthur Kennedy, governor of Hong Kong from 1872–77, Kennedy Town was laid out during his term in office. Built partly on reclaimed land, additional reclamation work in the area was undertaken in the late nineteenth century by a consortium which included the Armenian financier Sir Paul Chater.

This reclamation, around the end of the present tramway at Catchick Street (one of Chater's given names) and Kennedy Town New Praya, subsequently increased the total land area available for development by several acres. Kennedy Town Praya, as the new waterfront became known, remained as the waterfront until further reclamation in the mid-1990s. Until this later reclamation placed it inland, this was the last remaining section of Hong Kong Island in which the tramlines still ran along the coast.

Kennedy Town is also frequently known as Sai Wan among older residents, which occasionally causes some slight confusion as there is another Sai Wan at Hong Kong Island's eastern end. The China Merchants Wharf and Godowns to the west of the abattoir, which service the Kwangtung (Guangdong) coastal as well as West River ports, were all built on reclaimed land in the 1960s, and subsequently added to over the following three decades.

Shek Tong Tsui (Stone Pond Point) located between Sai Ying Pun and Kennedy Town, was a very popular area in the late nineteenth and early twentieth century for Chinese restaurants, high-class brothels, opium divans and gambling establishments, and had been a stone-quarrying area prior to the British arrival.

Aberdeen Main Road
香港仔大道

Formerly on the seashore, Aberdeen Main Road has changed little in recent years. Many of the businesses are the same as they have been for decades, and ship's chandlers and other maritime-related enterprises continue to make a reasonable living here. Moored offshore in the typhoon shelter for many years were a number of huge floating restaurants including the world-famous Jumbo. These were one of Hong Kong's most popular tourist sights for decades, perennially popular for a seafood dinner. There is only one left today, as another was sold some years ago and towed away to Manila. Now very expensive and somewhat eclipsed by other restaurants elsewhere in Hong Kong, the remaining floating behemoth still does a roaring trade, mainly among tourists from overseas.

① Staunton's Creek

Named after Sir George Staunton, who accompanied the Amherst mission to China in 1816–17, until the early 1970s Staunton's Creek was home to many thousands of fishing families, who lived all their lives on junks and sampans. A few still live

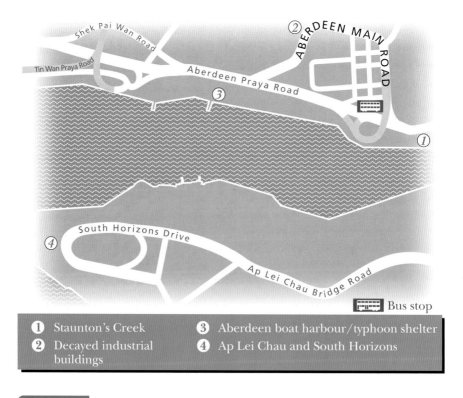

 Bus stop

❶ Staunton's Creek ❸ Aberdeen boat harbour/typhoon shelter
❷ Decayed industrial buildings ❹ Ap Lei Chau and South Horizons

waterborne lives, but the overwhelming majority have been rehoused on land over the last thirty years. Many old people in the area were born on junks and worked, married, raised families and lived most of their lives afloat.

Now partly canalized, Staunton's Creek is considerably less polluted than it was even a decade ago, due to the relocation of industry away from the Aberdeen area.

2 Decayed industrial buildings

Close to the city and surrounded — in the 1950s and 1960s — by densely populated squatter settlements, Aberdeen was transformed from a rather sleepy fishing port into one of Hong Kong's major industrial areas, with small export-orientated factories producing kitchenware, toys, garments and just about everything else imaginable.

With economic liberalizations on the mainland in the early 1980s, manufacturing activities — formerly the mainstay of the Hong Kong economy — increasingly moved across the border to Shenzhen and beyond, where wages are a fraction of Hong Kong's. As a result, industrial enterprises around Aberdeen drastically declined in importance and these days, many formerly active commercial buildings are semi-derelict and used mainly as warehouses.

③ Aberdeen boat harbour/typhoon shelter

Typhoon shelters are such a central feature of Hong Kong life that it seems hard to believe that many have not been around all that long. Yau Ma Tei's large typhoon shelter was only completed in 1915, while Causeway Bay's shelter was somewhat earlier, being finished in 1886.

For decades before that, the junk- and sampan-dwelling population were left largely to fend for themselves whenever the winds rose: massive typhoons generally caused considerable fatalities. Unofficial interests on the Legislative Council tended not to come to the defence of the boat people, in spite of many making their principal living from shipping and the import-export trade, all of which relied on boat people for off-lightering and cargo-handling.

Members of a Chinese ethnicity known as the Tanka (Egg People), boat-dwellers were — and for the most part still are — generally despised by land-dwelling Chinese. Some are Hoklo boat-dwellers originally, in the far-distant past, hailing from further up the coast in Fujian Province.

④ Ap Lei Chau and South Horizons

In many ways representative of Hong Kong's steadily rising middle-class expectations, the massive South Horizons residential was built in 1991 on the site of the former Ap Lei Chau power station, and additional phases were completed over the next few years. With a pleasant sea-front promenade, members-only gym, reasonably efficient transport links, residents' clubhouse facilities and a well-equipped shopping mall, South Horizons represents bourgeois arrival for many Hong Kong families.

Despite these perceived benefits, the development surrounds the increasingly polluted, foul-smelling Aberdeen typhoon shelter, brimming with all manner of floating *laap sap* (rubbish). South Horizons residents often complain about intolerable noise levels rising from the vessels moving about in the waters directly below their windows.

The island of Ap Lei Chau itself is a place of considerable contrast in terms of wealth, with a number of rundown public housing estates situated right next to what passes for one of Hong Kong's more desirable middle-class residential areas.

How To Get There

By Bus:	No. 70 from Exchange Square bus terminus, alight at Aberdeen bus terminus. Cross over to Aberdeen Praya Road and walk eastwards until you reach the creek.
By Taxi:	'Heung Kong Tsai Mong Kau Kup Bik Kau Chung Sum' ('Aberdeen Tennis and Squash Centre', which is next to Staunton's Creek).

Pok Fu Lam Road
薄扶林道

Permanently choked with roadworks over the last few years, Pok Fu Lam Road extends around the western end of Hong Kong Island from the University of Hong Kong campus to Aberdeen. This often hectic road around the western shoulder of Hong Kong Island wasn't always as busy as now.

Straddling the saddle between High West and Mount Davis, Pok Fu Lam was principally noted in the nineteenth century for quiet, out-of-town residences, and for the extensive Dairy Farm property in the early twentieth century.

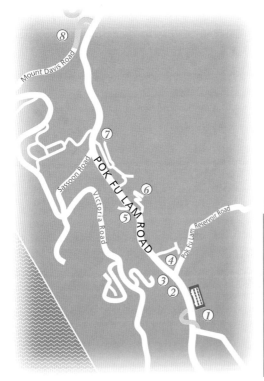

Bus stop

1 Pok Fu Lam village
2 Dairy Farm buildings
3 Bethany
4 University Hall
5 Ebenezer School for the Blind
6 Jessville
7 Queen Mary Hospital
8 Chiu Yuen Cemetery

Pok Fu Lam changed considerably after the Queen Mary Hospital was built and private motor transport became more common in the 1930s, and gradually more houses were built along here. It even attracted a few famous residents; in the late 1930s two of China's three famous Soong sisters, Madame Kung (Soong Ai-ling) and Madame Sun (Soong Ching-ling), both sisters of China's First Lady Madame Chiang Kai-shek (Soong May-ling), made their home on nearby Sassoon Road overlooking the sea — an important rendezvous for visiting politicians, journalists and China-watchers.

1 Pok Fu Lam village

These days looking more like a scruffy remnant of the extensive squatter settlements that characterized the territory in the 1960s than one of Hong Kong Island's original villages, Pok Fu Lam village straggles off up the hillside, with High West and Victoria Peak rising abruptly behind.

In 1865 the village had only 192 residents who lived mainly by subsistence farming, though today it numbers several thousand inhabitants. And believe it or not, there are still a few tiny well-tended vegetable plots there. Few genuinely old structures remain in Pok Fu Lam village, however, and most buildings here date from after the Pacific War.

For decades many of the Pok Fu Lam villagers worked as labourers on the Dairy Farm estate nearby; formerly very extensive, the farm produced most of Hong Kong's fresh milk cream until it finally closed in the 1970s.

2 Dairy Farm buildings

The driving force behind the establishment of a hygienically operated modern dairy farm in Hong Kong came from a Hong Kong doctor, Dr Patrick Manson. Manson arrived in Hong Kong in 1883, having previously lived at Takao (southern Taiwan) and later at

Amoy (Xiamen). Manson immediately recognized that the provision of an adequate fresh milk supply was essential to maintaining health for the European, Eurasian and Indian sections of the population who were accustomed to a diet that included it as a staple; at this time the overwhelming majority of Chinese refused to touch it. He was also astute enough to recognize an excellent business opportunity when he saw one, and backed by prominent local businessmen such as Armenian Sir Paul Chater, the Dairy Farm Company came into being in 1886 and rapidly prospered.

Heavily producing black-and-white Friesian cows were imported from Australia, and regularly replaced when they became worn down by the climate. Feed for the cattle was imported from Australia and Canada and transported from piers on the waterfront in Telegraph Bay up to the cowsheds by an ingenious means — a pulley-operated 'flying fox' hoist — that transported bales of lucerne up the hillside. In later years, motorists on Victoria Road often saw hay-bales slowly passing uphill over their heads as they drove along, a once common sight that has long vanished.

Dairy Farm's distinctive octagonal cowsheds are still there along Pok Fu Lam Road, a reminder of the time when much of this stretch of Hong Kong Island was considered remote enough from urban settlement to be extensively given over to dairying.

③ Bethany and the Missions Etrangères de Paris

Formerly part of the Missions Etrangères de Paris, this now crumbling building was used by the French priests as the chapel and printing press. The buildings were taken over by the University of Hong Kong in 1954 and were used for many years after that by Hong Kong University Press. The stained glass windows that formerly adorned the chapel were taken out when the French priests vacated the buildings and somehow became the property of Zetland Lodge, the Masonic Temple on Kennedy Road, where they are still to be seen today.

Just below Bethany, on the then wild Pok Fu Lam coast, Hong Kong's floral emblem, the vivid purple-mauve Blake's Bauhinia *(Bauhinea blakeana)* was discovered in 1908 by French fathers from the nearby mission. Very similar to the pink or white-flowered Camel's Foot flower *(Bauhinia variegata)*, a native of Burma, Blake's Bauhinia are planted on streets and roadsides all over Hong Kong. An extravagantly showy and very popular tree (a natural hybrid also known as the Hong Kong Orchid because of its distinctive, catteleya-like shape), the new species was named after Sir Henry Blake, governor from 1898–1903. The bauhinia flower has been in use as Hong Kong's floral enblem since 1965.

4 *University Hall (Douglas Castle)*

Now used as residential accommodation for students, this Gothic-inspired folly was originally built as an out-of-town retreat in the early 1860s by Douglas Lapraik, founder of the Douglas Steamship Co. Some time after Lapraik's death, the edifice became part of an imposing group of buildings used by the French Missions Etrangères de Paris (including Bethany, across the

road), who renamed the castle Nazareth and continued to use it until after the Pacific War.

Taken over by the University of Hong Kong in 1954, the castle was remodelled and is now used as student accommodation. The building's clock tower is a reminder of Douglas Lapraik — he was originally a watchmaker — who in typical Hong Kong-style branched out into other far more lucrative fields soon after he arrived in the colony. In the 1860s, Lapraik donated a imposing clock tower to Hong Kong, which stood for many years at the junction of Queen's Road Central and Pedder Street; it was finally demolished as a traffic hazard during the First World War.

(5) *Ebenezer School for the Blind*

Established in Hong Kong in 1897 by the German-based Hildeshiemer Blindenmission, this school for the visually impaired has been located on this Pok Fu Lam ridge for decades now and fills a very valuable — and often overlooked — social function, providing education and training for visually impaired children, and residential care for the visually impaired elderly. For many years the school was entirely supported by the Hildeshiemer Blindenmission, but since 1954 it has been subvented by the Hong Kong government as well as local charitable organizations, such as the Community Chest and the Hong Kong Jockey Club.

Many students from Ebenezer School have gone on to university and led fulfilling lives: a world away from the times, not so long ago, when all a blind person in Hong Kong could look forward to in life was a simple repetitive job like beadwork, knitting or working as a masseur, or for the truly poor and unfortunate, begging on a street corner.

(6) *Jessville*

High above Pok Fu Lam Road and mostly hidden by great old trees is one of the area's seeming oddities — a gracious old house from a former era, surviving almost unaltered and still lived in and surrounded by reasonably well-kept grounds.

High West rises steeply behind, the Lamma Channel with its magnificent vista of islands and sea stretches out in front, and the neighbouring high-rise buildings and busy road below somehow seem very far away. Coming from Aberdeen the house is clearly visible above the road — an incongruous link with the past that can make those unaware of Jessville's existence do a double-take.

7 *Queen Mary Hospital*

This large government hospital above Pok Fu Lam Road was built in 1937. Originally built in 1850, it was designed as a replacement for the old Government Civil Hospital in Sai Ying Pun. When it was completed, Queen Mary was the best-equipped hospital in the Far East. While it has been extended numerous times  since then, most of the original pre-war buildings, much renovated, are still there today. Queen Mary is the teaching hospital for the University of Hong Kong, and several of the departments in the Faculty of Medicine are headquartered there.

A School of Nursing opened in 1968 and throughout the 1960s Queen Mary continued to expand its services and facilities; today, Queen Mary has over 1,300 beds and offers the general public excellent, heavily subsidized medical services.

While the site enjoys spectacular views of islands and sea, the *fung shui* at 'Ma Lei Yee Yuen' is reputedly not all it could be — the hospital directly overlooks the densely crowded Chinese Christian Cemetery (itself established long before Queen Mary was built) and many patients comment that it is somehow *not* the most auspicious of all possible sites for a hospital!

8 *Chiu Yuen Cemetery*

Just below Pok Fu Lam Road, Chiu Yuen (meaning Clear and Distant) is Hong Kong's Eurasian cemetery. It contains the grave of many prominent early Eurasians, such as Sir Man-kam Lo and Sir Robert Kotewall. Usually overlooked today when the term 'local' is generally taken to mean Chinese, for over a century it was the Eurasians and the local Portuguese — and not the majority of Chinese residents — who were Hong Kong's truly local people.

STREETS

From the road, Chiu Yuen looks much like any other Chinese cemetery, and that sense of commonality was what the people who established it had in mind if only unconsciously; in death at least, they wanted to be the same as everyone else at last, rather than being on the margins, not quite one or the other, which was the fate of Hong Kong's early Eurasian community.

Chinese-style graves predominate and are generally very elaborate and well-maintained; perhaps unsurprising as among their descendants are some of Hong Kong's more prominent and wealthy citizens. Not as common but equally well maintained are the numerous more European-style headstones. Many graves have bilingual inscriptions, and some are only in English, even though the grave is traditionally Chinese in shape; a reminder that many early local Eurasians were not Chinese-literate.

How To Get There

By Bus:	No. 37A or 90B from Des Voeux Road Central, The Landmark bus stop, alight on Pok Fu Lam Road at bus stop outside Pok Fu Lam village. Minibus No. 22 from Central Star Ferry Pier, alight on Pok Fu Lam Road outside Pok Fu Lam village.
By Taxi:	'Pok Fu Lam Tsuen' ('Pok Fu Lam Village').

This dramatically scenic, winding road around the western end of Hong Kong Island was originally named Victoria Jubilee Road as it opened in 1897, Queen Victoria's Diamond Jubilee year. After a few years the name was shortened to Victoria Road, which it remains today. Most traffic going from Central across to Aberdeen uses Pok Fu Lam Road, which makes Victoria Road relatively quiet, except for the speed-demon minibus drivers who hurtle along here at really frightening speeds.

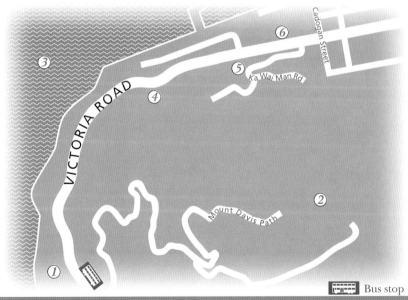

Bus stop

❶ Special Branch building
❷ Gun batteries at Mount Davis
❸ Sulphur Channel swimmers
❹ Mount Davis cottage area
❺ The Hong Kong Bayanihan Trust
❻ Bonky Parking Ltd.

Aberdeen • Pok Fu Lam

STREETS

Victoria Road

The stretch of road around Mount Davis runs above the last remaining length of rocky coastline on Hong Kong Island's northern shore, and even though it is only a few minutes away from Kennedy Town, it still manages to appear somehow remote from the city. The stunning vistas of sea and islands never fail to delight along here — at least on a pollution-free day and down along the seashore, the nearby urban area somehow seems very far away. Further along Victoria Road towards Pok Fu Lam are numerous substantial residences belonging to some of Hong Kong's super-rich: palatial dwellings behind massive gates nestling between the cliffside and the road.

① Special Branch building

Surrounded by barbed wire and watched over by security cameras, this unremarkable building along Victoria Road was originally used by the British army, and then subsequently for many years as an interrogation centre by the Royal Hong Kong Police Special Branch. Disbanded in 1995 in advance of the  handover, Special Branch had a number of notable successes in rooting out subversive elements, and during the 1950s kept a close watch on both Nationalists and Communists to prevent them from either fighting among themselves in Hong Kong or fomenting trouble in either Taiwan or the mainland, using Hong Kong as a base.

Close surveillance of both parties was especially vital after the *Kashmir Princess* incident in 1955, when Nationalist agents infiltrated themselves aboard a plane at Kai Tak that was supposed to be carrying Premier Chou En-lai to the Afro-Asian Conference in Bandung and sabotaged it. The *Kashmir Princess* crashed a few hours later with the loss of all on board, a tragedy that prompted increased police vigilance in Hong Kong.

The Special Branch building still looks very forbidding today, and it was only recently that its former internal security role was publicly acknowledged for the first time — in spite of this little 'secret' having been open for decades!

2) *Gun batteries at Mount Davis*

Looming above Victoria Road is Mount Davis, steep, forbidding, jungle-clad and almost wild in places, with dramatic views of islands and sea in every direction from the winding road to the summit.

Overlooking Sulphur Channel and commanding both the western harbour and the Lamma Channel, Mount Davis was very heavily fortified in the early twentieth century, with five 9.2-inch gun batteries being completed here in 1912. By the 1930s the strategic importance of Mount Davis had been downgraded, and two of the big guns had been relocated to Stanley.

After the Japanese attacked Hong Kong in December 1941, the fortifications at Mount Davis were badly damaged by

continuous aerial attack and were finally abandoned. Before the final British surrender, all remaining armaments and ammunition were destroyed.

In recent years Ma Wui Hall, a Jockey Club funded youth hostel was built near the summit, along with a microwave repeater tower. Otherwise, the gun batteries, bunkers and emplacements remain much as they were at the end of the war, overgrown and frequented by occasional hikers, visitors to the youth hostel and overcamouflaged war-gamers.

3) *Sulphur Channel swimmers*

Early in the morning and at sundry times during the day, swimmers come down here for a dip in the harbour. These are mostly old men, who are happy — or foolish — enough to brave both the numerous sampans and passenger ferries that pass through Sulphur Channel and the bacteria-rich waters of Victoria Harbour, for their daily exercise. Belonging to ad hoc swimming clubs such as the Golden Bell Swimming Club, these intrepid old fellows dodge all manner of

Aberdeen • Pok Fu Lam

flotsam and jetsam as well as passing passenger ferries and — one hopes — manage to avoid swallowing too much of Victoria Harbour's unappealing waters as they splash and frolic.

④ Mount Davis cottage area (squatter resettlement)

The hill slopes around Mount Davis became a temporary home to thousands of squatters in the early 1950s, all refugees from the civil war and subsequent communist takeover on the mainland. After living here for almost two decades, the new arrivals were gradually resettled elsewhere on

Hong Kong Island and their huts demolished; however, a nucleus of the original settlement still remains.

Down on the waterline a few village houses have small attractive gardens, along with views of islands and sea that many millionaires elsewhere in Hong Kong don't have and can't afford. While their homes seem somewhat dilapidated, the cottage residents around Mount Davis share with the palaces of nearby tycoons and multimillionaires that rarest of Hong Kong Island commodities — relative space, a patch of garden and a view.

5) *The Hong Kong Bayanihan Trust*

While the local Filipino community seems perhaps more in evidence in Statue Square on a Sunday than anywhere else in Hong Kong, there is a thriving Filipino community centre in Kennedy Town. Established in 1993, the Hong Kong Bayanihan Trust does much to assist the very large, but  often marginalized and discriminated against, migrant domestic worker community.

Low-cost or free courses are offered, teaching computer skills, hairdressing, baking, small business management and various other subjects. The centre offers welfare services and sporting facilities (volleyball is especially popular), and even has its own a Tagalog-language radio station. While originally established to offer support to the Filipino migrant worker community, Bayanihan also assists other migrant worker groups living in Hong Kong as well such as Thais, Indonesians, Sri Lankans and Indians. In addition to the Kennedy Town centre, there is another Bayanihan Community Centre at 78 Hak Po Street, Mong Kok.

⑥ Bonky Parking Ltd.

Signpost solecisms are commonplace all over Hong Kong and a constant source of amusement to many; one of the best is located here on Victoria Road not far from the former abattoir. The firm has several branches elsewhere in Hong Kong.

Wanko underwear, need I say more? Appetizing restaurants with names like Manky can't but raise a smile, and further beg the question: does no one *ever* gently point out that — just perhaps — there *might* be a double entendre lurking somewhere underneath?

How To Get There

By Bus:	No. 5A from Des Voeux Road Central bus stop outside The Landmark, alight on Victoria Road at the Felix Villas bus terminus. The Special Branch is across the road.
By Taxi:	'Wick Dor Lei Doh, Mor Sing Leng Ging' ('Victoria Road, Mount Davis Path').

According to the late K. M. A. Barnett, a Hong Kong government administrator and very capable linguist, Wong Chuk Hang — ostensibly meaning Yellow Bamboo Stream — is actually a layover from the times before Hong Kong was colonized by Han Chinese migrants. In the language of the now vanished Yao peoples, Wong Chuk Hang means 'left side'. Likewise, Wong Ma (Wong Ma Kok in Stanley) means 'right side', although 'yellow hemp' is the Cantonese meaning. Rock carvings, reminders of these vanished 'early Hong Kong people', were uncovered during an archaeological dig in 1984. With geometric patterns and images of animals, these carvings are similar in style and content to others found at Big Wave Bay, Po Toi and Cheung Chau.

Wong Chuk Hang is the site of one of Hong Kong Island's oldest villages, Hong Kong Wai. These days, although it is mainly an ugly, post-industrial area of blighted old factory buildings and squalid urban decay, Wong Chuk Hang still nevertheless has places of interest and charm.

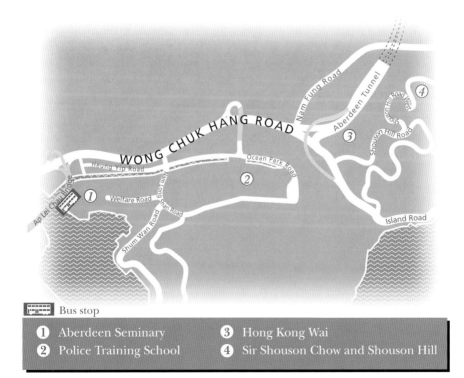

Bus stop

❶ Aberdeen Seminary	❸ Hong Kong Wai
❷ Police Training School	❹ Sir Shouson Chow and Shouson Hill

STREETS

1 Aberdeen Seminary

The Holy Spirit Seminary was established in 1931 to train Roman Catholic priests. The older building is a syncretic combination of Chinese palace architecture and Italian styles and was originally intended to be a Chinese courtyard-style structure; due to the great depression in the 1930s, only a third of it was completed. During the Japanese occupation, the seminary was closed and after 1949 the seminary was disbanded as there were no further catechists coming down from the mainland to train for the priesthood.

The seminary reopened as a school in 1957 and in 1967 several new classrooms were added to the southern side of the building. An especially well-known feature is a distinctive painting on one wall depicting the Virgin Mary and child surrounded by various Christian symbols. On one side is the Chinese legend 'descendants of the dragon' and on the other 'descendants of Christ' to remind them that they have a duty to remember their Chinese heritage and incorporate Christian and Chinese values.

② *Police Training School*

A Police School to train new entrants into the Hong Kong Police has been in operation since 1869. In 1920 the original school was replaced by a new and greatly reorganized Police Training School, based at the Central Police Station on Hollywood Road. Recruits were trained in a full syllabus of police subjects including criminal law, police regulations, drill and musketry as well as language courses. The Hong Kong Police at this time was very multi-ethnic, with British Europeans, Cantonese, Shantung men and White Russians, as well as some local Portuguese, and considerable numbers of specially recruited Punjabi Muslims and Sikhs.

In 1948 the Police Training School moved to new facilities at Wong Chuk Hang, taking over pre-war food storage godowns and a refugee camp. With expansion, the Police Training School has been based at this location since that time.

③ Hong Kong Wai

Before Hong Kong was established as a British colony, Wong Chuk Hang was a minor riverine port from where fragrant wood from Sha Tin (now part of the New Territories) and Tung Koon (now known as Dongguan and situated further into the Pearl River region) were exported.

One of Hong Kong Island's oldest remaining villages, Hong Kong Wai still has a number of old buildings; a few of them are over a hundred years old and still in quite a good state of repair. Like most of Hong Kong's other village areas, Hong Kong Wai is a rather jumbled mixture of new and old buildings, with little apparent planning involved in the placing of the newer structures.

④ Sir Shouson Chow and Shouson Hill

Perhaps now best remembered by many for the elite residential area of Shouson Hill named after him, Sir Shouson Chow was one of the leading figures in Hong Kong for over seventy years and the first Chinese appointed to Hong Kong's Executive Council. The Chow clan arrived in Wong Chuk Hang from Kwangtung (Guangdong) in 1759, over eighty years before the British landed in Hong Kong.

Born in Hong Kong in 1861, the Chinese government sent Chow, when he was thirteen, with a number of other promising scholars to study in America. He eventually studied at Columbia University and returned to China in 1881. After a long period on Chinese government service in Korea, he managed various commercial concerns with considerable ability.

After the 1911 Revolution, Chow returned to Hong Kong where his wide experience and obvious ability led him to being appointed to directorships in many firms and public utility concerns. Appointed a Legislative Council member in 1921, he was the first Chinese to be appointed to the Executive Council in 1926.

Chow finally died aged 98 in 1959 and was eulogized in the press as the 'Grand Old Man of Hong Kong'.

How To Get There

By Bus:	No. 90 from Exchange Square bus terminus, alight on Ap Lei Chau Bridge. A footpath from the bridge leads to the Holy Spirit Seminary.
By Taxi:	'Wong Chuk Hang, Sing San Sau Yuen' ('Wong Chuk Hang, Holy Spirit Seminary').

The steep hillside area extending westward towards the University of Hong Kong from Western Market is the oldest section of urban Hong Kong. Western District, incorporating Tai Ping Shan, Sai Ying Pun and Kennedy Town at the extreme western end of Hong Kong Island, encompasses a number of distinct

localities, some of which have changed little in recent years. Even the street layout in Western is fundamentally the same as it was in the 1850s, with new buildings gradually replacing the crumbling century-old tenements in the 1960s and 1970s.

Tai Ping Shan, immediately to the west of the Central business district, was the site of Hong Kong's first Chinatown, which gradually developed in the 1850s. While it may appear a contradiction to have a 'Chinatown' in such an overwhelmingly Chinese place as Hong Kong, during the nineteenth century the almost complete social segregation — and as a result residential separateness — of the various races that resided in the colony made Tai Ping Shan's largely divided development almost inevitable. Chinese-owned businesses increasingly congregated in the area and by 1855 there were no non-Chinese landholders or tenants remaining in Tai Ping Shan.

Many Chinese businesses, banks and organizations, with links to southern China and overseas communities in the 'Nanyang' or 'South Seas' (South-east Asian region), set up branches or had warehouses in the area. Important at this time in Hong Kong, and prominent and influential elsewhere in China, were representatives of various guilds, such as the Nam Pak Hong which dealt mainly with the import of rice and South-east Asian products, the Pawnbrokers Guild, the California Merchant's Guild which dealt with the lucrative West coast trade, the Chinese Medicine Guild and the Piece-goods and Silk Guild.

The area around Bonham Strand became colloquially known as the Nam Pak Hong (literally meaning the North-South Company), after the influential guild of the same name and because of the number of traders dealing in 'South Seas' produce that could be found in the area.

Timber, used for both construction and firewood, was imported from North Borneo, as well as medicinal products, bird's nests, dried seafood and other delicacies from elsewhere in South-east Asia. The mainstay of the Nam Pak Hong however was rice, imported mainly from Siam (now Thailand), and Cochin-China

- Belcher's Street
- Centre Street
- Des Voeux Road West
- High Street
- Ladder Street
- Tai Ping Shan Street
- Western Street

(now southern Vietnam). The rice trade from Siam was dominated by Chiu Chow merchants, natives of Swatow (Shantou) and its surrounding area further up the Kwantung (Guangdong) coast from Hong Kong. From Indochina it was dominated by Cantonese, based in Cholon, twin city to Saigon. Numerous trading firms established in the nineteenth century still maintain headquarters in the area, and while they have diversified their interests with the passage of time, the rice trade still remains very important.

The steep hillsides rising from the harbour on the western side of the city were rapidly taken up by a settlement, known as the Lower Bazaar. This developed between January 1841, when the British took possession of Hong Kong Island, and July 1843, when the island's status as a British Crown Colony was confirmed. During that period, European residential and business districts clustered in and about the Central area, whereas the military occupied a large area of prime ground east of Garden Road towards Wan Chai, which later became Victoria Barracks, and Chinese businesses congregated towards the west.

Thus, in the early 1840s, the hitherto sparsely populated western end of the city became transformed into what was effectively an unruly, barely planned, squalid and disease-ridden squatters' camp. Public health was such a concern that by 1881, a full-scale inquiry into sanitary conditions was ordered by the Secretary of State for the Colonies. The Chadwick Report, made public in 1882, recommended that numerous sweeping changes be made. The much-needed Sanitary Board was established, from which the Urban Council eventually developed.

But by the time plague broke out thirteen years later, most of the recommended sanitary reforms had still not been implemented. The Lower Bazaar was frequently devastated by fires and outbreaks of epidemic disease continued to occur every summer. Gradually more permanent buildings were erected after Crown Colony status was confirmed and further improved over the years. Buildings in this area have been demolished and rebuilt numerous times over the past century and a half, but the temporary and haphazard pattern of early settlement, in the physical form of narrow streets, quiet courts and interlinking stone steps, still persists today.

Western

Tai Ping Shan

Grossly overcrowded conditions in the Tai Ping Shan tenements led to repeated outbreaks of epidemic disease, the most serious of which were the bubonic plague epidemics of the 1890s. In this closely packed area, humans shared water supplies and living space with cattle, pigs and poultry. Conditions were ripe for a serious outbreak of disease, and had it not been the plague, it may well have been something else. Bubonic plague first made its appearance in the spring of 1894 and was to be a recurrent menace for the next thirty years. The disease surfaced in the early spring, after the coldest winter then recorded in Hong Kong. At its coldest, the Peak district down to 450 feet above sea level was ice-bound for three days. This had not previously happened since European settlement began.

Much of the Tai Ping Shan district was cordoned off during the outbreak, and three hundred soldiers from the Shropshire Regiment were brought in to assist in cleansing and disinfecting operations in Tai Ping Shan and elsewhere. Five servicemen became plague victims themselves, and were buried in the Colonial Cemetery at Happy Valley; their graves can still be seen there today. The Government Civil Hospital was overwhelmed by the number of victims and the Kennedy Town glassworks, a recently completed pig depot which had large airy sheds suitable for conversion to wards, and the Royal Navy hospital ship *Hygeia* were all pressed into action. Disinfecting stations were erected at Tai Ping Shan and Mong Kok and public bathhouses built at Pound Lane and Wan Chai.

The human cost of the plague was very high. On one day alone in June 1894, 109 plague victims were collected from where they had been abandoned to die. With no laws requiring the registration of deaths amongst the Chinese population, it proved impossible to accurately pinpoint the number of plague-related deaths taking place. Thousands of people decamped from Hong Kong to the mainland, encouraged to do so by the provincial authorities. Contemporary reports allege that over 100,000 people — half the population of the colony — departed for the mainland. The official figure however, given in the governor's dispatch to the secretary of state, indicated that some 80,000 people left.

The governor at the time, Sir William Robinson, felt the only effective long-term remedy was razing and rebuilding all unsanitary property. This would have entailed the demolition, according to one reliable estimate, of at least one-tenth of the entire city. After the plague epidemic abated, public bathhouses and lavatories maintained at government expense became a notable feature in Western, and remain prominent to this day in other parts of Hong Kong.

One such facility (since rebuilt) is still in use in Sai Ying Pun, next to the old Tsan Yuk Hospital on Western Street (now the Western District Community Centre). Bounties were issued for rats, whose fleas were a major contributor to the plague's rapid spread and for decades, black Phenyl-based disinfectant, appropriately named *chau shui* (stinking fluid in Cantonese), was issued free to the public.

As more than half the plague cases originated in Tai Ping Shan, a special Resumption Ordinance was passed empowering government to take over land and property deemed disease-stricken, against the predictably vocal objections of vested property interests on the Legislative Council. The worst and most decrepit tenements were demolished and land resumed on Kau U Fong was subsequently used to create Blake Garden (named after Governor Sir Henry Blake) a large, pleasant open space in the centre of Tai Ping Shan. Construction of the nearby Government Bacteriological Laboratory was authorized, and it was eventually built in 1906. One of the most attractive survivors from earlier times in the area, the building now houses the Museum of Medical Sciences.

Immediately to the west of Tai Ping Shan, the adjacent area of Sai Ying Pun was laid out in the 1860s. Sai Ying Pun's street layout follows a grid pattern, and is obviously better planned than Tai Ping Shan, which simply grew and developed from what was originally little more than a squatter settlement.

A number of educational institutes established themselves in the Western district, ranging from missionary schools such as St Paul's College to early government schools like King's College on Bonham Road. King's College remains today one of Hong Kong's most prestigious government boy's schools. The Hong Kong College of Medicine was established in 1887, and eventually the University of Hong Kong, established in 1912, developed from it.

Sai Ying Pun

Scholarly debate has occurred in recent years as to whether Sai Ying Pun actually refers to, as is generally believed, an early, British-era Western Soldier's Encampment, or an earlier settlement used by pirate leader Cheung Po-tsai in the first decade of the nineteenth century. Neither viewpoint has been conclusively proven.

In Sai Ying Pun a number of religious organizations were established, with many members of their congregations being drawn from Hakka settlers who migrated to Hong Kong in search of work from the East River districts in the 1850s and 1860s. German missionary organizations such as the Basel Missionary Society and the Rhenish Mission established themselves in Sai Ying Pun and built churches, schools and welfare organizations.

The Chinese community also established welfare organizations in Western at this time, most notably the Tung Wah Hospital, which opened in 1870. For its first thirty years as a British colony, Hong Kong lacked a hospital providing services that were either welcome or relevant to the vast majority of the population. The Government Civil Hospital was established in 1850, and at first catered mainly for the police force and the destitutes they picked up. Around 1864 it became accessible to private paying patients as well, though the then expensive fees of $1 discouraged most people and very few Chinese wished to use it anyway.

Part of this reluctance was due to a general distrust of foreigners and a deeply held belief that their intentions — however noble they may have seemed on the surface — were always ultimately evil. Western medicine in particular emphasized surgery and post-mortem examinations at a time when most Chinese devoutly believed that, after death, one should return to the ancestors with an unmutilated body. And nineteenth-century Western medical science, with its dirty, badly administered hospitals, poorly trained nurses and few specific cures for diseases did little to inspire public confidence — even amongst those familiar with its practices.

The Tung Wah Hospital on Po Yan Street is linked historically with the Kwong Fuk I T'ze, also known as the Pak Sing Miu ('Hundred Surnames' or Common People's Temple) on nearby Tai Ping Shan Street, built in 1851. These temple buildings were erected to house the *sun tsü pai* (ancestral tablets) of poor immigrant Chinese who died away from their *heung ha* (home districts). With no one to tend their spirit tablets, they ran the risk of becoming wandering malevolent ghosts, and the I T'ze was established to help prevent this unfortunate occurrence and the resultant menace to the wider community. Its successor repository, the Pak Sing Miu is still located on Tai Ping Shan Street today.

In the absence of anywhere else, the Kwong Fuk I T'ze eventually became a place where poor, terminally ill Chinese came to die. Inmates were usually single men living alone, who had been thrown out of their tenements by landlords or co-tenants when they became seriously ill, as it was deemed inauspicious that they should die in rented quarters. These beliefs, and the 'dying houses' that arose to cater for them, were quite common in immigrant Chinese communities elsewhere; Singapore had several on Sago Lane until the early 1970s.

By 1869 the sufferings of the desperately sick, who lay dying in appalling conditions at the I T'ze 'death house', had become a festering public scandal. Continuous adverse publicity finally shamed a number of influential Chinese into establishing a properly-run Chinese hospital. The Chinese community donated over $40,000 and the government contributed $115,000. The Tung Wah Hospital Ordinance defined the hospital as 'a Chinese hospital for the care and treatment of the indigent sick to be supported by voluntary contributions', and so it has largely remained till this day. Sir Richard MacDonnell laid the foundation stone in 1870 on a site granted on Po Yan Street in the Western district and the hospital opened to patients two years later. The Tung Wah Hospital is still located there today in newer premises, and the old foundation stone can be seen just near the entrance to the modern building.

Committee members were mostly drawn from the compradore (mercantile middleman) class, then at the height of their wealth, power and influence in Hong Kong and the Treaty Ports. The Tung Wah Hospital Committee's first Chairman was Leong On (Leung Hok-chau), compradore to Messrs. Gibb, Livingston and Co., one of the most important foreign firms at the time (over a century later absorbed into the Inchcape group). Another prominent early director was Lo Chen-kong, compradore of the Hongkong and Shanghai Banking Corporation.

Compradores of foreign firms at that time were among the wealthiest Chinese in the colony, but in time their influence on the Tung Wah Hospital Committee declined, as other Chinese began to engage independently in business, medicine or the law and gained social position. Later still, bankers, department store owners, rich overseas Chinese and émigrés from the 1911 Revolution also became influential on the committee. These latter groups formed a more diversified and somewhat more representative Chinese elite than existed in the nineteenth century, and eventually replaced the compradores as arbiters of power and influence within the Tung Wah Hospital Committee, and in the context of broader Chinese society within Hong Kong.

Western

STREETS

Belcher's Street
卑 路 乍 街

Thronged with vehicles and pedestrians at all hours, Belcher's Street was named for Captain Edward Belcher, RN, officer-in-charge of HMS *Sulphur*, a Royal Navy survey vessel which arrived at Hong Kong in January 1841.

Present at the flag-raising ceremony at Possession Point, further to the east, on 26 January 1841, Belcher later recorded the scene in his account, *Voyage Round The World*, published in 1843. ' ... The squadron arrived and the marines were landed, the union hoisted on our post, and formal possession taken of the island by Commodore Sir J. G. Bremer, accompanied by the other officers of the squadron, under a *feu de joie* from the marines, and a royal salute from the ships of war.'

Thereafter Edward Belcher and his ship fades from local history, but nevertheless the name of this otherwise largely known naval officer is commemorated in a street, a disused fort and now a lavish luxury apartment block; his vessel is in the Sulphur Channel, the narrow passage between Hong Kong and Green Island.

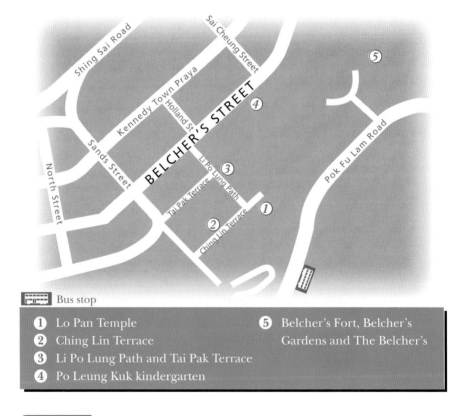

🚌 Bus stop

❶ Lo Pan Temple
❷ Ching Lin Terrace
❸ Li Po Lung Path and Tai Pak Terrace
❹ Po Leung Kuk kindergarten
❺ Belcher's Fort, Belcher's Gardens and The Belcher's

1 Lo Pan Temple (Lo Pan Miu)

Dedicated to the God of Carpenters, a temple was established on this site in about 1885. There is another temple to this deity found in Macao, near the Porto Interior. The sharply pointed, very distinctive roofline is perhaps its most striking feature, its ridge and eaves extremely busy with statues, paintings and carvings. The shady terrace in front of Lo Pan Miu is a quiet, atmospheric place to sit out on a hot summer's day, under the shade of spreading banyan trees that are almost as old as the temple itself.

Typical of so many hidden places in Hong Kong, one needs only to walk a few steps away from a busy road to find a quiet terrace with an old temple surrounded by trees that has changed little in many years. The only sounds you hear are birds, the rattle and clack of mah-jong tiles somewhere and the occasional distant radio. There are no crowds, no minibuses or trucks; it's green, peaceful, tranquil and — most unexpected of all — right in the heart of Kennedy Town.

2 Ching Lin Terrace

Ching Lin Terrace is one of a series of small terrace streets leading up the hillside above Belcher's Street to just below Pok Fu Lam Road. This quiet lane seems strangely rural, quite unlike its setting just above the busy traffic on Belcher's Street would at first suggest. This hillside terrace along with several others nearby has changed little over

STREETS

the years, and is a lingering reminder of what many of Hong Kong's steep backstreets looked like till the massive redevelopment and widespread prosperity of recent years. The complete absence of vehicles make Ching Lin Terrace and the terraces leading off it very pleasant and quiet residential areas, in sharp contrast to densely crowded Belcher's Street directly below.

(3) Li Po Lung Path and Tai Pak Terrace

A number of hillside backstreets in Kennedy Town recall the name of a long dead, mostly forgotten early businessman, and one of Hong Kong's first amusement parks. Li Po-lung was a wealthy Chinese entrepreneur who started an amusement park known as Tai Pak Yau Lok Cheung (Tai Pak Amusement Park), on the hillside above Belcher's Street.

Tai Pak Yau Lok Cheung opened for business in the early twentieth century and had extensive gardens, a number of teahouses, trinket stalls and, perhaps typically for the times, troupes of young girls who sang and played musical instruments such as the pipa (Chinese lute). Li Po-lung wished to commemorate the famous Tang dynasty poet Li Po (Li Bai) — his namesake — in the development and the surrounding streets: Hei Wong Terrace, Ching Lin Terrace and Hok Sze Terrace all drew their inspiration from phrases in Li Po's poetry. Tai Pak Yau Lok Cheung wasn't a great business success and eventually closed down; the site was — perhaps inevitably for Hong Kong — then redeveloped as a residential area, but barely audible echoes of the old amusement park, and of Li Po-lung himself, still persist in the street names extending steeply up the hillsides above Belcher's Street.

(4) *Po Leung Kuk kindergarten*

This pleasing, shuttered old building was the first fire station to be built in Kennedy Town and dates from the early 1920s. Now used as a kindergarten organized by the Po Leung Kuk, it is not subject to any protective legislation, despite being one of the few architectural reminders of the past still to be found in the area.

(5) *Belcher's Fort, Belcher's Gardens and The Belcher's*

The old Belcher's Battery site was redeveloped in the early 1950s as civil servants' subsidized housing and became known as Belcher's Gardens. This was the first planned development of its kind, though it was not the first to be completed, and along with similar developments helped alleviate the extreme overcrowding prevalent in Hong Kong during those years.

The Belcher's Gardens complex, extending from the northern side of Pok Fu Lam Road to Queen's Road West, was redeveloped in the late 1990s as The Belcher's, a massive, new luxury residential complex with what must be one of Hong Kong's most unfortunate-sounding names. Riding high, wide and very pink above the hillside behind, and a strikingly distinct landmark seen from any direction, The Belcher's

273

seems to epitomize the irrelevance of the surrounding landscape to many recent residential developments in Hong Kong.

As a reminder of the former gun battery that once stood on the site, a massive, old 9.2-inch naval gun was found on the site during the redevelopment; it is now in the Museum of Coastal Defence in Shau Kei Wan.

How To Get There

By Bus:	No. 3B from Connaught Road Central City Hall bus stop, alight at Pokfield Road bus terminus. Cross Pok Fu Lam Road, walk through a side gate near Block 1 of Academic Terrace until you reach Lo Pan Temple.
By Taxi:	'Pok Fu Lam Doh, Hok See Toi' ('Pok Fu Lam Road, Academic Terrace').
By Tram:	From anywhere in Central, take the west-bound tram marked 'Kennedy Town' and alight on Kennedy Town Praya near Kennedy Town Centre. On the Kennedy Town Centre side, walk against the direction of the traffic until you reach Sands Street. Walk up Sands Street until you reach the steps. Walk up the steps and turn left into Ching Lin Terrace. The Lo Pan Temple is at the end of Ching Lin Terrace.

This steep street leading down to what was once the waterfront has been a popular market street for generations of local residents. Just below Bonham Road, pedestrians in the old days would take off their *mook kek* (wooden slippers) and go barefoot to avoid falling over when walking down this very steep

Des Voeux Road West

③

Queen's Road West

First Street

Second Street

CENTRE STREET

Third Street

① Yu Lok Lane

②

High Street

Bonham Road

Western

Bus stop

① Yu Lok Lane
② Cheung Jan Ho Provisions Co. Cereals and Household Goods
③ Yuen Kee Tong Shui

STREETS

street. Old photographs taken from the top of the street show the expanse of the harbour stretching out below, but now only slivers of water can be glimpsed between the tower blocks.

Some of the area's oldest surviving buildings, dating from the late nineteenth century, can still be seen just off Centre Street around Yu Lok Lane, while the thriving street market spread out between Bonham Road and Queen's Road West always offers something of interest.

① *Yu Lok Lane*

Some of these old houses just off Centre Street date in parts from the 1880s, and originally housed a number of Chinese Christian converts who settled in the area during those years. The plot sizes along here are very narrow, making it very difficult to redevelop the street without first demolishing the entire block. Until the 1980s nearly every backstreet in Central and Western looked very similar to this one, but in most places they have long been cleared and redeveloped.

Most of these houses still have bucket-style sanitation to take away the *yeh heung* (night-soil) and this is not uncommon in other parts of Hong Kong too; shamefully primitive conditions, to say the very least, in what we are continually told is 'Asia's World City'.

While the little terrace houses here are cramped and facilities somewhat basic, for the mostly elderly residents the lane is nevertheless home and many have lived there most of their lives. Spreading trees shade the lane; there is a profusion of pot plants, and one can always find people sitting out in the cool. For all its back-alley decrepitude Yu Lok Lane retains a homely and strangely village-like flavour, in spite of being just a back lane right in the heart of the metropolis.

2 Cheung Jan Ho Provisions Co. Cereals and Household Goods

The quantity and sheer variety of goods on offer in this little shop almost defies description. Heavy dark green Canton glaze flowerpots deeply embossed with dragons are reasonably priced, with plainer ones being about half as expensive. This is one of the few remaining shops in Hong Kong that still stocks the solid, hard-to-break old-fashioned pots. Plaited palm-leaf fans popular with old ladies lie next to coconut-fibre *chee saw chaat* (toilet brushes) with split-bamboo handles. These are almost a museum piece these days, as like most household items they have been generally superseded by plastic. Mops, coarse and soft brooms, dustpans and so on hang from hooks overhead. All sorts of everyday porcelain and kitchenware, mostly blue-and-white are inside and spill out in neatly arranged piles onto the pavement.

③ Yuen Kee Tong Shui (sweet soup shop)

Really excellent walnut-cream soup, tasting slightly of bitter almonds, is one of the more popular items on offer at Yuen Kee. Various types of *tau sha* (red bean or green bean based soups) are also very popular. The sweet, heavy steamed chunks of *ma lai go*, so-called 'Malayan Cake' (in spite of the name you'll seldom *ever* find it in Malaysia), is a few dollars a thick spongy slice. Yuen Kee, like most other shops on Centre Street, has been here for decades and attracts a very loyal following. Even people who have moved away from Sai Ying Pun long ago still return to eat here from time to time — proof of its considerable popularity.

How To Get There

By Bus:	No. 3B from Connaught Road Central City Hall bus stop, minibuses No. 8 and No. 22 from Central Star Ferry Pier, alight on Bonham Road at the junction of Bonham Road and Park Road. You should be able to see an HSBC branch on your left and a Bank of East Asia branch on your right just before you reach the bus stop.
By Taxi:	'Goh Gaai, Jing Gaai loh hau' ('Junction of High Street and Centre Street').
By Tram:	From anywhere in Central, take the west-bound tram marked 'Kennedy Town' and alight on Des Voeux Road West after the Island Pacific Hotel. Centre Street is directly across the road from the hotel.

Des Voeux Road West
德輔道西

Des Voeux Road West follows the tramlines from Central towards Kennedy Town. It was the original waterfront praya from the early days of British rule until the 1890s, when the reclamation scheme gradually extended the seafront northwards. The road was renamed after Sir William Des Voeux, governor from 1887–91. Reclamation work was completed in 1904, leaving Des Voeux Road West a block away from the sea.

In the Central area Des Voeux Road is colloquially called *deen che lo* (tram road) while further west, past Wing Lok Street, it becomes known as *haam yu laan* (salt fish wholesalers). Many of its original inhabitants were Chiu Chow people, natives of Swatow (Shantou) and the surrounding districts in north-eastern

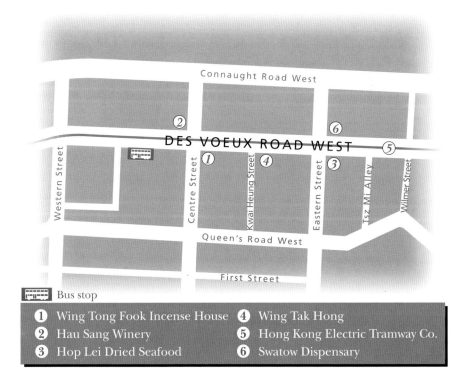

Bus stop

1. Wing Tong Fook Incense House
2. Hau Sang Winery
3. Hop Lei Dried Seafood
4. Wing Tak Hong
5. Hong Kong Electric Tramway Co.
6. Swatow Dispensary

STREETS

Kwangtung (Guangdong) province, further up the coast from Hong Kong. Prior to the Second World War, the staple diet of Hong Kong's working classes was rice and a little salted fish, which helped keep body and soul together but not much else. The distribution and retail marketing of salted fish in Hong Kong was in the hands of a powerful *laan* or wholesaler's cartel, which kept prices pegged at an artificial high. The domination of this influential monopoly was only broken in the late 1940s, leading to a corresponding drop in the price of salted fish amd more ready availability of fresh fish.

Today, there are dozens of shops along this road which specialize in Chinese food products. They range from pricey delicacies like shark's fin, abalone and dried conpoy (scallop), to less usual edibles such as dried sea slugs, sea cucumber and fish lips and other dried foods such as the humble but very popular *mui choy* (preserved vegetable). This is also the place to come if you are stocking up on *laap mei* (cured and dried meats), marvellous for making warming winter claypot dishes.

1 Wing Tong Fook Incense House

Wing Tong Fook Incense House stocks its own sandalwood incense sticks which are manufactured in Macao. Heung Gong, or 'Fragrant Harbour' as Hong Kong is still known, was originally named for the production of sandalwood incense at Aberdeen. Incense production costs in Hong Kong have risen dramatically  in recent years, leading to a decline in the local industry. Most of Hong Kong's incense is now imported from Macao and the mainland. The incense and joss-sticks in Wing Tong Fook are used mainly for religious purposes, and they come in various grades. Prices for a packet of 300 sticks range from $80 to $140 and beyond, depending on quality. Solid blocks of *tam heung* (sandalwood) and *chum heung* (agalloch eaglewood) are available as well.

2 Hau Sang Winery

This pre-war, four-storey shop-house is one of the last remaining examples of its kind on Des Voeux Road West. Until the 1970s the road was lined on both sides with buildings such as this; a few still remain, sandwiched like this one in among modern tower blocks. The ground floor is used for commercial premises, in this case a winery where one can get an empty bottle refilled with low-grade *sam su* (Chinese rice wine) for $10 or so. Above the shop are residential quarters where rooms are often very dark, due to the lack of windows on either side; this corner building is an exception. This tenacious old survivor will probably come down in the next few years, another marker of Hong Kong's past swept aside by the area's gradual transformation.

③ *Hop Lei Dried Seafood*

The dried seafood establishments along this road tend to be staffed by intimidating-looking toughs or cantankerous old men with tobacco-stained teeth, but some, such as Hop Lei Dried Seafood Company, employ attractive young women. But whoever is doing the selling, the products and prices remain generally the same from shop to shop.

Products on offer range from *ho see* (dried oysters) imported from Japan, *yue tsi* (shark's fin) from places as far away as Chile and Thailand, *yiu chue* (dried scallops), *ha mai* (tiny dried shrimps), 'super-lean' fat-free *laap cheung* (Chinese sausages) and *kum wah for toi* (Jinhua ham). And of course, they sell masses of *haam yue* (salted fish) in all shapes, sizes, qualities, and price ranges.

Western

STREETS

④ Wing Tak Hong

This little shop is one of the few places in Hong Kong that still stock a once ubiquitous item — the Hong Kong basket. Light and commodious, these open-topped baskets are woven from split rattan and come in various sizes from almost handbag-size up to the capacity of a medium-sized suitcase. Families travelling carried them instead of bags, office-workers brought a change of clothes to work with them in the days before air-conditioning, and housewives and amahs used them for marketing in the years before plastic bags became common.

Like many once universal household items, Hong Kong baskets have largely vanished from the local scene and only a few small shops, like this one, still sell them. A medium-sized one, just the thing for avoiding the plastic bag frenzy at the local supermarket, will set you back about $70.

⑤ Hong Kong Electric Tramway Co.

Hong Kong's much-beloved 'pollution solution' has been trundling along the northern coast of Hong Kong Island since 1904. The Hong Kong Electric Tramway had not been open for business a decade when it became the object of a major anti-colonial protest movement. This was sparked by the tramway company's refusal, shortly after the

collapse of the Ching (Qing) dynasty and the establishment of the Chinese Republic in 1912, to accept payment for fares with Chinese coins minted in China. A bitterly perceived slight to nationalist sentiments, the situation swiftly escalated to a sustained boycott of the tramway by large sections of the Chinese population. The stoppages to the tramways service lasted for several months and involved widespread violence and intimidation.

Since then, however, double-decker trams have become a local institution, and for almost a century they have provided a cheap and reliable, albeit at times rather slow, means of transport for the Hong Kong public. The fare must be one of Hong Kong's few remaining real bargains: at $2 per adult, it is the same for one stop or right to the end of the line at Kennedy Town in the west or Shau Kei Wan in the east.

6 Swatow Dispensary

Des Voeux Road West these days is no longer the almost exclusively Chiu Chow enclave that it remained until relatively recently, but the formerly dominant ethnic presence is reflected, in a small way, in the clientele of Swatow Dispensary. Despite the Chiu Chow reference in its name, Mr Fong the dispenser said that his customers these days include Cantonese, Europeans and Indians. A browse in the dispensary revealed that it still stocks various time-honoured, made-in-Hong Kong remedies like Shell stomach-ache powder ($15 a tin) and Five Photos Brand pills ($20 a pill) used for fractures, bruises and 'internal injuries'.

Western

How To Get There

By Bus:	No. 5B from Des Voeux Road Central The Landmark bus stop, alight on Des Voeux Road West at the bus stop after Island Pacific Hotel.
By Taxi:	'Dak Fu Doh Sai, Kong Doh Tai Ping Yeung Jau Deem' ('Des Voeux Road West, Island Pacific Hotel').
By Tram:	From anywhere in Central, take the west-bound tram marked 'Kennedy Town'. Alight on Des Voeux Road West after Island Pacific Hotel.

STREETS

This long, relatively level street in the upper section of Sai Ying Pun runs immediately below and parallel to Bonham Road for much of its length. There are a number of former institutional buildings scattered along its length, such as the old psychiatric hospital and methadone clinic, occupying sites left vacant when Sai Ying Pun was first surveyed and laid out for residential use in the 1860s.

In spite of recent redevelopments, the eastern end of High Street still retains something of the spaciousness inherited from its institutional part. King George V Park provides a popular green open area in the centre, while the western end of the street has a number of newer apartment blocks interspersed between a few surviving old terraced houses, and the occasional motor-mechanic's workshop or small sundry goods shop.

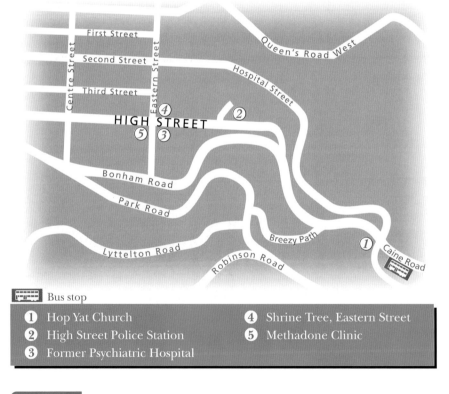

Bus stop

❶ Hop Yat Church
❷ High Street Police Station
❸ Former Psychiatric Hospital
❹ Shrine Tree, Eastern Street
❺ Methadone Clinic

1 Hop Yat Church

The Hop Yat Church's congregation is the oldest continuing Chinese Protestant group in Hong Kong. Its origins in Hong Kong begin with Dr James Legge and the converts who came with him when the Anglo-Chinese College moved from Malacca to Hong Kong in 1843. The congregation met in the successive buildings of the Union Church until 1888, when finally they occupied a building of their own on Hollywood Road, near the junction of Aberdeen Street.

In 1925, the congregation moved to the Caine Road site on which the Hop Yat Church now stands. Built in the neo-Gothic style, with an exterior of brick and pink-washed stucco, the Hop Yat Church is similar in style to the old Dairy Farm building in Wyndham Street (now used by the Foreign Correspondent's Club and the Fringe Club) with which it is a contemporary example.

2 High Street Police Station

This tree-shaded, whitewashed building is a direct successor to the old Upper Station Street Police Station, first built lower down the hill in Tai Ping Shan in the mid-nineteenth century. The police station on High Street was opened in 1935 and was originally known as No. 8 Police Station; the name was later changed to the Upper

Levels Police Station and the complex now accommodates the Regional Unit of the Hong Kong Island Crime Wing.

STREETS

Built in the 1930s in a pleasing, unadorned style eminently suitable to the tropics, police stations, barracks and other institutional buildings similar to this one can be seen all over the former British Empire, from Jamaica and West Africa to Singapore, North Borneo and Fiji.

(3) *Former Psychiatric Hospital*

Built originally as nurses' accommodation for the Government Civil Hospital on Hospital Road (across King George V Park and located where Prince Philip Dental Hospital is now), its size and extravagance was criticized when it was first built as only ten European nurses were to live in it. It was completed in June 1892 and was built of brick with a substantial granite-arched verandah running the full length.

The building was used for staff accommodation until the outbreak of war in 1941. Converted after the Second World War into a psychiatric unit, it remained in that function till 1961, when it became a day hospital and treatment centre for mental patients. When the new purpose-built facility at Castle Peak opened in 1971, this magnificent building was locked up and allowed to decay. The doors sagged, windows eventually broke allowing the elements to enter, floors rotted away and the roof eventually fell in — and shamefully all this neglect was entirely the result of governmental inactivity and interdepartmental buck-passing as none could be found to assume responsibility for the building and find a new use for it.

The remains were demolished about a year ago and a community centre/ 'singleton's hostel' tower block built in its place. The impressive stone facade has been retained and still stands in front of the new building, but seeing it one cannot but sadly wonder: was this *really* the best solution that the planners and 'responsible' government departments could come up with?

4) Shrine Tree, Eastern Street

This large old banyan tree on the corner of High and Eastern Streets has an incredible array of religious statues nestled among its buttressed roots. These are left by devotees who burn incense and leave daily offerings of fresh fruit, mainly oranges and bananas.

There are several porcelain Kwun Yum (Goddess of Mercy) statues and a number of fearsome-looking Kwan Ti (the general-god worshipped, perhaps surprisingly to some, by both the triads and the police — go into any police station in Hong Kong and somewhere you'll find an altar to Kwan Ti), among other lesser-known deities. There is even a statue of the Virgin Mary tucked away among the others, though you have to look hard and close to see just where she is.

5) Methadone Clinic

This attractive old red-brick building, with several tall Chinese fan palms growing in the forecourt, was opened in November 1891 as a 'Chinese Lunatic Asylum'. The asylum for European patients adjoined it to the south, just up the hillside, and had been opened six years earlier. The Chinese asylum only accommodated sixteen

patients at any one time. The small size was considered adequate because it was government policy at that time to repatriate mentally ill Chinese to Shek Lung (Shilong), near Canton (modern Guangzhou) to be cared for at Hong Kong

Western

government expense. Larger premises were not therefore required as the building was in effect only a transit centre. This policy remained in place until the communist takeover in 1949, after which time the mainland authorities would refuse to accept the return of what they uncharitably termed 'useless mouths'. From that time onwards Chinese psychiatric patients remained in Hong Kong, and were accommodated in the old nurses quarters across the road, until it became too overcrowded and a new facility was opened at Castle Peak in 1971.

The building has been used for the methadone treatment of heroin addicts since the 1970s, and in the late afternoon there are usually a number of people hanging around outside waiting to be attended to. Recently renovated and very well maintained, for all its undoubted usefulness in its present function, perhaps the wider community could derive more benefit if the building were converted to other purposes, such as a museum or community theatre, and the methadone clinic relocated somewhere else nearby.

How To Get There

By Bus:	No. 3B from Connaught Road Central City Hall bus stop, minibuses No. 8 and No. 22 from Central Star Ferry Pier, alight on Caine Road at the bus stop next to Caine Road Park and in front of Hop Yat Church.
By Taxi:	'Boon Haam Doh, Hup Yat Tong' ('Bonham Road, Hop Yat Church').

One of Hong Kong Island's most well-known backstreet locations, Ladder Street starts on Queen's Road Central near the junction of Lok Ku Road, passes the Man Mo Temple on Hollywood Road and extends straight up the hillside as far as Caine Road. The surrounding area has changed greatly in recent years, and even the old stones of the street have recently been realigned and some often replaced. The steep street is so named because it extends straight up and down, like a ladder. The Cantonese term for a staircase, *lau tai*, is broadly the same as for a ladder, so the naming of the street was probably the result of a mistranslation at some early point.

Ladder Street has a number of flat sections on the way up, which were originally built so that sedan chairs could easily traverse between the Bazaar area, lower down the hill, and the Mid-Levels above. The flat halts at various points along the steep street were to enable the sedan chair bearers to pause and realign their loads, a feature seen in many other parts of Hong Kong as well.

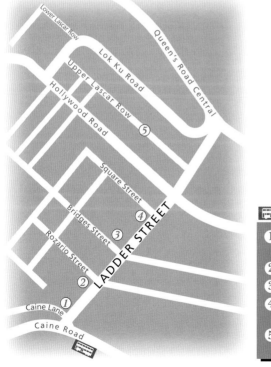

Western

 Bus stop

1 Museum of Medical Sciences

2 Rozario Street

3 Chinese YMCA

4 Kung Sau Funeral Service

5 Upper and Lower Lascar Row

STREETS

① Museum of Medical Sciences

This attractive survivor stands at the top of Ladder Street, on Caine Lane. Built in 1906, it was originally used as a Government Bacteriological Laboratory and designed by Leigh and Orange, still a leading architectural firm in Hong Kong. The site was part of the large area in Tai Ping Shan resumed by the government after a devastating outbreak of bubonic plague in

1894 claimed hundreds of lives. After serving as a laboratory for many years it was turned over to the University of Hong Kong, and for a time used by their Faculty of Medicine before eventually being fully renovated and restored.

The gracious old building now houses the Museum of Medical Sciences whose small but very interesting collection of displays and exhibits details of the development of medicine in Hong Kong. Looking down though the trees from Caine Road onto the building and grounds, one gets a rare glimpse of what much of the Mid-Levels once looked like, before serried ranks of generally undistinguished tower blocks made concrete canyons of the once pleasant tree-lined roads further up the hillside.

② Rozario Street

The name of this short street recalls the once prominent local Portuguese (sometimes known as Macanese) community, which has largely vanished from Hong Kong since the late 1960s.

Chinese converts to Catholicism in Macao were generally absorbed into the mixed-race Macanese community, taking on religious surnames as a mark of conversion. In due course they intermarried with other Macanese, and from the 1840s onwards some of their descendants settled in Hong Kong. Many among the local Portuguese community have Chinese forebears, even if quite distant; religious-sounding names, such as Rozario (Rosary), Cruz (Cross), Conceição (Conception) and Assumpção (Assumption) and others are a clue to this ancestry, as they are largely unknown as surnames in metropolitan Portugal.

③ *Chinese YMCA*

The Chinese Young Men's Christian Association stands on the corner of Ladder Street and Bridges Street. Bridges Street was named after a well-known barrister from Hong Kong's early days, Dr W. T. Bridges. He made a considerable fortune through moneylending and opium-dealing, in addition to his private legal practice. He was also Acting Attorney-General and Acting Colonial Secretary at various times between 1848 and 1859, official positions that gave him even further scope for graft-related personal profit.

The YMCA building here is the successor of earlier association buildings catering to Chinese members. The association opened on Des Voeux Road in 1901, and later moved to Queen's Road Central. However, these premises gradually proved inadequate as membership steadily grew, and in 1912 the governor, Sir Frederick Lugard, laid the foundation stone for the present Chinese YMCA in Tai Ping Shan. The building was completed and eventually opened in 1918, and has been of service to the local community ever since. It has a metal fire escape attached to one wall, a North American touch quite uncommon elsewhere in Hong Kong.

Built of red Canton brick with green Chinese tile decorations around the roof and eaves, the Chinese YMCA building is an eclectic combination of Chinese and European styles typical of many semi-missionary organizations in China during this period. Cast-iron lamps on the fence were originally designed for gas-fittings, but have long been electrified.

Western

4 Kung Sau Funeral Service

Scattered around the Ladder Street/Hollywood Road area there are numerous shops offering funeral services — some of them have been around for many years. Most specialize in Chinese-style funeral arrangements, but can also arrange a choice of Protestant and Roman Catholic funeral services as well. A whole 'package', including the casket, burial or

crematoria arrangements, flowers and the like, ranges from a few thousand dollars to tens of thousands. Chinese-style coffins made of tree-trunks are much more costly than Western-style caskets; the most expensive come from Liuchow (Liuzhou) in south-west China, renowned for centuries as the best place to obtain rot-resistant coffin-wood.

Many coffin shops — here and elsewhere in Hong Kong — perform a valuable and largely unsung social role by offering considerable discounts to poor families who otherwise could not afford to give their loved ones a decent send-off. Some shop proprietors say it's difficult to get staff; working in the 'death trade' is considered highly inauspicious and staff generally don't like to give out their names — many don't even tell their friends what they do for a living.

5 Upper and Lower Lascar Row

Commemorated in the name of these narrow lanes, but otherwise now largely forgotten, Lascars were Asian seamen, generally Bengalis or Malays, who worked on the many vessels that called through Hong Kong. A number of boarding houses were established along here in the 1850s that were often filled by sailors of all nationalities who found themselves based in Hong Kong for periods of time between contracts.

For many years these quiet back lanes had a local reputation as a thieves' market, with numerous temporary stallholders found kneeling behind their wares spread out over the pavement on mats. It was not uncommon for householders who had been burgled to come down here a day or two later and be able to buy back the item. In the 1950s excellent antique and curio bargains could sometimes be picked up here, as many refugees from the mainland, desperate for cash, sold off the few treasures they had managed to bring out with them. During these years the area around Upper and Lower Lascar Row was very popular with visitors to Hong Kong, who enjoyed the then authentic backstreet atmosphere. It was a distinctive feature of this corner of Hong Kong till the early 1980s, which has now almost completely vanished.

How To Get There

By Bus:	No. 3B from Connaught Road Central City Hall bus stop, minibuses No. 8 and No. 22 from Central Star Ferry Pier, alight at the bus stop at the junction of Caine Road and Ladder Street.
By Taxi:	'Geen Doh, Lau Tai Gaai' ('Caine Road, Ladder Street').

The name of this street means 'Great Peace Mountain', which was one of Hong Kong Island's names prior to the British arrival. As well as the mountainside upon which it was built, the name also commemorates Tai Ping Shan, Hong Kong's early 'Chinatown' which developed in the 1840s. A seemingly odd phenomena in an overwhelmingly Chinese place, the densely packed area became a Chinatown because after its first few years there were no other racial groups represented among its numerous, closely packed residents. In the very early days, there were only two European landholders living in Tai Ping Shan, who soon moved out, leaving the area an entirely Chinese enclave.

Gambling halls, illicit opium dens and sly brothels abounded and policing was largely left to the triads, despite periodic unsuccessful attempts to improve the area. In the interest of avoiding unnecessary confrontation, the government was reluctant to intervene in problems that were entirely Chinese in character, and people there were left largely alone to manage their own affairs as best they could. For decades afterwards Tai Ping Shan was an area where Europeans did not normally venture — many still don't — and the triad societies were the real

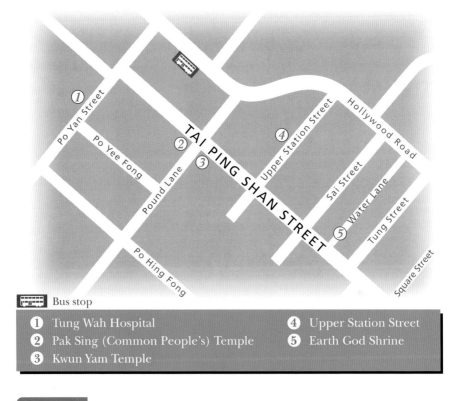

Bus stop

❶	Tung Wah Hospital	❹	Upper Station Street
❷	Pak Sing (Common People's) Temple	❺	Earth God Shrine
❸	Kwun Yam Temple		

locus of authority for local residents, much as they remain in some parts of Hong Kong today.

In the very early days, most buildings in Tai Ping Shan were matsheds, built of bamboo frames with *attap* (palm leaf) walls and roofing. These were eventually replaced by more substantial brick and timber structures, though generally the construction standards were very low. Even basically adequate sanitation remained a perennial problem until relatively recent times, and cholera, typhus, typhoid and other diseases were endemic.

As years went on, little real improvement was effected. In spite of a damning report into Hong Kong's sanitary situation in 1882, conditions in this area of densely packed buildings continued to deteriorate to dangerous

levels. Finally in 1894, there was a serious outbreak of bubonic plague which claimed hundreds of lives and at last prompted firm government action. Plague outbreaks continued to periodically occur until the mid-1920s.

Despite being extensively redeveloped in the 1970s, numerous pockets of interest still remain in the Tai Ping Shan area. But how many visitors to the antique shops and restaurants along nearby Hollywood Road, one wonders, never venture a mere block or so up the hill to this interesting reminder of early urban Hong Kong.

1 Tung Wah Hospital

The foundation stone of the Tung Wah Hospital on Po Yan Street was laid in 1870, and the building was opened in 1872. It has since been completely replaced, but the original foundation stone remains next to the front door. The Tung Wah Hospital grew out of a need for a Chinese hospital for destitutes. The Chinese prejudice against allowing persons unrelated to them to die in their premises meant that many poor people living in tenements were thrown out by their landlords when they became terminally ill, with only the Yi Chong (Pak Sing) Temple's limited facilities (mentioned below) to turn to as death drew near.

The Tung Wah Hospital Ordinance was passed in April 1870, paving the way

Western

for the hospital's foundation. Attempts by government to control and police gambling in Hong Kong led to monopolies being set up both to manage the vice and to extract a source of recurrent revenue from it. Part of the gambling revenue generated as a result was allocated for the expenses of the Tung Wah, in much the same way as Hong Kong Jockey Club surpluses endow numerous charities today. The Tung Wah Hospital Committee was composed of the great and the good from the Chinese community and wielded considerable influence behind the scenes, as it still does today.

Rebuilt in the 1920s, the Great Hall of the Tung Wah Hospital, used for committee meetings and ceremonial occasions, is very impressive and contains portraits of former committee members, though it is not usually open to members of the public without prior agreement.

② Pak Sing (Common People's) Temple

Hong Kong in its early days was an almost entirely immigrant society which nearly everyone of all races ultimately intended to retire from as soon as they were financially able to do so. Many Chinese who came to work in the early colony were unaccompanied men who either remained single or left their families back in the *heung ha* (ancestral village) on the mainland. They usually wished to be buried there eventually, but coffins often accumulated in storage in the temple's ante-room until it was possible to take them back. Those who died without issue, or without the means for returning their remains to the *heung ha* faced the distinct and fearful possibility of becoming a malevolent wandering ghost if there was no one to worship them and provide offerings at the appropriate festival times — a grave personal calamity for the individual and a source of menace to the wider community.

The Pak Sing Temple is a communal ancestral hall housing the spirit tablets of many people unrelated by birth or marriage. Pak Sing, literally meaning 'hundred surnames' is a term widely synonymous with the common people, and the temple performed common rituals offered for all those whose spirit tablets were enshrined within it — altogether a more satisfactory alternative for all concerned than becoming a peripatetic 'hungry ghost'.

The site was originally given to the Chinese community in 1851, but has been successively rebuilt and renovated a number of times. Before a hospital for Chinese patients was built, the temple assumed some of its functions. Hopeless cases were sent to the Pak Sing Temple, also known at this time as the Yi Chong, and it became widely known as a death-house, similar in function to death-houses formerly found on Sago Lane in Singapore, where immigrants without family to tend them also went to die. Conditions at the Yi Chong were described in 1869 as having 'the dead and dying huddled together indiscriminately in small filthy rooms'.

After repeated adverse press comment about conditions at the Yi Chong, prominent members of the Chinese community were shamed into action and the temple was renovated as a temporary hospital and relief centre for the very poor, providing food, shelter and medical treatment; its function was superceded by the Tung Wah Hospital the following year. At present it is a still used as a common ancestral temple, and the principal deity worshipped in the temple is Jai Kung, a god known for his eccentric ways. Numerous elderly beggars, mostly single women, often materialize in search of alms when visitors appear near the temple.

③ *Kwun Yam Temple*

One of a number of small temples along Tai Ping Shan Street between Upper Station Street and Po Yan Street, this temple is dedicated to Kwun Yam, the Goddess of Mercy. An interesting small building, it lacks many of the features normally associated with a Chinese temple, such as vents to let out the smoke from incense, and is fitted somewhat incongruously into the ground floor of a residential building.

The original Kwun Yam Temple on this site was relocated to Tai Ping Shan Street from the Western waterfront in 1894. The principal image of Kwun Yam found in the temple is said to have been carved from a piece of wood found in the sea in 1840 by the wife of one of the temple's founders. The altar table in the main hall has a very attractive gold-painted carved base, and highly polished brass oil lamps sit on this table and hang above it.

(4) Upper Station Street

An early police station was located at the junction of Po Yee Street and Upper Station Street. Redeveloped after the disastrous plague outbreak in 1894, the station was later removed to Hospital Road and subsequently relocated to High Street, where its attractive successor building, constructed in the late 1930s, still remains today. Po Yee Street was known in the past as Station Street and the first police station found there was built in around 1870.

Many of the policemen in Hong Kong at that time were recruited from the Indian subcontinent, and early photographs of the area show turbaned, uniformed Sikh policemen standing on the roadside. Early local Portuguese residents referred to the Indians as *moro* (meaning Moors or Moslems), which was corrupted into the local lexicon as *molo*. The surrounding area is still known in Cantonese as *Molo Gai*, 'Street of the Indians', while Indians in general are colloquially referred to as *molo cha* (a reference to the fact that most Indians in early Hong Kong were either Moslem policemen or soldiers).

5 Earth God Shrine

Set against the wall on the corner of Tai Ping Shan Street and Water Lane, locked behind a protective metal grille, is a red-painted shrine dedicated to the Earth God, or To Tei Kung. The Earth God has been worshipped in China on the second and sixteenth day of every lunar month for thousands of years. The To Tei Kung is believed to protect small communities and rule over neighbourhoods.

This To Tei Kung was stolen at one time, and — according to one long-time local resident — revealed his whereabouts in a dream to one of the people who regularly worshipped at the shrine. This devotee went out to Shau Kei Wan, as instructed in the dream, found the image and returned it to Tai Ping Shan Street. As a result of this episode, the To Tei Kung has been kept locked up ever since.

Testament to the strength of traditional customs brought by immigrants and still persisting to this day in quiet corners of the metropolis, the continuing presence of Earth God shrines all over Hong Kong is in many ways proof positive that the veneer of internationalism — so apparent in much of modern Hong Kong — is in fact very thinly overlaid on strongly enduring Chinese customs.

How To Get There

By Bus:	No. 26 from The Landmark, Des Voeux Road Central bus stop, alight on Hollywood Road at the bus stop next to Hollywood Road Park.
By Taxi:	'Po Yan Gaai, Dung Wah Yee Yuen' ('Po Yan Street, Tung Wah Hospital').

Western

Western Street
西邊街

Western Street extends straight up the hill from the former Western Praya (new Connaught Road West), past the Western District courthouse at the junction of Pok Fu Lam Road and up to Bonham Road. Walking up from the bottom, one can see the gradual changes taking place in building use the higher one gets up the hill. Lower down small shops and long-established trading companies abound, whilst midway there are a number of institutional buildings, such as the Kau Yan Church and the old Tsan Yuk Hospital, now used as the Western District Community Centre. At the very top of Western Street, the junction with Bonham Road marks the geographical beginning of the Mid-Levels at this end of Hong Kong Island.

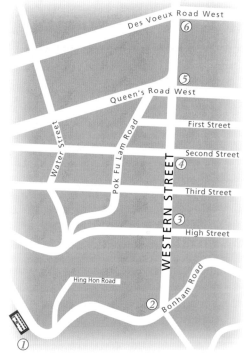

Bus stop

1. The University of Hong Kong
2. King's College
3. Kau Yan Church
4. Western District Community Centre
5. Tuck Chong Sum Kee Bamboo Steamer Company
6. Shwe Wer Southeast Asian Food Company

Disturbed conditions in South China in the 1850s during the Taiping Rebellion brought thousands of new immigrants to Hong Kong. To help cope with the influx, the area south of Queen's Road West, till then quite sparsely settled, was laid out and opened up to settlement. Streets in this new section of Sai Ying Pun followed a planned grid pattern, in sharp contrast to the earlier rather haphazard streetscape that developed in the early 1840s in nearby Tai Ping Shan, and still persists there today to some extent.

1) *The University of Hong Kong*

The main campus of the University of Hong Kong is located on Bonham Road, just around the corner from King's College. Built in 1910–12 and extensively added to since that time, the University of Hong Kong remained Hong Kong's only institution of higher learning for over half a century. The university grew out of the Hong Kong College of Medicine, established in 1888; early licentiates of this college included revolutionary Dr Sun Yat-sen.

The university opened in 1912, and its first degree congregation was held in 1916. Many students in the university's early years came from Malaya and the Straits Settlements. The two principal faculties at that time were medicine — developed from the old College of Medicine — and a School of engineering. An arts faculty opened in 1913 and graduated its first students in 1916. The first women students were admitted in 1921, a year or so after Yenching University in Peking admitted its first female candidates.

After remaining closed during the Pacific War, the university reopened in 1948, and has grown steadily ever since. Most of the older buildings have long been demolished and replaced, in some instances two or three times, but a few old favourites still remain, most prominently the Main Building and the old student's union building across from it, dating from 1919.

The university's attractive Main Building was partly paid for by a Parsee businessman, H. N. Mody, who was knighted for his contribution to the university

STREETS

and its establishment. The elegantly proportioned interior hall, originally used for degree congregations, concerts and other functions, was originally known as the Great Hall. These days, however, it is more commonly known as the Loke Yew Hall, after Loke Yew, a Cantonese entrepreneur who settled in Kuala Lumpur and made a massive fortune from rubber planting, tin mining, property speculation and numerous other business interests. Some of this largesse was eventually donated to educational institutions in Malaya, Singapore, Hong Kong and Canton (now Guangzhou), before his death in 1917. Other prominent local business figures, such as Stanley Ho and Li Ka-shing have been major donors to the university over the years, and major Hong Kong firms such as the Swire Group and the Bank of East Asia have contributed generously as well.

The general public often refers to the building as *Loke Yew Tong*— Loke Yew Hall — but to generations of students the gracious old university building has been fondly known as the 'West Point Ballroom' due to the large number of popular social functions the university's undergraduate societies hold in the building during the cooler weather.

② *King's College*

King's College, one of Hong Kong's premier government schools, is the successor to the Sai Ying Pun District School, which opened in 1891, originally on nearby Pok Fu Lam Road. The foundation stone for the present all-boys red-brick school was laid in 1923, and the first students enrolled in September 1926. King's College at that time was

one of the most modern schools in Hong Kong, with a swimming pool, well-equipped labs and a gymnasium.

In 1927 the Shanghai Defence Force, on their way to reinforce the British garrison in the International Settlement at Shanghai during the time of Chiang Kai-shek's Northern Expedition, briefly used part of King's College as a hospital. King's College was very badly vandalized by looters during the Second World War, who stripped out all the timber window frames, banisters and floorboards to burn for firewood, a fate suffered by almost all unoccupied buildings in Hong Kong at that time. The otherwise lightly damaged shell of King's College was refurbished in the late 1940s and has been a sought-after boys' school ever since.

King's College's old boys, like the alumni of other prestigious local schools remain influential in modern-day Hong Kong; perhaps the best-known old boy today is Convenor of the Executive Council, Leung Chun-ying.

3) *Kau Yan Church*

This gray, unadorned Lutheran church with a squat bell-tower, now dwarfed by surrounding modern tower blocks, was once a distinctive, immediately recognizable landmark seen from the western waterfront.

Built by the Tsun Tsin Mission, many of the Kau Yan Church's early parishioners were Hakka converts living in the nearby area. The interior of the church is very plain and unadorned, and nearby there is also a school run by the mission. Sai Ying Pun also has a number of other schools run by church or missionary organizations, all long established like this one. Other well-known local institutions located nearby include St Paul's College, St Stephen's Church School, St Clare's and of course the University of Hong Kong, whose main campus is just further along Bonham Road.

4) *Western District Community Centre (old Tsan Yuk Hospital)*

This attractive, solidly built institutional building was erected early this century to house the Tsan Yuk Hospital, Hong Kong's first Chinese maternity hospital. Tsan Yuk means 'assisting birth', which is what the hospital did in the process doing much to lower the formerly high infant mortality rates among working-class Chinese, who until then had to rely almost entirely on midwives, most of whom were completely untrained in modern methods of obstetrics and maternity care. The tragic result, when combined with poor standards of hygiene, was numerous unnecessary maternity deaths.

STREETS

The Tsan Yuk Hospital remained in use throughout the war years and continued as a hospital on the same site until the early 1960s, when a replacement Tsan Yuk Hospital was built on Hospital Road. The building then became the Western District Community Centre, which it remains today. The old hospital is very similar in style and construction to the new section of Central Police Station and the Magistracy, with solid granite foundations sloping up the hillside. The rooms and corridors within the old Tsan Yuk are still reminiscent of the building's former hospital role, with an attractive curving staircase linking the three floors.

⑤ Tuck Chong Sum Kee Bamboo Steamer Company

A family-owned business like many such enterprises, Tuck Chong Sum Kee Bamboo Steamer Company has been making household utensils from bamboo in Canton (Guangzhou) since the turn of the century. In 1945, the business moved to Hong Kong and today, five generations later, they have moved their factory *back* again to Canton, where bamboo steamers of all sizes are manufactured for much less than it would cost to produce them in Hong Kong.

Used mainly by restaurants and teahouses to steam buns, cakes, char-siu pao and the ubiquitous dim sum, these *loong* (baskets) come in dozens of sizes and prices. Part of the reason for their continued popularity is the taste that bamboo imparts to the food steamed within it: stainless steel or plastic simply cannot compete, and the shop itself has a wonderful fresh smell of split bamboo.

A medium-sized, attractive and functional steamer which fits comfortably into a domestic-sized *wok* costs $80 or so, while smaller ones can be had for about half the price. Other traditional culinary implements include Chinese pastry molds ($15 each) used for making *hang yun beng* (almond biscuits), bamboo spatulas, scrapers and mixing spoons ($6–8 each) and sharp-edged ginger graters ($6 each).

6 *Shwe Wer Southeast Asian Food Company*

The Penang-born co-proprietor of Shwe Wer Southeast Asian Food Company, Mr Yeo Chu Yok, travelled all over South-east Asia before he settled down in Hong Kong in 1969 and the contacts he made in his youth proved very useful when he set up shop in June 1998.

Mr Yeo's amazing little shop stocks everything a South-east Asian cook could possibly want, ranging from Vietnamese *pho* noodles, and frozen *lapu-lapu* (milkfish) from the Philippines, to traditional Indonesian *jamu* herbal remedies for 'ailments affecting ladies'. His best-selling product is a sachet of *bak kut teh* (pork rib soup) herbs and spices that he imports from — where else — Penang.

How To Get There

By Bus:	No. 3B from Connaught Road Central City Hall bus stop, minibuses No. 8 and No. 22 from Central Star Ferry Pier, alight on Bonham Road at Hong Kong University East Gate bus stop after passing King's College.
By Taxi:	'Heung Kong Dai Hok Dung Moon' ('Hong Kong University East Gate').
By Tram:	From anywhere in Central, take the west-bound tram marked 'Kennedy Town', alight on Des Voeux Road West at the Western Police Station. Turn right at the police station into Western Street.

Western

STREETS

Bibliography

A Record of the Actions of the Hongkong Volunteer Defence Corps in the Battle for Hong Kong, December 1941. Hong Kong, 1953, reprinted 1991.

Andrew, Kenneth. *Hong Kong Detective*. London, The Adventurers Club, 1962.

Angus, Marjorie Bird. *Bamboo Connection*. Hong Kong, Heinemann Publishers Asia Ltd., 1985.

Bard, Solomon. *Traders of Hong Kong: Some Foreign Merchant Houses, 1841–1899*. Hong Kong, Urban Council, 1993.

Bickley, Gillian. *The Golden Needle: The Biography of Frederick Stewart (1836–1889)*. Hong Kong, David C. Lam Centre for East-West Studies, 1997.

Birch, Alan and Cole, Martin. *Captive Christmas*. Hong Kong, Heinemann Educational Books, 1979.

Birch, Alan and Cole, Martin. *Captive Years*. Hong Kong, Heinemann Educational Books, 1979.

Bird, Isabella. *The Golden Chersonese and The Way Thither*. London, John Murray, 1883.

Blake, Robert. *Jardine Matheson: Traders of the Far East*. London, Weidenfeld and Nicholson, 1999.

Bowie, Donald C. 'Captive Surgeon in Hong Kong: The Story of the British Military Hospital, Hong Kong 1942–45', *Journal of the Hong Kong Branch of the Royal Asiatic Society*, Vol. 15, 1975.

Burkhardt, V. R. *Chinese Creeds and Customs* (in 3 volumes). Hong Kong, South China Morning Post Ltd., 1953.

Bush, Lewis. *The Road to Inamura*. London, Robert Hale Ltd., 1961.

Cameron, Nigel. *The Hong Kong Land Company Ltd: A Brief History*. Hong Kong, Hong Kong Land Company Ltd., 1979.

Cameron, Nigel. *Power: The Story of China Light*. Hong Kong, Oxford University Press, 1982.

Cameron, Nigel. *The Milky Way*. Hong Kong, The Dairy Farm Company Ltd., 1986.

Cheng, Irene. *Clara Hotung: A Hong Kong Lady, Her Family and Her Times*. Hong Kong, Chinese University Press, 1976.

Ching, Frank. *The Li Dynasty: Hong Kong Aristocrats*. Hong Kong, Oxford University Press, 1999.

Clarke, Nora M. *The Governor's Daughter Takes The Veil*. Hong Kong, Canossian Missions Historic Archives, 1980.

Coates, Austin. *A Mountain of Light*. Hong Kong, Heinemann Educational Books (Asia) Ltd., 1977.

Coates, Austin. *Whampoa: Ships on the Shore*. Hong Kong, South China Morning Post Ltd., 1980.

Coates, Austin. *China Races*. Hong Kong, Oxford University Press, 1983.

Coates, Austin. *Myself A Mandarin*. Hong Kong, Oxford University Press, 1988.

Coates, Austin. *Quick Tidings of Hong Kong*. Hong Kong, Oxford University Press, 1990.

Collis, Maurice. *Foreign Mud: An Account of the Opium War*. London, Faber and Faber, 1946.

Collis, Maurice. *Wayfoong*. London, Faber and Faber, 1965.

Cooper, John. *Colony in Conflict: The Hong Kong Disturbances May 1967– January 1968*. Hong Kong, Swindon Book Company, 1970.

Crisswell, Colin N. *The Taipans: Hong Kong's Merchant Princes*. Hong Kong, Hong Kong University Press, 1981.

Crisswell, Colin N. and Watson, Mike. *The Royal Hong Kong Police (1841–1945)*. Hong Kong, MacMillan Publishers (H.K.) Ltd., 1982.

Drage, Charles. *Taikoo*. London, Constable and Co. Ltd., 1970.

Eitel, E. J. *Europe in China*. Hong Kong, Oxford University Press, 1983.

Emerson, G. C. 'Behind Japanese Barbed Wire: Stanley Internment Camp, Hong Kong 1942–1945', *Journal of the Hong Kong Branch of the Royal Asiatic Society*, Vol. 17, 1977.

Endacott, G. B. *A Biographical Sketchbook of Early Hong Kong*. Singapore, Eastern Universities Press, 1962.

Endacott, G. B. *Government and People in Hong Kong 1841–1962: A Constitutional History*. Hong Kong, Hong Kong University Press, 1964.

Endacott, G. B. *A History of Hong Kong*. Hong Kong, Oxford University Press, 1993.

Endacott, G. B. and Birch, Alan. *Hong Kong Eclipse*. Hong Kong, Oxford University Press, 1978.

Endacott, G. B. and She, Dorothy E. *The Diocese of Victoria, Hong Kong: A Hundred Years of Church History 1849–1949*. Hong Kong, Kelly and Walsh Ltd., 1949.

England, Vaudine. *The Quest of Noel Croucher: Hong Kong's Quiet Philanthropist*. Hong Kong, Hong Kong University Press, 1998.

Evans, Dafydd Emrys. 'Chinatown in Hong Kong: The Beginnings of Taipingshan', *Journal of the Hong Kong Branch of the Royal Asiatic Society*, Vol. 10, 1970.

Field, Ellen. *Twilight in Hong Kong*. London, Frederick Muller Limited, 1960.

Ford, James Allan. *The Brave White Flag*. Glasgow, Richard Drew Publishing Ltd., 1985.

Gillingham, Paul. *At The Peak: Hong Kong Between the Wars*. Hong Kong, Macmillan, 1983.

Gittins, Jean. *Stanley: Behind Barbed Wire*. Hong Kong, Hong Kong University Press, 1982.

Gleason, Gene. *Hong Kong*. London, Robert Hale Ltd., 1963.

Goodwin, R. B. *Hongkong Escape*. London, Arthur Barker Ltd., 1954.

Hahn, Emily. *Hong Kong Holiday*. New York, Doubleday, 1946.

Hahn, Emily. *China To Me*. London, Virago Press, 1987.

Han Suyin. *A Many Splendoured Thing*. London, Jonathan Cape Ltd., 1952.

Harrison, Brian (editor). *The University of Hong Kong: The First 50 Years, 1911–1961*. Hong Kong, Hong Kong University Press, 1962.

Hase, P. H. (editor). *In The Heart Of The Metropolis: Yaumatei And Its People*. Hong Kong, Joint Publishing (HK) Co. Ltd., 1999.

Hayes, J. W. 'Old British Kowloon', *Journal of the Hong Kong Branch of the Royal Asiatic Society*, Vol. 6, 1966.

Hayes, J. W. 'The Nam Pak Hong Commercial Association of Hong Kong', *Journal of the Hong Kong Branch of the Royal Asiatic Society*, Vol. 19, 1979.

Hayes, J. W. 'Secular Non-Gentry Leadership of Temple and Shrine Organisations in Urban British Hong Kong', *Journal of the Hong Kong Branch of the Royal Asiatic Society*, Vol. 23, 1983.

Hewitt, Anthony. *Bridge With Three Men*. London, Jonathan Cape, 1986.

Hoe, Susanna. *The Private Life of Old Hong Kong: Western Women in the*

British Colony, 1841–1941. Hong Kong, Oxford University Press, 1992.

Hoe, Susanna. *Chinese Footprints: Exploring Women's History in China. Hong Kong and Macau*, Hong Kong, Roundhouse Publications (Asia) Ltd., 1996.

Hoe, Susanna and Roebuck, Derek. *The Taking of Hong Kong: Charles and Clara Elliot in China Waters*. London, Curzon, 1999.

Hong Kong Branch of the Royal Asiatic Society. *Hong Kong Going and Gone: Western Victoria*. Hong Kong, Hong Kong Branch of the Royal Asiatic Society, 1980.

Hong Kong Cricket Club Centenary 1851–1951. Hong Kong, Hong Kong Cricket Club, 1951 (no author).

Hong Kong Museum of History. *City of Victoria: A Selection of the Museum's Historical Photographs*. Hong Kong, Urban Council, 1994.

Hughes, Richard. *Borrowed Place Borrowed Time*. London, Andre Deutch Ltd., 1968.

Hutcheon, Robin. *The South China Morning Post: The First Eighty Years*. Hong Kong, South China Morning Post Ltd., 1983.

Hutcheon, Robin. *Wharf: The First Hundred Years*. Hong Kong, The Wharf (Holdings) Ltd., 1986.

Hutcheon, Robin. *The Blue Flame: 125 Years of Towngas in Hong Kong*. Hong Kong, The Hong Kong and China Gas Co. Ltd., 1987.

Hutcheon, Robin. *High-Rise Society: The First Fifty Years of the Hong Kong Housing Society*. Hong Kong, Chinese University Press, 1998.

Ingrams, Harold. *Hong Kong*. London, Her Majesty's Stationery Office, 1952.

Jarvie, I. C. (editor). *Hong Kong: A Society in Transition*. London, Routledge & Kegan Paul, 1969.

Jaschok, Maria. *Concubines and Bondservants: The Social History of A Chinese Custom*. Hong Kong, Oxford University Press, 1988.

Jones, J. R. 'Who Hoisted the Union Jack?', *Journal of the Hong Kong Branch of the Royal Asiatic Society*, Vol. 12, 1972.

Keswick, Maggie. *The Thistle and the Jade*. Hong Kong, Octopus Boooks Ltd., 1982.

King, Frank H. H. *The History of Hong Kong and Shanghai Banking Corporation.* Cambridge: Cambridge University Press, *Vol. 1, 1987; Vol. 2, 1988; Vol. 3, 1988 and Vol. 4, 1999.*

Ko, Tim-keung and Wordie, Jason. *Ruins of War: A Guide to Hong Kong's Battlefields and Wartime Sites.* Hong Kong, Joint Publishing (HK) Co. Ltd., 1996.

Lau, Alfred Y. K. 'An Outline of the Urban Development of Sai Ying Pun in the Nineteenth Century', *Journal of the Hong Kong Branch of the Royal Asiatic Society,* Vol. 35, 1995.

Lau, Chi-kuen. *Hong Kong's Colonial Legacy: A Hong Kong Chinese's View of the British Heritage.* Hong Kong, Chinese University Press, 1997.

Leiper, G. A. *A Yen For My Thoughts: A Memoir of Occupied Hong Kong.* Hong Kong, South China Morning Post, 1982.

Lethbridge, H. J. *Hong Kong: Stability and Change.* Hong Kong, Oxford University Press, 1978.

Li Shu-fan. *Hong Kong Surgeon.* London, Victor Gollancz Ltd., 1964.

Lindsay, Oliver. *The Lasting Honour: The Fall of Hong Kong 1941.* London, Hamish Hamilton, 1978.

Lindsay, Oliver. *At the Going Down of the Sun: Hong Kong and South-East Asia 1941–45.* London, Hamish Hamilton, 1981.

Lo Hsiang-lin. *Hong Kong and Western Cultures.* Honolulu, East West Center Press, 1963.

Luff, John. *The Hong Kong Story.* Hong Kong, South China Morning Post Ltd., n.d.

Maltby, C.W. Despatch by Major-General C. W. Maltby on Operations in Hong Kong from 8th to 25th December 1941, Supplement to the London Gazette of 27 January 1948.

Matthews, Clifford and Cheung, Oswald (editors). *Dispersal and Renewal: Hong Kong University during the War Years.* Hong Kong, Hong Kong University Press, 1998.

Mattock, Katherine and Cheshire, Jill. *The Story of Government House.* Hong Kong, Studio Publications, 1994.

McBain, Stuart (editor). *A Regiment at War: The Royal Scots (The Royal Regiment) 1939–45.* Edinburgh, Pentland Press, 1988.

Mellor, Bernard. *Lugard in Hong Kong: Empires, Education and A Governor At Work, 1907–1912*. Hong Kong, Hong Kong University Press, 1992.

Melson, P. J. (editor). *White Ensign – Red Dragon: The History of the Royal Navy in Hong Kong 1841–1997*. Hong Kong, Edinburgh Financial Publishing (Asia) Ltd., 1997.

Miners, N. J. *Hong Kong Under Imperial Rule*. Hong Kong, Oxford University Press, 1987.

Morgan, W. P. *Triad Societies in Hong Kong*. Hong Kong, Government Press, 1960.

Morris, Jan. *Hong Kong: Epilogue to an Empire*. London, Penguin Books, 1990.

Ng, Peter. *New Peace County*. Hong Kong, Hong Kong University Press, 1983.

Ommaney, F. D. *Eastern Windows*. London, Longmans, 1960.

Ommanney, F. D. *Fragrant Harbour: A Private View of Hong Kong*. London, Travel Book Club, 1962.

Pan, Lynn. *Sons of the Yellow Emperor: The Story of the Overseas Chinese*. London, Secker and Warburg, 1990.

Ride, Edwin. *British Army Aid Group: Hong Kong Resistance 1942–45*. Hong Kong, Oxford University Press, 1981.

Robinson, Spencer. *Festina Lente: A History of the Royal Hong Kong Golf Club*. Hong Kong, The Royal Hong Kong Golf Club, 1989.

Sayer, Geoffrey Robley. *Hong Kong 1862–1919: Years of Discretion*. Hong Kong, Hong Kong University Press, 1975.

Sayer, Geoffrey Robley. *Hong Kong 1841–1862. Birth, Adolescence and Coming of Age*. Hong Kong, Hong Kong University Press, 1980.

Selwyn-Clarke, Selwyn. *Footprints: The Memoirs of Sir Selwyn Selwyn-Clarke, Hong Kong*. Hong Kong: Sino-American Publishing Co. Ltd., 1975.

Sinn, Elizabeth. *Power and Charity: The Early History of the Tung Wah Hospital, Hong Kong*. Hong Kong, Oxford University Press, 1989.

Sinn, Elizabeth. *Growing With Hong Kong: The Bank of East Asia 1919–1994*. Hong Kong, Hong Kong University Press, 1994.

Smith, C. T. and Hayes, J. W. 'Hung Hom: An Early Industrial Village in Old British Kowloon', *Journal of the Hong Kong Branch of the Royal Asiatic Society*, Vol. 16, 1976.

Smith, Carl T. *A Sense of History: Studies in the Social and Urban History of Hong Kong*. Hong Kong, Hong Kong Educational Publishing Co., 1995.

Somers, Geoffrey V. (compiler). *The Royal Hong Kong Jockey Club: The Story of Racing in Hong Kong*. Hong Kong, The Royal Hong Kong Jockey Club, 1975.

Stokes, Gwynneth and John. *Queen's College: Its History 1862–1987*. Hong Kong, Queen's College Old Boy's Association, 1987.

Stericker, John. *A Tear for the Dragon*. London, Arthur Barker Ltd., 1958.

The Hong Kong Guide 1893. Hong Kong, Oxford University Press, 1982 (with an Introduction by H. J. Lethbridge).

Tong, Cheuk Man; Toong, David P. M.; Cheung, Alan S. K. and Mo, Yu Kai (compilers). *A Selective Collection of Hong Kong Historic Postcards*. Hong Kong, Joint Publishing (HK) Co. Ltd., 1995.

Tsai, Jung-fang. *Hong Kong in Chinese History: Community and Social Unrest in the British Colony, 1842–1913*. New York, Columbia University Press, 1993.

Waley, Arthur. *The Opium War Through Chinese Eyes*. London, George, Allen and Unwin. 1958.

Woodburn, Kirby S. et al. *The War Against Japan, Volume 1*. London, Her Majesty's Stationery Office, 1957.

Wright, Arnold and Cartwright, H. A. (editions). *Twentieth Century Impressions of Hong Kong*. Singapore, Graham Brash, 1990.

Wright-Nooth, George and Adkin, Mark. *Prisoner of the Turnip Heads: Horror, Hunger and Humour in Hong Kong 1941–45*. London, Leo Cooper, 1994.

STREETS

Photograph Credits

The page numbers are shown. Where more than one photograph appears on a page, 'a' denotes the upper and 'b' the lower one.

Richard Abrahall

13b, 14, 22, 23, 24a, 29, 37, 41, 48, 49, 65, 79a, 80b, 104, 110a, 118, 120, 131 137b, 140, 144, 164, 170a, 176, 182a, 194, 197ab, 202, 203, 207, 212, 264, 279, 282b, 286, 287a, 295, 300, 303, 304b, 305

Anthony Hedley

15, 17, 18a, 19, 24b, 25, 26, 32, 33, 43, 44a, 47a, 50, 53a, 58, 62, 63, 64ab, 70, 86, 89, 90b, 92, 95a, 99b, 103, 107, 110b, 115, 116b, 119ab, 121, 124b, 127ab, 128, 132, 133b, 134, 137a, 141, 142ab, 147ab, 148, 149, 151a, 152, 154, 156, 157ab, 160, 161ab, 162, 165, 166, 168, 174, 175, 177ab, 180, 181, 184, 185, 186, 188, 191ab, 192, 193, 195ab, 196, 198, 200ab, 201, 205ab, 206, 208, 209, 211, 213, 214, 215ab, 219, 220b, 221, 222, 224ab, 225, 226, 227, 230a, 232, 233ab, 235, 237, 239, 243ab, 244ab, 246, 247ab, 248, 249ab, 250ab, 251, 252, 253, 254, 255, 256ab, 257, 258, 260, 261, 262, 263, 265, 266, 268, 271ab, 272, 273ab, 275, 276, 277, 278, 283, 285ab, 287b, 290ab, 291, 292, 296ab, 297, 298, 299, 301, 302, 304a

John Lambon

12, 13a, 18b, 21, 27, 28, 30, 31, 34, 35, 36, 38, 39, 40, 44b, 47b, 52, 53b, 54, 57, 59ab, 66, 67, 68, 69ab, 71, 72, 73, 75, 76, 79b, 80a, 82, 83, 84ab, 85, 87, 88, 90a, 91, 93, 94ab, 95b, 96, 97, 99a, 100, 101ab, 102, 105, 108, 109ab, 112, 113, 114ab, 116a, 117, 122, 123, 124a, 125, 126, 129, 130, 133a, 135, 136, 138, 143, 151b, 153, 155, 159, 163, 167, 169, 170b, 171, 179, 182b, 220a, 228, 229, 230b, 280, 281ab, 282a